D0215754

Lenin

European History in Perspective

General Editor: Jeremy Black

Published

Benjamin Arnold *Medieval Germany*
Ronald Asch *The Thirty Years' War*
Christopher Bartlett *Peace, War and the European Powers, 1814–1914*
Robert Bireley *The Refashioning of Catholicism, 1450–1700*
Patricia Clavin *The Great Depression, 1929–1939*
Mark Galeotti *Gorbachev and his Revolution*
Martin P. Johnson *The Dreyfus Affair*
Peter Musgrave *The Early Modern European Economy*
J. L. Price *The Dutch Republic in the Seventeenth Century*
A. W. Purdue *The Second World War*
Francisco J. Romero-Salvado *Twentieth-Century Spain*
Matthew S. Seligmann and Roderick R. McLean *Germany
from Reich to Republic, 1871–1918*
Brendan Simms *The Struggle for Mastery in Germany, 1779–1850*
David Sturdy *Louis XIV*
Warren Treadgold *A Concise History of Byzantium*
Peter Waldron *The End of Imperial Russia, 1855–1917*
James D. White *Lenin*

European History in Perspective
Series Standing Order
ISBN 0–333–71694–9 hardcover
ISBN 0–333–69336–1 paperback
(outside North America only)

You can receive future titles in this series as they are published by placing a
standing order. Please contact your bookseller or, in case of difficulty, write to
us at the address below with your name and address, the title of the series and the
ISBN quoted above.

Customer Services Department, Macmillan Distribution Ltd
Houndmills, Basingstoke, Hampshire RG21 6XS, England

LENIN

THE PRACTICE AND THEORY OF REVOLUTION

JAMES D. WHITE

palgrave

First published 2001 by
PALGRAVE
Houndmills, Basingstoke, Hampshire RG21 6XS and
175 Fifth Avenue, New York, N.Y. 10010
Companies and representatives throughout the world

PALGRAVE is the new global academic imprint of
St. Martin's Press LLC Scholarly and Reference Division and
Palgrave Publishers Ltd (formerly Macmillan Press Ltd).

ISBN 0-333-72156-X hardback
ISBN 0-333-72157-8 paperback
This book is printed on paper suitable for recycling and
made from fully managed and sustained forest sources.

A catalogue record for this book is available
from the British Library.

Library of Congress Cataloging-in-Publication Data

White, James D., 1941 –
    Lenin : the practice and theory of revolution / James D. White.
        p. cm. – (European history in perspective)
    Includes bibliographical references and index.
    ISBN 0-333-72156-X – ISBN 0-333-72157-8 (pbk.)
        1. Lenin, Vladimir Ily'ch, 1870–1924. 2. Lenin, Vladimir Ily'ch,
    1870–1924 – Views on socialism. 3. Heads of state – Soviet Union –
    Biography. 4. Russia – History – Nicholas II, 1894–1917. 5. Soviet
    Union – Politics and government – 1917–1936. 6. Revolutions and
    socialism – Russia. 7. Revolutions – Russia – Philosophy. I. Title. II. Series.

DK254.L4 W375 2000
947.084'1'092–dc21   00-062593

10   9   8   7   6   5   4   3   2   1
10   09   08   07   06   05   04   03   02   01

Printed in China

For
Andrew White
1918–80

CONTENTS

PREFACE

Lenin is one of the undeniably outstanding figures of modern history. It was the Russian revolution and the founding of the Soviet state, with which his name is associated, that shaped international politics for most of the twentieth century, and whose repercussions are still being felt in our own day. Lenin's impact on world history has been so profound because ostensibly he was able to overthrow the existing social order in Russia and put in its place the kind of socialist order that Karl Marx had advocated in his theoretical writings in the previous century. After Lenin, the communism which had haunted Europe in a ghostly form acquired real physical shape.

In one of his lectures E. H. Carr, the historian of Soviet Russia, explained the uniqueness of the Russian revolution, and by implication Lenin's contribution to it, in these terms. 'The Russian revolution', he states, 'was the first great revolution in history to be deliberately planned and made. It was this element of self-consciousness which gave the Russian revolution its unique place in modern history' (*1917: Before and After* (London, 1969), pp. 8–9). It is Lenin as the deliberate planner and maker of the Russian revolution that the present work sets out to investigate.

It is not the intention of the present work to be a complete biography of Lenin. Such a work has yet to be written, and would be extremely extensive. What the author intends to do is to concentrate on the key episodes of Lenin's life and examine these episodes in conjunction with Lenin's major works on socialist theory.

Because Lenin's claim to fame is the combination of what he thought and what he did, it is appropriate to discuss simultaneously Lenin's ideas and his activity as a revolutionary. Perhaps surprisingly, this approach has not been adopted previously. Existing works about Lenin deal predominantly either with his life and activities or with his ideas. Yet neither of these aspects can be profitably treated in isolation.

A central question in the study of Lenin as a theoretician and political activist is whether he was, as he claimed, a faithful follower of Marx, or whether he diverged from Marx's ideas in substantial ways. With this question in mind the introductory chapter attempts to place Lenin in the context of how Marxist ideas developed up to the time that Lenin encountered them in the late 1880s.

A related question is Lenin's place in the history of the revolutionary movement in Russia. This is a more complex problem than it might at first appear, because this history was itself moulded to meet the needs of ideological polemics first by Plekhanov, then by Lenin, and finally and most decisively by Stalin. Placing Lenin in the context of the Russian revolutionary movement thus involves the attempt to reconstruct the actual evolution of this movement and the interconnection of the parties involved.

The student of Lenin should never lose sight of the fact that a serious problem is created by another interrelationship between political practice and theory. That is the way in which even primary source material on Lenin's life has been slanted by the imperatives of Soviet politics at various times. The historian can never be sure whether he or she is reading fact or propaganda. For that reason the concluding chapter sets out to track the influence of the various political considerations which had an impact on the presentation of Lenin's biography. This is a way to highlight the succession of distortions which were introduced into the various episodes of Lenin's career and the context in which they took place. This kind of investigation is in its way the obverse side of reconstructing the history of the Russian revolutionary movement and Lenin's place in it.

A word should be said about a matter of terminology which has an important bearing on understanding the politics of Bolshevism. Before 1918 it is an anachronism to speak of the Bolshevik 'party'. Prior to that time the Bolsheviks were a *fraktsiya* of the Russian Social Democratic Labour Party. Unfortunately English has no exact equivalent for the Russian word *fraktsiya*, which is a borrowing from the German *Fraktion*, meaning 'party group'. Thus, the German Social Democrats would have a *Fraktion* in the Reichstag. Some authors render *fraktsiya* into English as 'faction'. But the connotation of disapproval present in English is absent in the original Russian and German, which are entirely neutral. The term has therefore been translated as 'fraction' throughout the present work.

Bibliographical data in the endnotes and in the Bibliography are given in the modified version of the Library of Congress transliteration system which is the one in common use in libraries. To transliterate Russian words and proper names in the text I have used the *Europe–Asia Studies* system, which gives a better idea of pronunciation than the

Library of Congress method. Where an accepted spelling of a Russian proper name existed I have retained it. Proper names of non-Russians have been given in the modern forms of the languages in which they appear. This is not only for accuracy, but also because the content of the present work requires that national affiliations be established. Dates prior to 14 February 1918 are given according to the Russian (old-style) calendar, which was twelve days behind the Western (new-style) calendar in the nineteenth century and thirteen in the twentieth.

My thanks are due to the series editor, Professor Jeremy Black, and to Terka Bagley of the publishers for their critical comments and for the help and advice they have given me.

JAMES D. WHITE

INTRODUCTION

Marx, Lenin and the Russian
revolutionary movement

Much of what Lenin did and wrote, especially in his early political career, was determined by the previous development of the Russian revolutionary movement and by the history of Marx's ideas in Russia. His approach to revolutionary practice and theory are also to be explained by the peculiar way in which Marxist doctrine and the Russian revolutionary movement interacted in the period during Lenin's childhood and youth. It was at that time that Marx's ideas began to circulate in Russia, and their implications discussed for the country's future economic development and for the tactics which revolutionaries might adopt. Lenin entered the Russian revolutionary movement at a time when both its politics and its ideology were in a state of flux. As a result he was able to make a profound impact on both. Examining historically the interrelationship of Marxism and the Russian revolutionary movement provides the political context in which Lenin operated and gives an insight into what Lenin's relationship to Marx was.

The history of Marxism in Russia is a very broad and complex subject, so that it is possible here to sketch out only the barest outlines.[1] It is further complicated by the fact that this history was itself part of a polemic waged by Lenin and his mentor Plekhanov against their political opponents, whom they termed 'Narodniki'. They wished to imply that the Narodniki were a current of socialist thought in Russia, inspired by Alexander Herzen and Nikolai Chernyshevskii in the 1850s, who wished Russia to escape the capitalist phase and build socialism directly on the basis of the peasant commune, whose egalitarian and democratic constitution had first been described by the German visitor to Russia August von Haxthausen at the end of the 1840s. Plekhanov and Lenin maintained that these ideas were

utopian and were being superseded by the scientific socialism represented by Marx, which recognised that capitalism was already developing in Russia and that socialism would come about following a
successful revolution by the Russian working class. This version of
events was not history but ideology, though it has been accepted by
many historians of the period. The 'Narodniki' in fact had no less
claim to be followers of Marx than Plekhanov or Lenin.

In speaking of the introduction of Marxism into Russia one should
not imagine that Marx first formulated his ideas and then these were
somehow transported into Russia. In fact the influences were recipro-
cal, and Russian economic conditions and the way they were described
by Russian writers influenced the direction of Marx's thinking. Marx
needed materials on the Russian economy to complete the second volume of *Das Kapital* and this stimulated his interest in Russia and the
Russian revolutionary movement. Russian revolutionaries in their turn
looked on Marx as an authority on their country's economic future.

Why Marx should begin in 1870 to learn Russian and study the
Russian economy is explained by the nature of the project he was
working on for most of his adult life, his 'Critique of Political
Economy' of which his published work *Das Kapital* in its three volumes was to form the first part. In the much-quoted statement that
'It is impossible to understand Marx's *Das Kapital*, and especially its
first chapter, without having thoroughly studied and understood the
whole of Hegel's *Logic*',[2] Lenin showed an appreciation that Marx
had set out to treat political economy in a manner comparable to
how Hegel had approached philosophy in his *Science of Logic*; or – to
be more exact – an appreciation of how Marx had originally set out
to treat political economy, because the first chapter of *Das Kapital*
Lenin was referring to was the first chapter of the first edition of the
work and the edition from which the Russian translation had been
made. Marx rewrote the chapter for subsequent editions of his book
and in those the Hegelian language had been removed.

The reason for the resemblance that Lenin noted was that Marx
had intended his 'Critique of Political Economy' to emulate Hegel's
Science of Logic. Hegel had set out to show that creative thought did
not come from unconscious inspiration, as many of his contemporaries believed, but from systematic reasoning. He argued this – in a
manner calculated to convince his contemporaries at least – by
demonstrating that there was a necessary progression from the most
rudimentary forms of awareness to thought at its highest possible

level, Absolute Knowledge. The *Science of Logic* links together all the philosophical conceptions of the day, the 'categories' of philosophy, beginning with the simplest and ending with the most complex. The progression from one category to the next is effected by the three-stage movement, or 'dialectic' of the Concept, through its phases of Universality, Particularity and Individuality. It was this kind of terminology that Lenin found in the first chapter of Marx's *Das Kapital*.

In his 'Critique of Political Economy' Marx intended to link together the categories of political economy in the same way that Hegel had linked together the categories of philosophy. He would begin from the most elementary category, the commodity, and proceed to show how the commodity implied all other categories of capitalism including: money, capital, landed property, wage labour, the state and international trade. The culminating point of capitalism would be the world market. He would show that 'the tendency to create the world market is directly given in the Concept of capital itself'.[3] The point of proving that the commodity led inevitably to the world market was that having reached this point of culmination the capitalist system, having nowhere further to go, would then give way to a higher form of economic and social organisation.

Marx's project was a very ambitious and extremely arduous and intricate one. Unlike Hegel, he was not working only with abstractions, but with real economic data, because he expected the real capitalist system to follow the dynamic which he was elaborating in his book. He expected capitalism to expand throughout the world, form a world market, and become the Universal economic system. Marx worked first on the section of his 'Critique' dealing with Capital. This had three sections: (1) Capitalist Production, (2) The Circulation of Capital and (3) Income from Capital. Most attention was given to the first section, which went through several drafts, and was finally published as the first volume of *Das Kapital* in 1867. The third section was completed in a single draft, but remained unpublished in Marx's lifetime. It was when he came to make a full version of the second section, on the circulation of capital, that Marx ran into serious difficulties with his project, which prevented its ever being completed.

The circulation of capital was crucial for Marx's vision of how the capitalist system operated. He believed that as capital circulated it 'reproduced' itself, so that its circuits were perpetuated. He also thought that as it circulated capital broadened its sphere of operation, giving rise to 'expanded reproduction'. This would cause it

eventually to permeate throughout the entire world. The third function capital carried out as it circulated was to make its transactions
swifter and smoother by removing more and more obstacles in its
way. These obstacles were the remains of any earlier economic or
social systems. This was the means by which capitalism made the
environment in which it operated more and more capitalist.

The reason which sent Marx back to the drawing-board was the
realisation that in the real world the circulation of capital did not act
in this way. It did not necessarily expand into new areas, nor did it
inevitably destroy earlier forms of social and economic organisation.
Capitalism could happily coexist with traditional, communal types of
social order, as was proved by the example of Marx's native region
of Westphalia. This discovery caused Marx to revise the manuscript
of *Das Kapital*, Volume I, removing references it contained to the
inevitable expansion of capitalism and its destruction of earlier forms
of economic organisation. He did not succeed in eradicating these
completely, and some passages remained which suggested the earlier
direction of his thought. Moreover, the first chapter, which contained
the philosophical framework for the scheme of the 'Critique of
Political Economy', still stood. This was only removed in the second
edition of *Das Kapital*, Volume I which appeared in 1872. For the
French translation of the same year Marx rewrote substantial sections, removing all trace of the philosophical framework, and adding
passages to make it clear that he did not envisage an inevitable
onward march of capitalism throughout the world. It was this French
translation that Marx would cite in reply to Russian socialists who
raised the question of Russia's future economic development.

One significant passage Marx had left in the first edition of *Das
Kapital* was the passage in the Postscript concerning Alexander
Herzen. Herzen in the 1850s had written about the possibility of
socialism in Russia based on the communal attitudes of the peasant
community. Marx had ridiculed the idea because it was at odds with
his own conception of socialism as a world system. After 1868 Marx
began to see that Herzen might have a point, and in subsequent editions of *Das Kapital* the scornful remarks about Herzen were removed.

Despite these efforts to prevent giving the impression that *Das
Kapital* propounded the doctrine that all countries were fated to
undergo capitalist development, that was precisely the way his work
was first received in Russia. This was due largely to the fact that the
pamphlet on economics he had published in 1859, *A Contribution to*

the Critique of Political Economy, had argued in this way, and had contained the memorable scheme of successive types of economic development: the Asiatic, classical, feudal and capitalist. The first person to propagate Marx's ideas in Russia was the professor of economics at Kiev University Nikolai Sieber, who in 1871 published a perceptive commentary on Marx's theories under the rather ponderous and misleading title of *David Ricardo's Theory of Value and Capital in Connection with the Latest Contributions and Interpretations*.[4] Sieber took the view that Marx considered capitalism to be a universal system and that he expected it to take root in Russia. His book was to provide Plekhanov and subsequently Lenin with their early conceptions of Marx's economic ideas.

After 1870 Marx started to collect materials on how capitalism was beginning to circulate in Russia. In that country he had the perfect model to hand. In 1861 serfdom had been abolished and it was anticipated that in due course a market economy would develop in Russia, as it had in the more advanced countries of Western Europe. Marx was assisted in his task by the group of people who translated *Das Kapital*, Volume I into Russian, especially by Nikolai Danielson and Herman Lopatin. Danielson and Lopatin were followers of the Russian socialist thinker, Nikolai Chernyshevskii, who himself had independently written a work comparable to Marx's *Das Kapital*. This was a commentary on John Stuart Mill's *Principles of Economics*, which took a critical view of the individualism that capitalism fostered.[5] Like Herzen, Chernyshevskii thought that Russia ought to avoid capitalism and, taking advantage of the fact that the peasant commune was still viable, go directly to socialism.

In Russia Marx was looking to see what peculiar combination of circumstances were necessary before capital began to circulate. Danielson supplied him with materials on the history of the peasant commune, the legislation of the 1861 land reform, and statistical publications on the post-reform Russian economy. Many of the notes and manuscripts Marx wrote on the basis of Danielson's materials were later published.[6] They constitute an interesting source, because in the 1890s Lenin was also to investigate the development of capitalism in Russia, and with these materials one can compare how Marx and Lenin approached the same subject.

In his studies of pre-capitalist forms of economic and social organisation, Marx was aided by research carried out by the young Russian scholar Maxim Kovalevskii, whom he had first met in 1875.

Kovalevskii made a comparative study of how peasant communities had been destroyed in countries other than Russia, such as India, South America and Algeria. This research was published as a monograph entitled *Communal Landownership: The Causes, Course and Consequences of its Dissolution* in 1879.[7] Kovalevskii confirmed what Marx had already observed: that traditional agrarian societies showed considerable resilience and did not succumb to the inroads of capitalism; the cause of their disintegration came as a consequence of policies deliberately designed to achieve that result. It was the action not of economic but of political forces that destroyed communal forms of social organisation. This conclusion was at considerable variance with what Marx had assumed when he first conceived of the circulation of capital. Consequently, he could no longer be so definite that capitalism would spread to every country, nor could he be dogmatic about how socialism would come about.

Marx did not succeed in incorporating the results of his Russian studies into a revised version of *Das Kapital*, Volume II. But his conclusions were reflected in two letters which he drafted, one in 1877 to the editorial board of *Otechestvennye zapiski* in reply to the Russian socialist writer Nikolai Mikhailovskii,[8] and the other to the young Russian revolutionary Vera Zasulich in 1881.[9] Both Mikhailovskii and Zasulich had raised the question of whether Russia must inevitably pass through the capitalist stage and whether socialism might be introduced in Russia on the basis of the peasant commune. In both cases Marx denied any suggestion that he believed all countries had to undergo the capitalist phase, and that if Russia could indeed avoid the horrors of capitalism he saw no reason why the peasant commune could not serve as the basis for a socialist order. The letter to the editorial board of *Otechestvennye zapiski* was not sent and was only published in 1886.[10] The letter to Vera Zasulich did reach its intended destination, but was not made public, and was first published in 1924.[11]

Although Marx personally did not publish any systematic work which incorporated the conceptions of capitalist development he had formed as a result of his Russian studies, such works were published by Danielson. Danielson not only supplied Marx with materials on the Russian economy, but also carried out research on these materials in conjunction with Marx. A result of this parallel research was Danielson's article 'Studies in our Post-Reform Economy' which was published in 1880.[12] This article was expanded into a book with the same title which appeared in 1893.[13] In his analysis of the

Russian economy Danielson observed that capital was circulating in Russia not in a regular, but in an imbalanced way. Peasants were being uprooted from the land by the fiscal policies of the government, but they were not being turned into proletarians, because industry had developed insufficiently to absorb them. In 1882 the Russian economist V. P. Vorontsov published his *Fate of Capitalism in Russia*,[14] which elaborated on Danielson's article and came to the same conclusions as Danielson had. Unlike Danielson, however, Vorontsov had not been in contact with Marx, and had the impression that 'socialists of Marx's school believed that capitalist production was bound to triumph in Russia'.[15] In the 1880s that was clearly the public perception of what Marx's teaching was.

A curious situation had come about in which Marx's ideas entered Russia in not one, but two forms. One was Marx's original scheme that capitalism was necessarily a worldwide phenomenon and that every country would be brought within its ambit. The other form derived from Marx's later conception of capitalism based on empirical evidence. This was of a system that did not necessarily expand into all countries, or even into all areas of a given country. It was not necessarily a purely economic phenomenon and might require political intervention to initiate and even to perpetuate its operations. It might function, moreover, in a very crude fashion wasteful of human life. The first variant of Marx's ideas came to be known in Russia as 'Marxism', while the second was given the designation 'Narodism' by Plekhanov. Both Plekhanov and Lenin as 'Marxists' devoted a great deal of energy to combating 'Narodism' which they saw as inimical to the socialist cause.

Georgii Plekhanov was the teacher from whom Lenin learnt his Marxist theory. Plekhanov had taken part in the 'going to the people' movement in the 1870s, when young intellectuals had gone among the peasants, some to educate them in socialist ideas through 'propaganda', others, through 'agitation', to stir them to rebellion against the tsarist regime. In this movement Plekhanov had been a follower of the anarchist Mikhail Bakunin, who believed that the Russian peasantry had no need to be schooled in the ideas of socialism, because they already possessed socialist instincts, instilled into them by their lives in the commune. For the Bakuninists the revolutionaries' agitation would be sufficient to release the peasants' innate revolutionary energies and cause them to bring about a social revolution that would sweep away the existing regime.

The idea of the social revolution was fundamental for Plekhanov and his revolutionary contemporaries. They aimed not just to bring about a change in government but to effect a radical transformation of the entire social and economic order. The corollary of this position was that political action was futile and a betrayal of revolutionary principle. This view was bolstered by reference to the passage in Karl Marx's *Contribution to the Critique of Political Economy* which spoke of the economic base of society determining the political superstructure. It seemed to follow from this that even changes in the political order should be effected through the social and economic foundation on which it was built.

The 'going to the people' movement met with little success. The peasants proved impervious to socialist propaganda, and attempts to agitate them into rebellion left them unmoved. Mass arrests of the young revolutionaries took place followed by long terms of imprisonment and exile to Siberia. The lesson drawn by the revolutionaries was that their efforts needed better coordination and that an organisation should be established for the purpose. The organisation which was created as a result was known as 'Land and Liberty'.

Because the members of Land and Liberty thought of themselves as championing and articulating the immediate desires and aspirations of the common people, rather than pursuing policies which they personally believed to be in the interests of the people, they referred to themselves as 'Narodniki' (from the Russian word *narod* – people, nation).[16] The most common formulation of this principle was: 'The emancipation of the working classes must be conquered by the working classes themselves.' This was the original meaning of 'Narodism', and in view of the Slavophile connotation later attributed to this term, it is worth noting that the dictum which embodied the principle was actually the opening words of the constitution of the First International, which had been drawn up by Karl Marx. Land and Liberty supported the programme of the International because of the adherence to it of the Bakuninists.

Conflict arose within Land and Liberty when some of its membership began to favour using political terror as a revolutionary tactic. The question had arisen when, as a reprisal for the maltreatment of a political prisoner, Vera Zasulich had made an assassination attempt on the Governor of St Petersburg. She had been tried and acquitted in 1878 to the great delight of her many sympathisers. To some members of Land and Liberty Zasulich's popularity showed that political terror was capable of arousing great support among the public for the revolutionary cause. Plekhanov, however, vehemently opposed this tactic because as a political act it infringed the principle that revolutionaries should abstain from politics and concentrate on furthering the social revolution. In 1879 Land and Liberty split into two groups. The one which favoured a more political orientation and countenanced the use of terror took the name 'People's Will'. The other, representing the non-political Narodnik orthodoxy, called itself 'Black Repartition'. From 1880 it operated as an *émigré* group based in Geneva, where Plekhanov had fled to avoid arrest by the tsarist police. Somewhat ironically, Black Repartition was the group that Zasulich herself joined. It was from Geneva that she addressed her letter to Karl Marx in 1881. Consequently, she and other members of the group would be aware of Marx's opinions on the prospects for socialism in Russia. As it happened, these opinions were not to their liking and they kept them to themselves.

The year 1881 was an important landmark in the history of the Russian revolutionary movement. On 1 March of that year members of People's Will succeeded in assassinating the 'tsar reformer' Alexander II. The act brought People's Will to public attention and enhanced its prestige enormously among the revolutionary community. In the longer term, however, it was disastrous for the organisation, as the tsarist authorities tracked down and arrested its members. Within a short time the organisation was almost entirely destroyed. Nevertheless, the brief glory of People's Will was sufficient to overshadow Plekhanov's Black Repartition. In 1883 Plekhanov launched a new group, the 'Liberation of Labour'. This organisation was conceived by Plekhanov as a Marxist one, and held that the socialist revolution in Russia would come after capitalism had developed in the country and would be carried out by the working class.

Plekhanov explained the views of his new group in the pamphlet *Socialism and the Political Struggle*.[17] He now accepted the political struggle, and, by implication, terrorism, as a legitimate revolutionary tactic, though he insisted that this did not mean that he had in the slightest way departed from Narodnik principles. He remained a critic of People's Will, though now not for its use of terror, but for its attitude to Russia's future economic development. He thought People's Will mistaken for imagining that Russia might succeed in avoiding the capitalist stage. In Plekhanov's view there was no point in pinning any hopes on basing socialism on the peasant commune, as this was being undermined by the inroads of capitalism, and in the future Russia's economic development would take a course identical to that of Western European countries. Plekhanov considered these views to be thoroughly Marxist in character.

Lev Tikhomirov replied to Plekhanov's pamphlet on behalf of People's Will. He thought Plekhanov's vision of the socialist revolution incongruous, because since Russia was not a capitalist country and the working class only existed in a rudimentary form, it meant giving up all thought of socialist activity and waiting until capitalist development had taken place. This development, moreover, Tikhomirov pointed out, would be by no means a smooth and rapid one because Russian capitalism would have to face obstacles that its counterparts in Western Europe had not encountered. Because it was emerging later, Russian industry had little in the way of an internal market and on external markets it had to face the formidable competition of European and American producers.[18]

Plekhanov continued his offensive against People's Will in the pamphlet *Our Differences* published in 1885.[19] Again he emphasised that Russia's economic development would take the same course as that in Western countries. As his opponents did not accept this view, and thought that Russian development might not be identical to the West's, Plekhanov accused them of having derived their mode of thought from the Slavophiles of the 1840s, who had maintained that Russia differed fundamentally from the West. Having established the Slavophile ancestry for this view, he then traced it through Herzen and Chernyshevskii to contemporary writers who believed capitalism would have difficulty in establishing itself in Russia, like Vorontsov, Mikhailovskii and the members of People's Will. Plekhanov's greatest coup, however, was to provide the neo-Slavophile school of thought he had invented with a name. Whereas in *Socialism and the Political Struggle* he had accused People's Will of 'a complete and all-round denial of Narodism',[20] in *Our Differences* he now applied the term 'Narodnik' not to himself or his group, but to his ideological opponents in its changed connotation. The manoeuvre was extremely successful, and the term later gained the kind of currency Plekhanov had intended.

In 1886 Marx's letter to the editorial board of *Otechestvennye zapiski* was published, undermining any suggestion that Marx subscribed to the theory that the economic development of countries must be everywhere alike. In 1892 Mikhailovskii wrote an article confronting

Plekhanov with this evidence that Marx's own position was very different from what some of his disciples in Russia maintained. But what Mikhailovskii found most objectionable in the attitude of Russian Marxists was that they had taken the doctrine of 'economic materialism' to a bizarre conclusion. During the famine of 1891 they had tried to stop aid being given to famine victims on the grounds that such aid would obstruct the process of capitalist accumulation.[21]

While making no specific reference to Plekhanov's attempt to classify every writer who denied the inevitability of capitalist development in Russia as a 'Narodnik', Mikhailovskii made it quite plain that he himself did not accept the designation. He later added that having investigated the matter, he had discovered only two writers who actually did describe themselves as 'Narodniki'. One was Vorontsov and the other was Yuzov-Kablits. From a comparison of their writings, however, it emerged that each meant something entirely different by the term 'Narodism'.[22]

It was mainly in reply to Mikhailovskii that Plekhanov wrote his major work of the period, *The Development of the Monist View of History*, published at the end of 1894.[23] One of its objectives was to argue away the contents of Marx's letter to *Otechestvennye zapiski*. Plekhanov did this by saying that being written in 1877, the letter referred to a situation that had now passed; that Russia was now well on the way to capitalism. Probably as a result of Mikhailovskii's remarks on the subject, the term 'Narodnik' appeared rather infrequently in *The Monist View*, and then usually in the phrase 'Narodniki and subjectivists'. The implication was that those who did not wish to countenance the fact that Russia would have a capitalist future were 'subjectivists' who did not face up to reality as it existed. This served to identify 'Narodism' with 'subjectivism', and once made, the connection was to prove remarkably constant.

One reason for Plekhanov's eagerness to classify the 'Narodniki' as subjectivists was that he had discovered a convenient way of discrediting subjectivist thinking. This was by reproducing the criticisms Marx had made of the brothers Bruno and Edgar Bauer in the book *The Holy Family*, published in 1847. He asserted that the ideas of the Bauer brothers were identical to those of the Russian 'subjectivists'. The implication was that this was a refutation of 'Narodism' from Marx's point of view.

Because Marx had given a sympathetic exposition of eighteenth-century French materialism in *The Holy Family*, Plekhanov took this to signify that Marx was in part at least an adherent of this philosophy. But since he also knew that Marx had belonged to the Young Hegelian movement, he concluded that Marx's philosophy must be an amalgam of these two elements – a synthesis of metaphysical materialism and dialectical idealism. Consequently, in Plekhanov's view, the correct description of Marx's philosophy was 'dialectical materialism'. It was a term which Marx had never employed, though Lenin for one was always convinced that he had.

Lenin made his literary debut in 1894, shortly before Plekhanov's *Monist View of History* was published. His essay, *What the 'Friends of the People' Are and How They Fight the Social Democrats*,[24] was clearly influenced by Plekhanov's earlier writings, which are referred to in the text. Lenin joined Plekhanov in his campaign against the 'Narodniki', though, probably in response to Mikhailovskii's disavowal of the term, he tended to avoid its use. In fact, the caution he exercised in this respect probably accounts for the somewhat curious title of the essay.

As an opponent of the 'Narodniki' Lenin threw his considerable energies behind the particular ideological current in Russia represented by Plekhanov. It was a current which sought to propagate a 'Marxism' which was the remains of a system that Marx himself had abandoned since it embodied a serious misapprehension about the nature of capitalism. On the other hand Plekhanov's ideological current strove to discredit and eliminate the line of inquiry which Marx had pursued from 1870 and which took a more realistic approach to understanding the peculiar combination of circumstances that were necessary to form a market economy. Plekhanov and Lenin's campaign against the Narodniki was not the debate between Marxism and populist agrarian socialism that it has often been portrayed as, but the battle of one part of Marx's ideological heritage against another. Lenin would ensure that the scheme Marx had rejected would become the dominant ideology of the Russian revolutionary movement.

1

THE MAKING OF A REVOLUTIONARY

The Ulyanov family

Writing in 1927, Lenin's sister Anna recalled that when she was four years old or thereabouts, in 1868 or 1869, her parents took her and her little brother Alexander on a steamer trip down the Volga from Nizhnii Novgorod to Astrakhan, the home of her father's relations. She remembered the small two-storey house in which her grandmother and her uncle Vasilii lived, the warm welcome they received there, and the great fuss made over Alexander and herself. The trip stood out in Anna's memory because it was the first and last visit ever paid by the Ulyanovs to the Astrakhan branch of the family.[1]

When Anna visited Astrakhan her grandfather Nikolai Vasilevich Ulyanov (1768–1836) had been dead for over thirty years. He had started life called not Ulyanov but Ulyanin and as a serf in the village of Androsovo in the Nizhnii Novgorod province. It is possible that, while Nikolai belonged to the Orthodox faith, he might have been not a Russian but a Mordvinian or a Chuvash.

The village of Androsovo, like most peasant settlements of the time, would have been a self-contained community or *mir*, in which the heads of households met to decide collectively on how to divide and cultivate the land at their disposal, how to keep order, how to support those in need, and how to meet the obligations imposed on them by the landowner. Androsovo formed part of the estate of the landowner Stepan Brekhov, whose property embraced not just the village and the lands surrounding it but its peasant population as well. Nikolai Ulyanov was one of Stepan Brekhov's possessions.

As a landowner, Stepan Brekhov might demand two types of service from his serfs. He might require them to provide the labour needed to cultivate his fields. This kind of labour service was known as *barshchina*. Or he might demand that the serfs provide his household with a variety of goods, such as agricultural produce or items of local handicraft manufacture. This payment in kind was known as *obrok*. In this way the estates could be largely self-sufficient with little need to buy goods on the open market. Nevertheless, the payment of *obrok* in money could be demanded, and in that case the landowner might hire his serfs out to work for another employer and was paid some of the wages they received. This is what Stepan Brekhov did, and in 1791 he hired Nikolai Ulyanov out to work on *obrok* down the Volga in the Astrakhan province. The move turned out to be a fortunate one for Nikolai, because by the terms of a decree issued by the Astrakhan authorities he was freed from serfdom in 1799. He then settled in the village of Novopavlovsk, where he eked out a living as a tailor. In 1803, having received the consent of the provincial governor, Nikolai was able to move to Astrakhan and become a townsman (*meshchanin*), enrolled in the tailors' guild.[2]

In 1811 Nikolai married Anna Alexeevna Smirnova, a baptised Kalmyk, nineteen years younger than himself. The couple had four children, Ilya, Lenin's father, being the youngest. Although Nikolai's earnings were extremely modest, the family were able to acquire a two-storey house of their own, albeit in the poorest district of Astrakhan. Perhaps in keeping with his new status as a homeowner, Nikolai began to have his name entered on official documents no longer as 'Ulyanin', but as the more solid-sounding 'Ulyanov', the form subsequently used by the family.[3]

Nikolai Ulyanov died in 1836 when Ilya was only five, leaving the family to be supported by the 18-year-old elder son Vasilii. Vasilii found employment as a salesman with a commercial firm in Astrakhan and earned enough money to support his mother, his brother and his unmarried sister. At the cost of working hard all his life and denying himself an education and a family life of his own, he was able to send Ilya to school and then to see him through Kazan University.[4]

On the recommendation of his teacher at Kazan, the famous mathematician N. I. Lobachevskii, Ilya Ulyanov was appointed principal teacher of mathematics and physics at the Penza Nobles' Institute. When the Institute was closed in 1863 he moved to Nizhnii Novgorod to become principal teacher of mathematics and physics at the high school there. Throughout his life Ilya remained grateful to his brother Vasilii for the education he had received, and Vasilii for his part was highly gratified by Ilya's success. Seeing Ilya, when he came on a visit to Astrakhan with his pretty young wife and his two little children, it must have seemed that all the self-sacrifice and the hard work had been worthwhile.[5]

Ilya's wife Mariya also came from a family that had come up in society in the course of a generation. Mariya's grandfather, Moishi Blank, had been Jewish and lived in the village of Starokonstantinov near Zhitomir in the Ukrainian province of Volhynia. Moishi had been a truly remarkable man with an exceptionally cantankerous nature. Moishi did not get on with his neighbours in the local Jewish community and, in pursuit of his vendetta, reported them to the police for neglecting to say prayers for the tsar in the synagogue.

Moishi was not a popular man in Starokonstantinov, and when a fire broke out in the village in 1808, the Jewish community assumed that Moishi once again had started it as some kind of reprisal against them. They reported him to the police and Moishi was arrested and imprisoned. But when the case was brought to trial Moishi was cleared of all charges and was set free. He then claimed damages from the people who had signed the letter accusing him of arson. The court eventually found in Moishi's favour, and in 1828 the movable and immovable property of Moishi's accusers was sold off to raise the money to pay his damages.[6]

To distance himself further from his Jewish neighbours, Moishi took the Orthodox faith and was baptised with the name of Dmitrii. He had his two sons enter the Orthodox church as well, Israel taking the name Alexander and Abel taking the name Dmitry. The two boys were sent to the Russian school in Zhitomir, to be educated as Orthodox Russians. This, on the one hand, cut them off from their Jewish community, but, on the other, it opened up career prospects which would otherwise have been closed to them. In 1820 Alexander and Dmitry went to study medicine at the prestigious St Petersburg Medical–Surgical Academy from which they graduated in 1824.

In 1846 Moishi – now Dmitrii – Blank sent a long letter in Yiddish to Tsar Nicholas I offering him advice on how to deal with his Jewish subjects. There was, Moishi said, a great deal of animosity shown by the Jewish population of the Russian Empire towards Orthodox Christians like himself. But there was a simple means by which the Jews could be made to convert to Orthodoxy. Since the Jewish faith prohibited its adherents to milk cows, start fires and so on on the Sabbath, the Jews had to rely on the cooperation of their Orthodox neighbours to perform such tasks. It only required the government to ban this type of cooperation and the Jews would be starved into conversion. This policy, seemingly, was too extreme even for the ultra-conservative government of Nicholas I, and Moishi Blank's scheme was not followed up.[7]

Between 1824 and 1832 Mariya's father Alexander Blank (1799–1870) served as a police surgeon in St Petersburg, and thereafter as a medical practitioner for various public bodies and business concerns in the provinces. In 1829 he married Anna Johannovna Grosschopf (1801–40), the daughter of a German father and a Swedish mother. Alexander Blank had the theory that it was very beneficial for women to have many children, but Anna Grosschopf gave up the ghost after her fifth. She had one son and four daughters, her third daughter Mariya being Lenin's future mother. The son, Dmitry, for a time studied in the faculty of law at Kazan University, but committed suicide in 1850 at the age of nineteen.[8] It fell to Anna Grosschopf's widowed sister Ekaterina von Essen to bring up the girls. She gave them an education which went well beyond that which daughters of the nobility traditionally received. She taught them German, French and English besides giving them piano lessons. The seriousness with which these studies were undertaken is indicated by the fact that in 1863 Mariya Blank was able to pass the examinations which qualified her as a teacher of Russian, French and German.[9]

The year after his wife died, Alexander Blank took up the post of inspector of the medical board in Perm and moved there with his family. For a short time he acted as the doctor for the Perm high school, where he befriended its Latin teacher Ivan Dmitrievich Veretennikov, who in 1850 married his eldest daughter Anna. Subsequently Veretennikov became inspector of the Perm Nobles' Institute. It was on a visit to her married sister's home in Perm that Mariya Blank met the mathematics teacher at the Institute, Ilya Ulyanov, her future husband. Teaching colleagues of Veretennikov's, Alexander Ardashev, Iosif Lavrov and Andrei Zalezhskii, also provided spouses for the remaining three of Alexander Blank's daughters.[10]

Alexander Blank took early retirement in 1847 and, in respect of his standing in the medical hierarchy, was granted hereditary nobility some years later. Just before his retirement he bought the estate of Kokushkino near Kazan. Blank's social standing was enhanced considerably by this purchase, as he now entered the ranks of the landowning aristocracy and had become the owner of serfs, the traditional mark of wealth and substance in Russia. Unlike many landowners, however, Blank treated the peasants on his estate with compassion and consideration, holding clinics for them in the manor house. When Russia's defeat in the Crimean War brought home to the government the need to modernise the country and strengthen it internationally, it was decided that serfdom should be abolished. To avoid the social upheaval that might result when the 22 million former serfs began to use their freedom to roam about the country, it was resolved to retain the peasant commune and to provide the peasants with at least a small allotment of land and the opportunity to purchase additional amounts by 'redemption payments' spread over 49 years.

Many landowners tried to cling on to as much land as possible, making use of the regulations allowing them to keep at least one- third of their former estates. This could be done at the expense of peasants' allotments, and the portions of these 'cut-offs' (*otrezki*) tended to include the most fertile and valuable tracts of land. Their removal often left the peasants with less land to cultivate than they had had at their disposal before emancipation and caused them considerable hardship as a result. Alexander Blank, however, was not a landowner of this type, and when his serfs were liberated he gave them the maximum allotments of land allowed for in the 1861 Liberation Edict.[11]

In retirement at Kokushkino Alexander Blank helped Ekaterina von Essen with the upbringing of his daughters. He saw to it that they understood the value of taking cold baths, avoiding tea and coffee, and of having numerous children when they got married. These injunctions were dutifully carried out, so that all five daughters had large families, each having something between six and ten children.[12] All of Alexander Blank's daughters and their families congregated at Kokushkino during the summer holidays, so that the ex-doctor had to extend his house to accommodate the rapidly multiplying Veretennikovs, Ardashevs, Zalezhskiis, Ulyanovs and Lavrovs. Alexander Blank died in June 1870, having lived long enough to see his daughter Mariya's second son Vladimir, the future Lenin, who had been born on 10 April of that year.

It is worth remarking that although the Ulyanov family was untypical of Russian families as a whole in the value it attached to educating the children, it was entirely typical of the families of Alexander

Blank's daughters. In these it was common for both boys and girls to go to university and enter the professions, usually schoolteaching, but also medicine and the law. The Veretennikov girls were especially notable for entering professions that were traditionally practised by men. Anna Veretennikova studied medicine at the St Petersburg Women's Medical Institute and subsequently worked as a doctor in the Ufa province, being one of the first women doctors in Russia. She died, however, in 1888 when she was only 33, at Kokushkino. Her younger sister Ekaterina studied at the St Petersburg Bestuzhev Courses, becoming a schoolteacher in Simbirsk, before moving to St Petersburg and there opening first a primary school and a kinder-garten and subsequently a high school for girls. In 1906 she was to open the Juridicial Higher Women's Courses to prepare women for the legal profession. Ekaterina was supported in these endeavours by her husband, the influential liberal journalist Matvei Leontevich Peskovskii, who was to rally to the aid of the Ulyanov family when Alexander and Anna were arrested for their part in the attempted assassination of the tsar in 1887.[13]

By the time young Vladimir was born the Ulyanov family had moved from Nizhnii Novgorod to Simbirsk. After fourteen years as a schoolmaster Ilya Ulyanov had secured the post of inspector of pri-mary schools for the Simbirsk province. This was a major challenge because the Simbirsk province was comparable in size to a small country, and in 1870 had a population of 1 million 300 thousand people, one-third of whom were Chuvash, Mordva or Tatars. There were – at least on paper – 460 primary schools, with an average of 21 pupils per school. But as Ilya soon discovered, some of these schools were fictitious, and of those that actually existed, most were of a very rudimentary nature and staffed by people with no proper teacher training. It was Ilya's job to bring these schools up to stan-dard and to increase educational provision in the province. Ilya threw himself into the task with enthusiasm and dedication, travel-ling around the primitive roads of the province in all weathers, being absent from home for months on end. In recognition of his services he was promoted in 1874 to director of primary education for the Simbirsk province, first with two assistants and then five.[14]

One of Ilya Ulyanov's proudest achievements of this time was the part he had played in advancing teacher training in the province, in particular the establishment of the teachers' training college in 1872 in the village of Poretsk, 100 miles from Simbirsk.[15] The measure was to prove controversial, however, because the college was to be criticised by the more conservative representatives of the local clergy and the nobility for its emphasis on the natural sciences rather than religious instruction. It was feared that teachers produced by the college might spread subversive ideas amongst the peasantry. These fears were not unfounded, since in the 1870s the role of village schoolteacher was one ideally suited for young socialist intellectuals to 'go to the people' and spread socialist propaganda. Two graduates of the Poretskii college were arrested and imprisoned for doing precisely that, causing Ilya Ulyanov considerable embarrassment and the college to be threatened with closure.[16]

Ilya Ulyanov himself had no sympathy for revolutionaries, and was badly shaken by the news of Tsar Alexander II's assassination by People's Will in 1881. He had every reason to be well-disposed towards Alexander II, as his own career and the educational policies he had implemented had been made possible by the reforms of the early 1860s Alexander had inspired. Alexander's assassination was to be the prologue to a long period of political reaction in the country, one in which education would be one of the principal victims. From 1884 onwards the initiative in primary education passed to the clergy, and in the school curriculum religious knowledge was given prominence at the expense of Ilya's beloved natural sciences.[17]

Just before the conservative I. D. Delianov became Minister of Education, in January 1882 Ilya Ulyanov was awarded the Order of St Vladimir 3rd class for 'outstandingly diligent service' in education. This was a much sought-after decoration because it gave the recipient the right to hereditary nobility. It was only after her husband's death, however, that Mariya Ulyanova enrolled herself and her children in the genealogical register of the Simbirsk nobility.[18]

The Ulyanovs had six children in all who survived beyond infancy. Anna, born in 1863, was a slim, dark and serious girl, to whom it fell in later years to be the chronicler of the Ulyanov family. We are indebted to Anna for much of what we know of the Ulyanovs' life in Simbirsk, but because she spoke rarely of herself, Anna remains a rather shadowy figure. Alexander (Sasha), who had inherited his mother's fine features and was a year younger than Anna, was the member of the family to whom Anna devoted most attention in her reminiscences. The picture of Sasha which emerges is perhaps idealised, but it is clear that he was a gifted boy, sincere, earnest and with a highly developed sense of integrity.

Vladimir (Volodya), who was four years younger than Sasha, was extrovert and boisterous. He had inherited his father's high cheek-bones, his inability to pronounce the sound 'r', and in later life a rapidly receding hairline. Olga, who was born the year after Lenin, was a petite, vivacious and imaginative girl. Being of much the same age, she and Lenin had shared the same closeness as Anna and Sasha. The two youngest children, Dmitrii, born in 1874, and Mariya, in 1878, formed the youngest pair of the Ulyanov children.

As their father was so frequently away from home the Ulyanov children were brought up by their mother with the help of a nanny. The household, while not affluent, was certainly comfortably off, and did not suffer any want. Relations between parents and children were invariably warm and affectionate, and in later years Lenin's brother and sisters would look back on their childhood as being a very happy time of their lives. The Ulyanovs were a close-knit family whose friends and acquaintances tended to belong to the world of education and to be colleagues and associates of Ilya, a category which overlapped with the in-laws and their families who milled around at Kokushkino every summer.

In keeping with Ilya Ulyanov's belief in education all the Ulyanov children – boys and girls – were encouraged to apply themselves seriously to their studies from an early age. In this sphere both parents were able to give very substantial guidance, Ilya showing how to write essays and Mariya Alexandrovna passing on her knowledge of French, German and English. Even before they went to school the children were tutored by teachers that Ilya had hired for the purpose. With their native intelligence, their capacity for hard work and the advantage of having trained teachers within the home, it was natural that the Ulyanov children should distinguish themselves at school.

Sasha and Lenin attended the Simbirsk high school, at which Fedor Kerensky, the father of Alexander Kerensky, was headmaster. Alexander quickly developed a passion for the natural sciences, but found languages, particularly the classical languages, difficult. Lenin was quite the opposite. Though he had no taste for the natural sciences, he mastered all his school subjects with apparent ease, showing a special aptitude for Latin and Greek.

Alexander Ulyanov

Instead of going to the nearby Kazan University, Alexander chose to study at St Petersburg University, as the natural science faculty there was better. He took up residence in the capital in August 1883 where he was joined a month later by his sister Anna, who had come to study at the Bestuzhev Courses for women. Alexander worked well at university in his first two years and won a gold medal for his study on annelid worms. Misfortune struck the Ulyanov family in January 1886, when Ilya died suddenly from a brain haemorrhage at the age of 54. An even greater tragedy was to come the following year when Sasha was hanged for his part in an attempt to assassinate Tsar Alexander III.[19]

Lenin's biographers have tended to deal rather cursorily with the plot to assassinate Alexander III in which Sasha Ulyanov was involved, on the grounds that it was an isolated incident embracing a small group of immature students and that, in Trotsky's words, 'it contained no seeds of the future'. A closer examination, however, shows that the assassination attempt represented an important phase in the emergence of Social Democracy in Russia, and provided the starting point from which Lenin's theory and practice of revolution were to evolve.

The way in which Alexander Ulyanov came to be involved in revolutionary politics was initially through the student societies of which he was a member. In Russian universities in the 1880s student societies were organised as associations of people from the same locality – *zemlyachestva*. On arrival in St Petersburg Alexander Ulyanov joined the Simbirsk *zemlyachestvo* on the invitation of his flatmate Ivan Chebotarev, whom he had known since his schooldays in Simbirsk. Cooperation between different *zemlyachestva* for various purposes brought Alexander into contact with representatives of similar student societies from different parts of Russia, and in particular with members of the Don and Kuban *zemlyachestva*, whose members tended towards radicalism in politics. Some of Alexander Ulyanov's fellow conspirators in the assassination attempt, such as Orest Govorukhin, Andreyushkin and Generalov, came from this student association.[20]

Another *zemlyachestvo* inclined towards radical politics was the Polish society, the Koło (Circle), to which many Poles and Polish-speaking Lithuanians from the Vilna area belonged. Among these was Jozef Lukasiewicz, several of whose family members had taken part in the Polish uprising of 1863. Even as a schoolboy in Vilna Lukasiewicz read the banned publications of the Polish and Russian revolutionary organisations. He entered St Petersburg University in 1883 to study mathematics and physics, and soon joined a study group composed of Polish students who had contacts with the Polish socialist party 'Proletariat'. He recalls that he would have joined the Russian terrorist group People's Will, but was unable do so because its organisation had been destroyed. Lukasiewicz was to be one of the driving forces behind the assassination attempt of 1887 and the designer of the bomb to be used in the enterprise.[21]

Polish students were the first organisers of workers' circles in St Petersburg which began to be formed in 1887. Bronisław Lelewel, Gabriel Rodziewicz and his wife Julia were the organisers of an influential workers' circle which was taken over by the Russian Mikhail Brusnev, one of the pioneers of Social Democracy in the St Petersburg labour movement.[22] Brusnev recalls that in 1887 in preparation for the assassination of Alexander III he held in his apartment for safe keeping a complete laboratory designed for the manufacture of nitric acid.[23]

Lukasiewicz had connections not only with the Polish student radicals in St Petersburg, but also with a revolutionary group in his native Vilna led by Antoni Gnatowski and Isaak Dembo. It was the Gnatowski group that was to supply the essential bomb-making materials.[24] The group is also significant because some of its members would later become prominent in the Russian revolutionary movement. Among these were Charles Rappoport, later to be a leading figure in the French socialist movement, Lyubov Akselrod-Ortodoks, who became a Marxist philosopher, Leo Jogiches, a pioneer of Polish Social Democracy and lifelong associate of Rosa Luxemburg, and Timofei Kopelzon, later a founder member of the Jewish socialist party, the Bund. The group also included Bronisław Piłsudski and his more famous brother Józef, later to be the Polish head of state.

According to Akselrod-Ortodoks, the group's two leaders Gnatowski and Dembo were followers of People's Will. But the ideological outlook of the membership as a whole was less strictly defined. The group was familiar with Plekhanov's two main works of the period, *Socialism and the Political Struggle* and *Our Differences*. These were regarded with general disdain in the Gnatowski circle, since the views developed in them were held to be a betrayal of the revolutionary cause. The members of the group tended to agree with the criticism of Plekhanov's ideas which had been voiced by Lev Tikhomirov. Nevertheless, Akselrod could discern a movement towards Social Democracy in the group, and a gradual abandonment of the tactics associated with People's Will.[25]

In Akselrod-Ortodoks's view, this transformation was dictated not so much by theoretical as by practical considerations. While continuing to believe in the efficacy of terrorism, the members of the Gnatowski circle began to organise study groups for the workers in Vilna, and this activity led to the acceptance in practice of the kind of Social Democratic principles which Plekhanov and his Liberation of Labour group propounded.[26]

The economics study group was one of the student societies that Sasha Ulyanov joined during the 1886–87 academic year along with his friends Mark Elizarov and Ivan Chebotarev. The group's founder member Viktor Bartenev and Chebotarev are among those to leave memoirs of what the group did. From these one learns that in its first year the group read Chernyshevskii's commentary on J. S. Mill's *Principles of Political Economy*, progressing in the second year to studying Mill, Adam Smith and David Ricardo. In that year the members of the group presented papers on aspects of the contemporary Russian economy. There was a paper, for example, on the development of capitalism in Russia, criticising V. P. Vorontsov's *The Fate of Capitalism in Russia*. This was a subject in which Alexander Ulyanov was especially interested and read a great deal about. Chebotarev states that for a long time he kept the notes that Alexander had made from Vorontsov's book along with lengthy extracts from the contemporary press on the development of large-scale industry in the south of Russia. Chebotarev recalls that in reading over these notes he could observe that Alexander Ulyanov had an extensive and profound understanding of economic questions, that he saw capitalism developing rapidly in Russia, that he took a critical attitude towards Vorontsov's ideas and that he was dubious about the vitality of the Russian peasant commune as a basis for social regeneration. Chebotarev thought that perhaps Alexander's ideas had been influenced by Plekhanov's book *Our Differences* which had appeared a little earlier, and of which Alexander had formed a favourable impression.[27] Marx's *Das Kapital* was not read in the study group because of its difficulty, but individual members of the group had tackled it. Alexander Ulyanov read it in 1885.

Some members of the economics study group took the 'Marxist' approach to Russian economic development, believing that capitalism was fast developing in Russia, that the peasant commune was in decline and that the key role in the revolutionary movement would be played by the proletariat. Those who disagreed with this approach Bartenev termed 'romantics', emphasising that in the period 1885–90 there was no definite division into 'Marxists' and 'Narodniki'. Nor was the term 'social democrat' in wide usage. There was also a division of opinion between those who advocated terrorism and those who did not. But what emerges clearly from the memoirs is that it was impossible to make the generalisation that the followers of 'Marxism' opposed terror and vice versa. To Bartenev in fact it seemed the other way round: that it was the 'Marxists' who were the most ardent advocates of terror, although they also referred to themselves as adherents of People's Will.[28]

The same kinds of divisions which existed in the economics study group were to be found among the group of conspirators who intended to assassinate Alexander III. The group called itself 'The Terrorist Fraction of People's Will' (though they had no formal connection with that organisation). The programme which the group members drew up showed how an approach to Russian economic development that was inspired by Marx's writings could coexist with a political strategy of terrorism. Having stated that 'Every country inevitably arrives at the socialist order by a natural course of its economic development', the programme went on to argue that the working class was the natural bearer of socialist ideas and a decisive force in the revolutionary movement. Workers must therefore form the nucleus of the socialist party, the main aim of which would be to conduct propaganda among the working class as a whole to prepare it for the task of transforming society.[29]

However, the programme argued, under the present political regime it was impossible to conduct propaganda among the workers without freedom of speech. Thus, the necessary preliminary to propaganda work was the campaign for elementary civil rights. Acquiring these rights was a function which the intelligentsia could undertake. And since the intelligentsia was deprived of any possibility to campaign peacefully, and since access to any form of legal oppositional activity was closed to it, the only avenue which remained was terror.

An event which had brought home to Sasha Ulyanov and his friends just how little freedom of expression there was under the tsarist regime was the demonstration held at the Volkovo Cemetery on 17 November 1886. This was a gathering to mark the 25th anniversary of the death of N. A. Dobrolyubov, a radical literary critic and friend of Chernyshevskii's. The demonstration was obstructed by the police and some 40 arrests were made. In response to this action by the police Alexander Ulyanov produced a leaflet for distribution around St Petersburg, deploring the lack of civil rights in the country. Anna Ulyanova believed that the Dobrolyubov demonstration was the episode that inclined her brother towards the assassination attempt.[30]

The economics study group had contacts with Social Democratic workers' circles in St Petersburg. Bartenev had come across such a group in 1886 and some of these Social Democrats held discussions with members of the economics study group.[31] Echoes of these discussions are to be found in the Terrorist Fraction's programme.

The Terrorist Fraction made preparations to assassinate the tsar at the end of February 1887. The police, however, had intercepted the correspondence of one of the Fraction members, Andreyushkin, and were able to forestall the event and arrest those they thought were most closely involved, including Sasha Ulyanov and his sister Anna, who had been the unwitting recipient of a coded communication from one of the conspirators in Vilna. Fifteen people were brought to trial, five of whom, including Alexander Ulyanov, were eventually sentenced to death. The sentences did not reflect the scale of involvement in the conspiracy. Sasha Ulyanov had only become one of the leaders at the last moment when one of the main instigators, Petr Sheveryev, had dropped out. Lukasiewicz's role was played down at the trial because he and other members of the group feared that the involvement of Poles would be seized upon by the police and the gutter press to imply that the assassination attempt had been inspired by the Poles, and in this way its character as a general protest against the existing regime would be lost.[32] As a result, the impression was created that Alexander Ulyanov had been a major figure in the assassination attempt.

Apart from the relatively small number of people brought to trial the authorities made mass arrests of those they suspected of having any connection with the assassination attempt, whether in St Petersburg, Vilna or other provincial centres. By the autumn of 1887 the number of such arrests reached over 100. About 50 were sent to Siberia without trial, and the remainder given lesser penalties such as prison sentences, expulsion from the university or placement under police surveillance. Through the intercession of her cousin Ekaterina's husband Matvei Peskovskii, Anna Ulyanova's Siberian exile was commuted to a term of banishment under police surveillance at Kokushkino. There was little hope that these measures would evoke a new revolutionary upsurge; the forces of the radicals had been so severely depleted, and, according to V. V. Bartenev, of those who remained few had the inclination towards terrorist action.[33]

The few surviving adherents of People's Will among the students of the Technological Institute, a group consisting of Gabriel and Julia Rodziewicz, M. V. Petrovskii and V. N. Ivanov, resolved to continue terorist activities, and to that end to recruit more members of the intelligentsia and to set up some workers' circles. When Bronisław Lelewel was asked to join this group, he – with the fate of the 100 students in mind – consented only on condition that it renounce its tactic of terror and concentrate on organising the workers for mass political action in the future. This was agreed, and Lelewel along with Kosiński, Bańkowski, Cywiński, V. S. Golubiev, M. I. Brusnev and V. V. Bartenev began to organise workers' circles throughout St Petersburg.[34] As Lelewel points out, this was the organisation joined by Herman Krasin in 1890 and by Lenin in 1894. In other words, there was a high degree of continuity between the organisation Alexander Ulyanov had belonged to and that joined by his younger brother.

Both in the capital and in Vilna those revolutionaries who had escaped arrest had now become convinced of the futility of terrorist action. It was not worth the risk of so many arrests and wasted lives. Thenceforth attention turned increasingly to peaceful propaganda in workers' study circles, which already had been found to be a successful and rewarding activity.

Developments in Vilna were to be especially significant for the development of Social Democracy in Russia. Leo Jogiches managed to escape arrest, and along with Wacław Sielicki he formed a group whose members included I. O. Khlopov, M. I. Kovalevskii and Evgenii Sponti.[35] In May 1888 Sielicki travelled to St Petersburg to negotiate with the revolutionary groups there, declaring that the members of the Vilna group had adopted a Social Democratic programme and were opposed to the terrorist struggle. In May 1889 Sielicki was arrested and in the following year Jogiches, using his contacts abroad, escaped first to Germany and thence to Switzerland.[36]

The loss of its two most active members did not entirely disrupt the Vilna group. It carried on its propaganda among the workers under the direction of Evgenii Sponti, who was discharged from the army in 1889. He was joined by Alfons Morawski, and in 1890 by the Polish Social Democrat Stanisław Trusiewicz (Zalewski). He found the socialist organisation there consisted of two groups, one Russian–Jewish and the other Polish–Lithuanian.[37] Because propaganda among the workers in Vilna tended to be conducted in Yiddish, it was natural that there should emerge a current of opinion calling for a separate Jewish organisation. This current, represented by Kopelzon and Gozhanskii, led to the formation of the Bund.[38]

The more internationalist wing of the Russian–Jewish group, whose most illustrious representative was Julius Martov, joined the Russian Social Democratic Labour Party (RSDLP). The Polish–Lithuanian group also divided, giving rise to nationalist and internationalist currents. The nationalist current was represented by the Lithuanian Social Democratic Party founded by Morawski and Andrej Domaszewicz, and the internationalist wing by the Social Democracy of the Kingdom of Poland and Lithuania (SDKPiL), which had among its members Leo Jogiches, Rosa Luxemburg and Feliks Dzierżyński.[39]

In the mid-1890s the Jewish Social Democrats Samuel Gozhanskii, Julius Martov and Arkadii Kremer, finding that teaching a small number of workers in study groups – propaganda – did not develop a large-scale workers' movement, decided to employ the tactic of 'agitation'. This was the attempt to appeal to wide sections of the workers on a more short-term basis, using literature specially designed for the purpose.[40] The success of this tactic in Vilna was to lead to its adoption in other parts of the country.

In 1924 Lenin's youngest sister Mariya claimed that on receiving the news of his brother's execution, Vladimir exclaimed: 'No, we won't go that way; that is not the way to take.' The implication was that 17-year-old Lenin had concluded that terrorism was not an effective revolutionary tactic and that a more productive one was that which he eventually adopted. Trotsky was the first to question this story, pointing out that Mariya was hardly a reliable witness, being not quite nine years old at the time,[41] and subsequent historians have repeated Trotsky's critical observation. But what renders the story improbable is not Mariya's age, but the fact that it embodies a stylised interpretation of the Russian revolutionary movement's history that had become accepted by 1924 but which could not have existed in 1887.

The statement is misleading because the shift from terrorism to propagandising the workers did not come about through a decision by Lenin or any other individual; it was brought about by activists on the ground in the wake of the failed assassination attempt of 1887.

When Lenin joined his first workers' organisation in St Petersburg in 1894 it had long ago decided that assassination was not the way to take. Also misleading is the implication in Mariya's statement that the young Lenin dissociated himself from his brother's act. Quite the contrary is the case. The Ulyanovs' teacher friend Kashkadamova recalls that when Lenin spoke of Sasha to the younger members of the family he would repeat: 'So you see, he had to do what he did; he could have done no other.'[42] Anna Ulyanova records that Sasha's arrest and execution served to revolutionise both Lenin and – more noticeably – Olga.[43] The actions of Lenin and Olga in the period following Sasha's execution suggest that they had resolved that their brother's death would not be in vain and that they would serve the cause for which he had sacrificed himself – just as soon as they could discover what that cause had been.

The problem facing the Ulyanov family was that Sasha's involvement in the revolutionary movement had come as a complete surprise to them. It compounded the tragedy of Sasha's loss that they did not understand what had led him to become a terrorist. Even Anna had been unaware of what her brother was planning, because he had tried not to compromise her. (That he had not succeeded in doing this caused him extreme anguish in his last days.) The task facing Lenin and Olga was to piece together what the ideas were that had inspired Sasha to become a revolutionary.

Some light would be thrown on this by Sasha's friend Mark Elizarov, who had also become Anna's fiancé. Both Mark Elizarov and Ivan Chebotarev had been expelled from the university. Chebotarev recalls that when he returned to Simbirsk at the beginning of June 1887 he went to visit the Ulyanov family and was questioned by them, especially by Lenin, about the last days he spent in Sasha's company. Chebotarev says that Lenin was especially interested to know about what had made his brother a revolutionary.[44] We know what Chebotarev thought about this question because he wrote about it in his memoirs published in 1927. In those memoirs he gave prominence to Sasha's membership of the economics study group, and must certainly have mentioned this to the Ulyanovs forty years earlier. What he said could be supplemented by Mark Elizarov, who had also been a member of the study group. From these sources it would be possible to establish Sasha's programme of reading and what the direction of his thinking had been. These were the tracks that Lenin and Olga were to follow.

The 'elders'

Sasha's execution came just at the time Lenin was taking his leaving-certificate examinations at Simbirsk high school. Despite his inward distress, he was able to score top marks in all subjects and earned a gold medal for his distinguished performance. Olga took her leaving-certificate examinations at her school in the same year, and she too came top of her class and was awarded a gold medal. Instead of choosing to study the classical languages or the natural sciences as his family expected, Lenin decided to enter the law faculty at Kazan University. As he explained to his cousin Nikolai Veretennikov, it would enable him to study political economy.[45] Olga planned to go to Helsinki to study medicine. She had taught herself Swedish to this end, but had finally to admit defeat when she discovered that a knowledge of Finnish would also be a requirement. In 1891 she went to study at the Bestuzhev Courses in St Petersburg.

Lenin commenced his studies at Kazan University in August 1887. Within a matter of weeks he had joined the Samara–Simbirsk *zemlyachestvo* and made contact with a revolutionary group that had continuity with the one to which Sasha had belonged. After the demonstration in honour of Dobrolyubov, which Sasha had helped organise, some of the students arrested were sent to Kazan where they formed a revolutionary group. Although the leaders of this group were removed to Siberia following the assassination attempt, some, like Konstantin Vygornitskii (who, as the police noted, was a friend of the executed Andreyushkin), were able to remain in Kazan. The group also attracted new members such as Ospianov's friend Vadim Kalinin, as well as Lazar Bogoraz and Alexander Skvortsov, both from Taganrog and both with People's Will connections.[46]

On 4 December this group led a student demonstration at Kazan University which made a number of demands including the abolition of the existing oppressive University Statute, the right to form associations and the right to collect funds for student welfare. Lenin was reported to be among the most prominent and vociferous of the demonstrators. Following this demonstration a number of arrests took place, Lenin spending some days in gaol before being expelled from the university and banished to the family estate at Kokushkino.

For the younger brother of an executed terrorist to associate with possible accomplices in the conspiracy and to cooperate with such subversives in organising a student demonstration was for Lenin

uncharacteristically foolhardy behaviour, behaviour that was to cost
him dear. His sister Anna's explanation is that local radicals would
tend to seek out the brother of a martyred revolutionary, and that in
the wake of his brother's execution Lenin himself felt very antagonistic towards the Russian government.[47]

Lenin later recalled that during the year that followed his banishment from Kazan he read more intensively than at any other time of
his life. He read all of Chernyshevskii's articles on the peasant question and his commentary on J. S. Mill's *Principles of Political Economy*.
He observed in retrospect that reading Chernyshevskii's attack on
bourgeois economics was a good preparation for his later study of
Marx.[48] But that is also something he would know at the time. He
would have learnt from Mark Elizarov and Ivan Chebotarev that
Sasha and the other members of the economics study group had
approached Marx by way of Chernyshevskii precisely because they
found that the commentary on Mill helped make Marx's *Das Kapital*
more accessible. Marx was Lenin's destination, because he knew that
his brother had valued and even translated him.

A parallel, and to some extent a coordinated, reading programme
was being undertaken simultaneously by Olga. This is clear from her
letters to Lenin when she left the family in 1890 to live in St
Petersburg. By that time she and Lenin had progressed to studying
Marxist economics and their application to the Russian situation, to
the way in which the development of capitalism was affecting peasant
agriculture and social institutions. Their reading had included Sieber's
study of Ricardo and Marx, Maxim Kovalevskii's comparative study of
peasant communities and V. P. Vorontsov's *The Fate of Capitalism in
Russia*. More detailed statistical works on peasant agriculture were now
being sought, and Olga's correspondence shows that to help in track-
ing down material of this kind she had enlisted Viktor Bartenev, the
founder-member of the economics study group to which Sasha had
belonged. Bartenev was at that time closely connected with Mikhail
Brusnev's social democratic workers' organisation in St Petersburg.[49]

Lenin spent almost a year of banishment in Kokushkino before
being allowed to return to Kazan in the autumn of 1888. But despite
repeated applications to the authorities, he was not allowed to return
to the university. He used his time to pursue his programme of reading, and, sometimes along with Olga, studied *Das Kapital*, Volume I
and other writings by Marx and Engels. In Kazan he joined a study
circle at which Marx's writings were discussed. The study circle was

organised by Nikolai Fedoseev, one of the first Marxists in Russia, a young man Lenin was to hold in high regard, but whom he never actually met. In July Fedoseev and several members of the circle Lenin had attended were arrested. Lenin escaped because by that time he and his family had moved to the estate of Alakaevka in the Samara province, which his mother had bought with the proceeds of the sale of the house in Simbirsk.[50]

In the spring of 1890 Lenin was allowed to take the law exams at St Petersburg University without attending lectures. He set himself the objective of graduating at the same time as his former classmates at Kazan University. This involved working intensively to cram a four-year course into a mere eighteen months. He was able to do this with the help of his cousin Vladimir Ardashev, who had himself completed a law degree, and took his examinations in the spring and autumn of 1891. He passed with flying colours and was awarded a first-class diploma. But his success was marred by the death of Olga, who fell victim to typhoid fever in May of 1891 aged only 19.

At the end of January 1892 Lenin was called to the bar and in March he began to practise law in the Samara circuit court as assistant to the lawyer A. N. Khardin, in cases defending local peasants against charges of petty larceny and wife-beating though with none too great a degree of success.[51] A more congenial pursuit in Samara was discussing points of Marxist theory with a group of young radicals including A. P. Sklyarenko, I. Kh. Lalayants and A. A. Belyakov, sometimes on boating trips on the Volga. Belyakov's reminiscences reveal Lenin at this time eager to display his newly acquired mastery of Marx's economics and demonstrate the superiority of Marx's thought over the ideas of Lavrov and Mikhailovskii, whom Sklyarenko and other members of the group had until then held in high esteem. Lenin had by now assimilated Plekhanov's conception of 'Narodism', which held that Russia's historical development would be different from that of the West because of its communal peasant institutions. He had already begun to campaign against this Narodism. This was logical, because if Marxists aspired to represent the working class, this was only feasible in a country which had a proletariat, that is, in a capitalist country. Belyakov's memoirs show that while in Samara Lenin was looking for evidence that the commune did not play a major role in the peasant economy and that the Russian agrarian social structure was beginning to show the same class divisions as in the West.[52]

It was while in Samara that Lenin began to correspond with Fedoseev. This was prompted by a polemic between Fedoseev and Mikhailovskii on the pages of the journal *Russkoe bogatstvo* (Russian Wealth) in 1892. This was the occasion on which Mikhailovskii had expressed his indignation that during the great famine of the previous year some Russian Marxists had tried to stop aid being given to the victims on the grounds that this might impede the process of capitalist accumulation. Mikhailovskii went on to deplore the doctrine of 'historical materialism', which left economic processes to take their natural course, despite the suffering this might involve. He recalled that he had criticised Russian Marxists for this attitude some years before, but now he was able to refer to Marx's reply to these criticisms, which had been published in 1885. There Marx had dissociated himself from any general scheme of historical inevitability and denied that for Russia a capitalist stage was obligatory.

Fedoseev had been stung by this criticism of Russian Marxists and had secretly circulated a letter against Mikhailovskii protesting that not all Russian Marxists had been against helping famine victims, though admittedly he knew some who had, and he conceded the foolishness of their position. He himself did not condone the break-up of the peasant economy accompanied by the division of the peasantry into a richer and a poorer stratum, the growth of peasant unemployment, and the spread of hunger and disease among the rural population. Fedoseev thought that measures ought to be taken to halt these processes and to turn the destitute peasants into independent proprietors. Mikhailovskii printed Fedoseev's letter, remarking that there was nothing particularly Marxist about his views and that more typical of Russian Marxism was the insistence that economic progress depended on dispossessing the peasants and turning them into proletarians.[53]

Against the background of the coming campaign of Russian Marxists against 'Narodism', Fedoseev's interchange with Mikhailovskii was a significant one. In it Fedoseev was attempting to show that the differences between himself and Mikhailovskii were not as great as might appear, and that these had their origins in Mikhailovskii's imperfect understanding of the Marxist case. Nevertheless, Lenin was apparently impressed enough with Fedoseev's stance to make contact with him in prison through Fedoseev's fiancée Mariya Hopfenhaus. It was Mariya Hopfenhaus who brought Lenin Fedoseev's extensive dissertation on the reasons for the abolition of serfdom in Russia.[54]

Fedoseev's essay has not survived, but his correspondence of the period is sufficient to show what the character of the work would have been. It was intended as an examination of the causes prompting the 1861 legislation, an analysis of the legislation itself and a consideration of what the consequences of the legislation would have been. In fact, it would have been a project very like the one Marx had embarked upon some twenty years earlier. Moreover, Fedoseev used some of the same sources as Marx had done. Like Marx, he made use of the four-volume collection of documents on the 1861 reform compiled by Alexander Skrebitskii, and he drew heavily on Kovalevskii's researches, just as Marx had done.

Unfortunately, Lenin's comments on Fedoseev's work are not extant, but a good indication of their content is given by Fedoseev's remark in a letter to his friend P. P. Maslov that: 'I do not agree with V. I. on the origins of the commune, and I don't think you will either. On the basis of the facts, few as they are, it seems to me that M. Kovalevskii's hypothesis is more correct than Chicherin's.'[55] The implication is that Lenin had sided with Chicherin in considering the commune to be the creation of the government, against Kovalevskii, who believed the agrarian commune to have evolved organically out of more primitive forms of social organisation. In fact the refusal to recognise the existence of communal relations was to be characteristic of Lenin's own later writings on agrarian matters. It was to become typical of Russian Social Democrats in general, as in the course of their campaign against 'Narodism' they moved away from the position adopted by Fedoseev, and earlier by Marx.

In the summer of 1893 the Ulyanovs left Samara for Moscow. Lenin, however, moved to St Petersburg in order to have greater scope for revolutionary activities. Sasha's friend Ivan Chebotarev had married and now lived with his wife Alexandra in the capital. On moving to St Petersburg Lenin was a frequent guest at the Chebotarevs' home. He made contact with the circle of students, mainly from the St Petersburg Technological Institute, known as the 'elders' (*stariki*) who were the successors to the Brusnev group, with which his brother Alexander and his sister Olga had had connections. The chief organiser of the group was the accomplished conspirator Stepan Radchenko, and its main theoretician was his fellow student at the Institute Herman Krasin. Its membership included three other members of the Institute, Vasily Starkov, Gleb Krzhizhanovskii and Peter Zaporozhets as well as the three young

women teachers at evening and Sunday schools for workers – Olga
Ulyanova's two friends from the Bestuzhev Courses, Zinaida
Nevzorova and Appolinaria Yakubova, and Lenin's future wife
Nadezhda Krupskaya.[56]

As one of its subjects for discussion the group chose to examine
the market question. The topic had an important contemporary
ideological significance, because V. P. Vorontsov, and more recently
Danielson in his book on the Russian economy, had highlighted the
lack of internal and external markets as an obstacle to the development of capitalism in Russia. Lenin acted as discussant to a paper on
the subject by Herman Krasin and impressed the group with a
lengthy refutation of Krasin's ideas, illustrated by mathematical for-
mulae taken from the second volume of Marx's *Das Kapital*.[57] The
version of Lenin's paper published many years later with its precise
definitions and its esoteric terminology conveys what the lure of
Marx's economics would have been for young Russian intellectuals.
One might easily believe that such a paper showed a consummate
mastery of the subject if one did not know that ultimately it was
the product of self-delusion. For the paper could not possibly do
what it set out to do, that is, to demonstrate on the basis of *Das
Kapital*, Volume II that capitalism in Russia would develop through
expanded reproduction. If Marx had been able to do that his
'Critique of Political Economy' would have been published in his lifetime and his researches into the Russian situation would have been
unnecessary.

Encouraged by his friends in the study group, in the spring of
1894 Lenin began to write a critique of Mikhailovskii and other critics of Russian Marxism which was published under the title of *What
the Friends of the People Are and How They Fight against the Social
Democrats*. The three-part essay (of which only two sections are
extant) is written at considerable length. As in Plekhanov's writings,
the tone is sarcastic and concerned with scoring discrete debating
points. Individual statements are taken from the opponent's work
and ridiculed. In this process the overall argument of the opponent
is never expounded and tackled head-on. The work was also meant
to have a positive side, to expound Marx's ideas. But although Lenin
was able to demonstrate considerable erudition in this regard, the
exposition of Marx's ideas was diffuse and piecemeal.

This, however had a certain advantage: two mutually contradic-
tory stages in Marx's thought could be defended within the confines

of a single essay. Thus, in the opening pages of the work Lenin propounded the ideas Marx had elaborated in the 1850s and early 1860s, when he had believed that capitalism must inevitably become a universal system. These ideas included the conception that society should be understood in terms of 'natural laws', of 'historical necessity' and 'determinism'. In this connection Lenin reproduced the famous passage from *A Contribution to the Critique of Political Economy* in which Marx referred to the economic base and the legal and political superstructure of society, and designated the Asiatic, classical, feudal and capitalist modes of production as successive epochs in the economic formation of society.[58]

But some pages later, with Marx's letter of 1877 to *Otechestvennye zapiski* in mind, Lenin denied vehemently that any Marxist had ever regarded Marx's theory as an obligatory philosophical scheme of history. None could, he asserted, because Marx himself had denied having such a scheme. Lenin added that if Mikhailovskii had heard anyone doing so, he should not regard them as proper Marxists.[59] One may surmise that Lenin was not entirely comfortable with Marx's declaration in the letter to *Otechestvennye zapiski*, because although he referred to it on two occasions, on neither of them did he mention that Marx had conceded that a non-capitalist course of development for Russia was possible.

The difficulty for Lenin was that to all appearances Marx had propounded a doctrine of historical necessity and of successive economic formations. This would seem to imply that all countries, Russia included, would pass through the capitalist stage. Marx himself had declared in his preface to *Das Kapital* that: 'The country that is more developed industrially only shows, to the less developed, the image of its own future.'[60] But it was impossible to say that Marx's theory determined a capitalist future for Russia, because it was with regard to Russia that Marx had gone out of his way specifically to deny that he had any such theory. A systematic examination of Marx's ideas would have pointed up this contradiction and seen it as a question to be investigated; but for the requirements of the polemic, both sides of the contradiction were incorporated into the exposition of Marx's ideas regardless.

Since it was impossible to claim, on the basis of Marx's theories, that the development of capitalism in Russia was inevitable, an argument of another order had to be deployed. This was that empirically capitalism *had* developed in Russia. Plekhanov had already argued in this way, and Lenin had determined to follow his example. It was a method that required the painstaking accumulation of statistical evidence, an activity which Lenin had been engaged in since his days in Samara, and which would culminate in the publication of his major work *The Development of Capitalism in Russia*.

Lenin's *What the Friends of the People Are* was circulated in a small hectographed edition, in this way avoiding the problems of getting it past the censor. But the same year saw the legal publication of Peter Struve's *Critical Remarks on Russia's Economic Development*, a book written from a Marxist viewpoint against 'Narodism'. Struve took a completely different approach to Lenin on the question of why capitalism would develop in Russia. Struve had no doubt that Marx did indeed have a 'whole historico-philosophical theory' which embraced '*all possible changes in social forms*, both in the past and in the future'; it was 'a bold attempt to explain the whole historical process from a single principle'.[61] Struve believed that Marx's doctrine still lacked a 'purely philosophical basis', but this was a deficiency that he intended to make good from the works of sociologists and philosophers of his day.[62] Lenin welcomed Struve's attack on Narodism, but he was irritated by Struve's patronising attitude to Marx and Engels and what Lenin considered to be the superficiality of Struve's critique of Narodism. Lenin joined forces with Struve in publishing a collection of articles criticising Narodnik views. His own contribution to the collection, however, a lengthy essay under the pseudonym of 'K. Tulin', was more concerned with demonstrating the alleged errors of Peter Struve than those of his ostensible opponents. The publication was seized by the police and burnt, only 100 copies being saved.

At the end of 1894, Plekhanov's book *The Development of the Monist View of History* was published legally in St Petersburg. This was also a reply to Mikhailovskii's attack on Russian Marxism, as well as an attempt to expound the variety of Marxism predicated on the development of capitalism in Russia. Lenin found himself much more in sympathy with Plekhanov's interpretation of Marx than with Struve's.

In terms of political activity, the lesson Radchenko had derived from the arrests which had destroyed the Brusnev circle in 1891 was that the direction of all socialist propaganda should be in the hands of a highly conspiratorial body consisting exclusively of members of the intelligentsia. This conception was at odds with the doctrine of the Brusnev and all previous Social Democratic groups, that the role of the intellectual revolutionaries was essentially an auxiliary one to the workers' movement, that 'the liberation of the working class was the task of the workers themselves'. To prevent the collapse of the entire organisation if the police should light on one of the workers' study circles, Radchenko's group kept the workers at arm's length. Isolated workers' circles were supervised by an intellectual delegated by a directing centre to which no worker was admitted. The workers for their part had their own separate organisation, the Central Workers' Circle, made up of representatives from the workers' circles in various parts of the city.[63]

At the time Lenin joined the 'elders', dissatisfaction within the Social Democrat organisations was growing with the tactic of 'propaganda', the relatively thorough and long-term teaching of workers in small clandestine study circles. The activity seemed to yield no perceptible development of the Russian labour movement. Social Democrats now aspired to proceed to 'agitation' and induce workers to go on strike by capitalising on the concrete grievances suffered in their workplaces, using the methods so successfully employed in Vilna. Sponti had brought the tactic to Moscow from Vilna in 1894 and in March of the following year he and Kopelzon came to St Petersburg to meet the 'elders' and discuss introducing the Vilna programme in the capital. The tactic would require publications specifically written for workers, and it was decided to send Sponti and Lenin to Geneva to ask Liberation of Labour's assistance in producing this kind of literature. Lenin left St Petersburg on his first trip abroad in April 1895, returning to Russia in September.[64]

Lenin's sojourn in Switzerland, France and Germany allowed him to accomplish a number of objectives. In the course of carrying out his mission to arrange for the production of agitational literature by the Liberation of Labour group he was able to make the acquaintance of the great figures of Russian socialism, including Plekhanov, Paul Akselrod and Vera Zasulich. He also went to introduce himself to Paul Lafargue and Wilhelm Liebknecht. From Plekhanov and Akselrod he was able to gain recognition as a budding Marxist theoretician, presenting each of them with a copy of the book in which his essay on Struve had appeared. Lenin must have received Plekhanov's encouragement to pursue his theoretical writings, since he spent much of his time abroad in the Berlin Imperial Library where, presumably prompted by Plekhanov, he copied out extensive extracts from Marx and Engels's book *The Holy Family*.[65]

When Lenin returned to St Petersburg in September 1895, the 'elders' were being reinforced by the addition of a small group of intellectual revolutionaries headed by Julius Martov, who had just returned from exile in Vilna, where he had co-authored with Alexander Kremer the influential pamphlet *On Agitation*. Guided by the man who was at the very fountainhead of the tactic, the 'elders' were now in an excellent position to carry on agitation among the workers. There was, however, some reluctance among them to implement the tactic, not least from Radchenko himself, who considered that the higher profile it would require would expose the group to discovery by the police. Veterans too of the Central Workers' Circle were apprehensive lest the tactic would lead to the sacrifice of the conspiratorial workers' circles. Younger workers, however, were more enthusiastic because they believed that they would be able to play the part of agitators.[66]

Lenin did nevertheless contribute to writing pamphlets aimed specifically at workers and dealing with their everyday concerns. One of these was *Explanation of the Law on Fines Imposed on Factory Workers*. This work dealt with the law in such a manner that the workers would be able to see the connection between the industrial regulations which oppressed them and the state which had passed the legislation. In this way the workers would be shown the necessity for the political struggle – as the authors of *On Agitation* had envisaged.

In November the 'elders' had an opportunity to put the tactic of agitation into practice when a dispute broke out at the Thornton Woollen Mill about wage rates. The workers themselves wanted to present a petition to the city governor, but the Social Democrats drew up a leaflet which was distributed round the factory. This leaflet and others, as well as pamphlets written and distributed by Lenin and his fellow-members of the group in the factories and working-class districts, visibly increased workers' militancy in St Petersburg.[67] The group's success in this direction, as well as Lenin's trip abroad, attracted the attention of the police. On 8 December Lenin and other members of the 'elders' were arrested and sent to the Remand Prison. After more than fourteen months' imprisonment, on 13 February 1897, Lenin was sentenced to three years' exile in Eastern Siberia.

Prison and exile were common experiences for those who took up the career of revolutionary in tsarist Russia. But in many respects Lenin was an unlikely revolutionary. There was nothing in his family background or upbringing that would have inclined him in that direction. The Ulyanovs were a family that had flourished under the tsarist regime, and the Ulyanov children could look forward to careers which would build on their father's success. After the death of Alexander Ulyanov his sister Anna went over in her mind for many years what it could have been in his early life that had inclined Sasha towards terrorism, but could find nothing of significance. Neither Sasha nor Lenin became revolutionaries through any personal grievance. Sasha became a revolutionary through his sense of loyalty to friends, and Lenin became a revolutionary through his loyalty to his brother.

From the time of Sasha's death Lenin tried to model himself on his brother. He had associated with the same people as Sasha, had read the same books as Sasha, joined the same revolutionary organisations as Sasha. He could not be a terrorist like Sasha, because the revolutionary organisations that he joined had rejected terrorism, largely as a result of Sasha's unsuccessful attempt. It cannot be any coincidence that Lenin took the same approach to the future of the Russian economy as Sasha had as conveyed to him by Chebotarev, Elizarov and Bartenev. He knew that Sasha had been impressed by Plekhanov's arguments and that he shared Plekhanov's views on the imminent disintegration of the peasant commune and the prospective development of capitalism in Russia. Lenin's first major theoretical work, his study of the development of capitalism in Russia, would adopt these views and give them a polemical edge.

2

A PARTY OF A NEW TYPE

The development of capitalism in Russia

Lenin was in prison when in July 1896 30 000 St Petersburg textile
workers went on strike. The 'elders' helped the strikers by printing
and distributing leaflets for them. For her part in this activity
Krupskaya was arrested and imprisoned. In May of 1897 Lenin
arrived at his place of Siberian exile, the village of Shushenskoe in
the Minusinsk district of the Enisei province. Krupskaya, who had
been sentenced to three years' exile in the Ufa province, requested a
transfer to Shushenskoe, describing herself for this purpose as
Lenin's fiancée. The permission was given on condition that the
marriage take place immediately after Krupskaya's arrival in
Shushenskoe. Lenin and Krupskaya were duly married on 10 July
1898 in the local church.[1]

Even while in prison in 1896 Lenin had begun working on the
book that would eventually be published as *The Development of
Capitalism in Russia* in 1899. It is significant that the first person to
whom he turned for materials was Chebotarev, the person who had
preserved Alexander Ulyanov's notes on the subject.[2] In exile in
Shushenskoe work on the book was to be Lenin's main intellectual
activity. His sister Anna Elizarova was kept busy sending him statistical materials and other books he needed for his research.

The way Lenin went about investigating the development of capitalism in Russia was strikingly different in scope from that of his predecessors. The parameters of both Marx's and Fedoseev's studies
had been much broader. It had seemed to both Marx and Fedoseev
that the subject had three interrelated aspects. These were the

character of the peasant commune, the provisions of the 1861 Reform and Russia's post-Reform economic development. This scheme revealed the dynamic of Russia's economic development within its social context, investigating whether the peasant commune was being fragmented as market relations replaced attitudes of social solidarity and cooperation.

On the grounds of making the subject more manageable, Lenin set out in the Preface four limitations which determined the parameters for his study: (1) the question of the development of capitalism in Russia was treated from the standpoint of the home market, leaving aside the problem of the foreign market and data on foreign trade; (2) the study was restricted entirely to the post-Reform period; (3) almost exclusively the interior, purely Russian, provinces of Russia were covered; (4) only the economic aspect of the subject was investigated.[3] These limitations, when stated in the Preface, no doubt sounded reasonable enough, to be explained by the caution of a writer anxious to keep his project within feasible bounds. But in fact they are used to justify an approach which skews the study in the direction Lenin desired.

The Development of Capitalism in Russia consists of three main sections. The first is a theoretical section in which Lenin attempts to show that Russia is a capitalist country in Marx's sense of the term. In particular he argues that a home market has been created for Russian commodities. The second section deals with the differentiation of the peasantry, and is an attempt to demonstrate that the inequalities among peasant families are leading to the formation of a peasant bourgeoisie on the one hand and a peasant proletariat on the other. The third section is concerned with Russian industry, and surveys the three main types of industry to be found in Russia at the end of the nineteenth century. These are handicraft industries, manufacture industries, in which workers are brought together within a single establishment, and modern machine industry, where division of labour has taken place and industry has finally become separated from agriculture. The conclusion is that Russia has become a capitalist country, though one which is relatively little advanced.

Because the timescale is restricted to the post-Reform period, Lenin's presentation of the Russian economy has the character of a snapshot. There is very little indication in it of temporal sequence, of what has always been there and what is new. Thus, when Lenin presents his reader with statistical tables showing inequalities among peasant families, the implication is that this inequality is a new phenomenon. But there are no data to show this is the case; there are no corresponding tables demonstrating that at a certain point of time in the past there had been greater equality among peasant families. In any case it would have been surprising if such equality had existed because the periodic redivisions of land within peasant communes presupposed an inequality among families.

As regards Russian industry, one might easily believe that Lenin's depiction of handicraft, manufacture and machine industry was a historical progression of types. In fact, all of these forms of industry existed simultaneously when Lenin was writing, and Russian industry was still overwhelmingly small-scale handicraft industry. If one supplies the historical dimension to Lenin's description of Russian industry, by comparing it with say Tengoborski's *Commentaries on the Productive forces of Russia* published in 1856,[4] it would appear that not a great deal had changed in the post-Reform era. The same categories of industrial undertaking, for example, can be found.

The inclusion of a historical perspective would have raised an insoluble question for Lenin. It is that since many of the phenomena he classifies as capitalist can be found in pre-Reform Russia, for example, the production of goods for sale, it requires Lenin to determine at which point these phenomena acquired a capitalist character. In the case of the production of articles for sale it requires Lenin to say when and why these goods took on the character of commodities. This was a conundrum Marx had avoided by restricting his investigation to societies in which the capitalist mode of production prevailed. This, however, was not a solution that Lenin could adopt.

Lenin's approach to the question is legalistic. It was sufficient for his purposes to show that the economic categories which Marx had used in his analysis of the capitalist system could be applied to Russia. Thus, all economic phenomena are interpreted as manifestations of capitalism; in particular all goods produced for sale are regarded as commodities. What is missing is some criterion for judging whether goods are or are not commodities. It is missing for good reason. The criterion of commodity production would be the context in which it occurred. Goods produced for sale would be commodities if production for the market were generalised, if commodity production were the system which prevailed. But at the time Lenin was writing not even he would have maintained that capitalism was the predominant economic system in Russia.

Lenin also focused his study on the question of the home market for polemical purposes, believing that on this question his opponents were particularly vulnerable. But the focus on exclusively internal economic developments had a bizarre consequence. It was that the question of foreign investment in Russia was left out of the reckoning almost entirely. In the whole lengthy work only two sentences refer to foreign capital. *The Development of Capitalism in Russia*, moreover, was written and published while Sergei Witte was Minister of Finance and when foreign investment was being encouraged by government policy. For Lenin to have discussed the question of foreign investment, and the tariff policy which encouraged it at any length, would have meant conceding his opponents' case that the development of capitalism in Russia was artificially stimulated. Vorontsov in *The Fate of Capitalism in Russia*, for example, had given the question of foreign investment in Russia considerable prominence.[5] By avoiding mention of foreign investment, however, Lenin ignored one of the main sources of capitalist development in Russia at the time, and underestimated the amount of modern machine industry in Russia, because that machine industry originated outside the country.

The most significant of all the limitations that Lenin mentioned in his Preface was the intention to deal 'exclusively with the economic aspect of the process'. This looked innocuous enough, because Lenin did not spell out what it was that he was excluding by this particular restriction. By classifying the commune as a social or ethnographic phenomenon, it could be left out of all consideration of the treatment of the peasantry. This means that the commune, its dynamics, or how communal life influenced the economic situation of the peasantry in the post-Reform era, is not discussed. From reading Lenin's book one would never guess that most Russian peasants continued to live in village communities.[6]

Lenin's manoeuvre begs the question of capitalist relations in Russia, for it is tantamount to a refusal to recognise the existence of social institutions in which cooperation, mutual aid and the pooling of resources take place. By a stroke of a pen Lenin, for purposes of his book, has abolished the peasant communes and has put atomised civil society in their place. The implication is that the structure of Russian society corresponds exactly to the statistical tables of land-ownership, horse-ownership and agricultural implement ownership which give such a scientific appearance to Lenin's argument. But the presupposition of these tables is that every proprietor of a horse, a plough, a morsel of food, cleaves to their piece of property and resolutely refuses to share it with any living soul. One is required to believe that no borrowing or lending, no cooperation or pooling of resources takes place. But it was precisely mutual aid that was the characteristic feature of peasant life in the agrarian village communities.

Lenin's notes for *The Development of Capitalism in Russia* show that he was unwilling to countenance the possibility that life in village communities might be any less egotistical than elsewhere. One of the authors Lenin consulted, S. Kapustin, had pointed out that commune members ploughed or harvested the land of those who were unable to do so themselves, provided horses for those who had none of their own, paid taxes for those who had become impoverished, took care of orphans and so on. In contrasting urban and rural society, Kapustin remarked that 'among us nobody considers it his duty, for example, to feed the hungry and shelter the homeless'. Lenin in a marginal note enquired: 'And is it any different in the peasant commune? Where are the facts?'[7] The facts were in almost every work written on the peasant commune from Haxthausen's onwards, none of which were cited in Lenin's book.

The Development of Capitalism in Russia has been called the fullest, best-documented and best-argued examination of the crucial period of the evolution of capitalism out of feudalism in the literature of Marxism.[8] In relative terms, this might well be the case, since there are rather few works of that particular genre. But in absolute terms it is a highly misleading work. It is a very poor guide to the social and economic situation in Russia at the time. It also gives a false idea of what Danielson and Vorontsov were arguing and from what standpoint. It does not address squarely the problems they raised.

It is interesting to note that when Marx had examined the question of how capitalism developed in Russia in the 1870s, he had approached it in quite a different way. For Marx the question of how capitalism originated was identical to the question of how capital began to circulate. This involved establishing all the links in the chain which made the circuits of capital possible. He found that the links included the taxation policy of the government which on the one hand ruined the poorer peasants and on the other provided funds with which the exchequer financed the railway companies. Marx had been assisted in his studies of the Russian economy by Nikolai Danielson who had supplied him with the necessary statistical materials, and who had himself worked on the problem of capital circulation in Russia. Marx in fact had summarised Danielson's findings and incorporated them into his own manuscripts.[9] When Danielson and Vorontsov later published studies of the Russian economy which stressed the part played by the Russian government in fostering capitalism in the country, this was condemned by Lenin as being characteristic of Narodnik ideology. Essentially Lenin was using one part of Marx's intellectual heritage to try to refute another.

An essential element in the development of capitalism for Marx was the dissolution of traditional social bonds and their replacement by civil society, the fragmented aggregate of atomised individuals, and the subsequent grouping of these individuals into antagonistic classes. This dimension is absent from Lenin's thinking entirely. There is no investigation of whether and in what ways economic development in the post-Reform era has eroded the social cohesion that characterised peasant village life. Lenin never recognised that such social cohesion existed. For Lenin, the characteristic of capitalism is not the growth of individualism, but the stratification of peasant society. The bulk of *The Development of Capitalism in Russia* consists of commentaries on tables of statistics showing the distribution of land, livestock and other resources between peasant families in various parts of the country. These purport to show the emergence on the one hand of a wealthy group of peasants destined to form an agrarian bourgeoisie and on the other of a stratum of poor peasants, well on the way to becoming the proletariat. Marx had noted the emergence of differences in economic status among the Russian peasantry, but he had not regarded this as central to the problem of how capital began to circulate in the country.

'Economism'

While Lenin was in prison and Siberian exile important developments were taking place in the revolutionary movement in European Russia. After the arrest of the 'elders', Martov and the surviving members of the group put out a defiant leaflet to create the impression that the organisation was still viable. To enhance the impact of the leaflet Martov issued it in the name of the 'Union of Struggle for the Liberation of the Working Class', the name by which the group was subsequently to be known.[10] At the beginning of January, however, a second wave of arrests took place, carrying off Martov and many of the Social Democrats still at liberty as well as most of the Central Workers' Circle. The Union of Struggle was now reduced to the great survivor Radchenko and a sprinkling of elders and members of Martov's group. It was precisely at this time that the strike movement in St Petersburg reached unprecedented heights. In May of 1896 a strike of textile workers spread to several factories in the industry and reached a scale that signalled to the rest of Europe that the workers' movement in Russia had come of age.[11]

The depleted Union of Struggle worked hectically along with other revolutionary groups in St Petersburg to issue leaflets to advise and encourage the textile workers in their dispute with the employers. But it was too small and weak to direct the entire movement. The leadership of the strike was largely in the hands of the workers themselves; factories set up their own strike funds. After the strike had collapsed two of the St Petersburg social democratic groups merged with the Union of Struggle. These were the so-called 'youngsters' (*molodye*), who had from the outset shown more enthusiasm for the tactic of agitation than had the elders, and the small group led by Konstantin Takhtarev, the future husband of Appolinaria Yakubova and the author of detailed memoirs of the period. Takhtarev and his friends followed the traditional doctrine of Russian Social Democrats that the role of intellectual revolutionaries was to be auxiliaries to the workers' movement, that the liberation of the working class should remain the affair of the workers themselves.

According to Takhtarev, it was during the strike that the existing relationships between the controlling group of intelligentsia in the Union of Struggle and the Central Workers' Circle came under strain. The workers' leaders who had shown such organisational flair during the strike were no longer content to submit to the direction of the intellectuals in the Union of Struggle, but wished themselves to join the Union's central group. The demands of the workers' leaders plunged the Union into dispute. Some, like Radchenko, insisted that things should remain as before and that the central group should consist only of intellectuals. Others, including Takhtarev and Yakubova, were convinced that in order to retain its credibility the Union of Struggle had to reckon with the presence of an advanced stratum of workers which was capable and willing to take its place in the most responsible positions in the Union of Struggle. They believed that such aspirations should not be thwarted.[12]

These discussions were still rumbling on when Lenin had the opportunity to have a brief meeting with the members of the Union of Struggle in February 1897. Before being sent to Siberia, Lenin, along with other elders and Martov, was allowed three days' grace to put his affairs in order. The encounter with the Union of Struggle, as it was now constituted was not entirely amicable, and was to leave Lenin with a lasting sense of irritation.

Lenin, Martov and the elders arrested during the previous winter all took the side of Radchenko and opposed admitting workers to the Union of Struggle's central group. In the absence of Takhtarev, Yakubova valiantly put the case for the other side, insisting that it was absurd to draw a distinction between a worker and a revolutionary. In the event it was decided at the end of February to admit two worker representatives to the Union's central group, but a wave of arrests occasioned by the renewal of the strike movement the previous month removed Yakubova and other supporters of workers' participation from the scene, and the old order of things was restored in the Union of Struggle. Frustrated in their aspirations, some of the workers' leaders bent their efforts to publishing a newspaper, *Rabochaya mysl* (Workers' Thought),[13] whose defence of workers' autonomy and disdain for the intelligentsia were to be a target for the most biting of Lenin's sarcasm in the pamphlet *What Is To Be Done?*

The controversy which had racked the Union of Struggle had its counterpart in the debates which engulfed the *émigré* Liberation of Labour group, as a rising generation of Russian Marxists began to challenge the preeminence in the Russian Social Democratic movement that Plekhanov and Akselrod had hitherto enjoyed. The challenge was a serious one, because it came from experienced revolutionaries who had been involved in workers' circles and who were capable of providing the Liberation of Labour group with links to the Social Democratic movement within Russia. The practical perspective of these 'youngsters' tended to make them impatient with the Liberation of Labour's preoccupation with theoretical questions. For while these might be of consuming interest to intellectuals, they had little relevance for the real workers' movement. In the opinion of the 'youngsters' it would be much more useful if the group published literature designed specially for workers to read, as had been done so successfully by the Polish socialists. The 'youngsters' also believed that the activity of Social Democrats ought to be channelled in a direction which had a bearing on the genuine needs and concerns of the workers.

The 'youngsters', who formed the majority of the Union of Russian Social Democrats Abroad founded in 1895, included such people as Kopelzon from the Gnatowski group in Vilna, B. N. Krichevskii, V. P. Akimov and V. P. Ivanshin, P. F. Teplov, S. N. Prokopovich and his wife E. D. Kuskova. The Liberation of Labour group undertook to edit and publish revolutionary literature on behalf of the Union of Russian Social Democrats Abroad, and among these was the essay *On Agitation* which was circulating in Russia at that time in manuscript. The Liberation of Labour group published it in 1896, Akselrod, however, adding a preface and a postscript in which he defended Liberation of Labour from the criticisms of it contained in the pamphlet. He said that the issues raised by the authors of *On Agitation* were by no means new, and went back to debates on tactics which had taken place in the 'going to the people' movement of the 1870s.[14] By November 1898 tensions between Liberation of Labour and the 'youngsters' had reached such intensity that at the First Congress of the Union of Social Democrats Abroad the Liberation of Labour group left the organisation and refused to edit or publish anything more for the Union. In consequence the 'youngsters' themselves began to publish the newspaper *Rabochee delo*, whose editors were Krichevskii, Ivanshin and Teplov.[15]

These developments were the background against which Plekhanov and Akselrod launched their campaign against the 'youngsters' at the end of the 1890s. It was a campaign to reassert the authority of the veterans and was carried on as a struggle against 'Economism'. It bore striking parallels to the campaign against Narodism that Plekhanov had conducted in the previous decade. Just as nobody (except Vorontsov) had admitted to being a 'Narodnik', so nobody admitted to being an Economist and espousing the kind of doctrines that Plekhanov and Akselrod attributed to them. Moreover, the Economists were not criticised for any actual wrong actions or activities. It was their public and private utterances that were scrutinised for propositions that could be represented as showing that their views on the workers' movement would cause that movement to go in the wrong direction. The assumption was (despite abundant recent evidence to the contrary) that the views held by intellectual revolutionaries could determine the course the workers' movement took.

The veterans' offensive against the 'youngsters' was launched by Akselrod in a pamphlet entitled *On the Question of the Present Tasks and Tactics of the Russian Social Democrats* published in 1898. In it Akselrod elaborated on his objections to the tactic of agitation, and in so doing voiced for the first time some of the key ideological points on which the anti-Economist case would be based. It rested on emphasising the limitations of the tactic of agitation, namely that it 'revolved almost entirely round the direct economic exploitation of the workers by the employers'; it was a confrontation devoid of political character. It did not involve the struggle to overthrow the autocratic regime. Certainly, the authors of *On Agitation* had argued that the tactic would eventually lead in that direction but, Akselrod maintained, there was nothing to indicate that this would necessarily be the case. Similarly, the contention that through the pursuit of the economic struggle the workers gradually acquire the consciousness of a social ideal Akselrod found unconvincing on the evidence of the history of the workers' movement in Western countries. He believed that ideals of this kind had to be supplied by those members of the intelligentsia who were sympathetic to the proletariat's cause.[16]

The idea that the workers' movement on its own could go no further than the struggle for economic aims, and that an awareness of socialist objectives had to be supplied by the radical intelligentsia, was a doctrine of Akselrod's invention. It cannot be said, as some writers have claimed, to belong to 'Marxist orthodoxy'. Indeed, it represented something of a revolution in the thinking of the Liberation of Labour group itself. In 1889 Vera Zasulich had written a pamphlet entitled *Studies in the History of the International Working Men's Association* which discussed Marx's conception of how the workers' movement ought to be organised. In speaking of the circumstances in which the constitution of the International was drawn up at the inaugural meeting in 1864, Zasulich recounted how the supporters of both Blanqui and Mazzini had favoured some kind of centralised and conspiratorial organisation. Marx, on the other hand, was against this proposal, predictably so, Zasulich thought, because much earlier, in the *Communist Manifesto*, he had already enunciated the principle that the communists 'had no interests separate from those of the proletariat as a whole'. They did not 'set up any sectarian principles of their own by which to shape and mould the proletarian movement'. It was, therefore, Zasulich believed, entirely consistent that Marx should draft a constitution for the International embodying the principle that 'the liberation of the working classes must be achieved by the working classes themselves'.[17] This pamphlet had been published by the Liberation of Labour group, which seemed to find Zasulich's views uncontroversial at that time. Apparently, the group's opinion had altered to meet the needs of the power struggle in hand.

When Martov read Akselrod's pamphlet in his Siberian exile he was at first inclined to compose a refutation of it. Lenin, however, wrote to caution him against such an action, since he had heard that in St Petersburg some of the young activists were interpreting the tasks of the Social Democrats in a strange way, that in some issues of *Rabochaya mysl* there was a tendency to play down the political struggle, and that in Geneva the young *émigrés* (including Takhtarev) were conducting a systematic campaign against the Liberation of Labour group. These tidings taken together sounded ominous to Lenin, and he advised Martov against entering the fray until the picture had become clearer.[18]

In emigration in Berlin S. N. Prokopovich did answer Akselrod's pamphlet in a serious investigation of the kind of contribution the Social Democrats could make to the workers' movement in Russia. The principle Prokopovich set out to uphold was the idea that the 'liberation of the working classes must be achieved by the working classes themselves'. This was a formula, he argued, which presupposed initiative among the workers and an understanding of their own needs and objectives. Akselrod, on the other hand, refused to countenance the fact that the workers possessed any consciousness and initiative, and believed that this had to be supplied by people like himself. Seemingly, the Liberation of Labour group had determined *a priori* what the objective of the revolution should be: the overthrow of the autocracy. The proletariat would serve as the means by which this objective was to be achieved.

Prokopovich thought it essential to distinguish between the interests the intelligentsia attributed to the workers and the interests which the workers actually had. The consciousness of the workers was not a dough which the intellectuals could mould according to their own image and liking. Intellectuals could only supplement what the workers learnt from their own experience. The workers, moreover, were quite capable of initiative to further their interests without any contribution from the intellectuals, as the summer strike in St Petersburg in 1896 had shown. So far there had been no instance of the workers demanding political rights. This, Prokopovich thought, was not surprising as no one had suggested any means by which the workers might struggle against the autocratic state. Political activity would be possible only when an arena for this kind of struggle had been created, when, for example, there were elections to contest. This led Prokopovich to the generalisation that the freer a country was the sooner the workers' movement would become political; the more despotic the country, the longer the workers' movement within it would be deprived of a political character.[19]

In Prokopovich's view Akselrod had a highly unrealistic conception of what a political revolution would involve. He seemed to envisage it as a handful of energetic revolutionaries at the head of a few thousand St Petersburg workers overthrowing the autocracy. Prokopovich thought that the workers' political campaign against the autocracy would arise as an autonomous movement in the same manner as the mass economic strikes had emerged in St Petersburg in 1896, without the direct involvement of the intelligentsia. It would be pointless, Prokopovich thought, for the Social Democrats to impose political agitation on an unreceptive workers' movement. His conclusion was, therefore: 'The interests of the Russian revolution itself compel us for the time being to limit ourselves to political propaganda, avoiding political agitation at all costs.'[20]

Plekhanov was infuriated by Prokopovich's ideas, and with his anathema ringing in their ears Prokopovich and his wife E. D. Kuskova returned to Russia. In St Petersburg Kuskova continued to argue with the 'orthodox' Social Democrats of Plekhanov's persuasion. Following one debate she was requested to set down her ideas so that her adversaries might be able to refute them more effectively. This she did in a short note which summarised in a shorthand fashion the arguments that Prokopovich had put forward in his reply to Akselrod.

In the note Kuskova argued that there were important differences between the way the workers' movement had developed in Western countries and the way it had developed in Russia. In the West the freedom to engage in political activities had been won by the liberals before the workers' movement had emerged, and as a result the workers had been able to engage in the political struggle with relative ease, though it proved much more difficult to pursue the economic struggle. The political struggle had now been pushed to its limits, and the resulting dilemma of how to proceed further had manifested itself in Bernstein's revisionism in Germany. In Russia, on the other hand, the oppressive regime had precluded political activity by the workers' movement. But, while extremely difficult, it was at least possible to wage the economic struggle, and by doing so, the Russian workers would come into collision with the political regime and would eventually create forms of organisation best suited to Russian conditions. Russian Marxists, therefore, should not borrow patterns of behaviour imported from abroad, but should participate in the economic struggle of the proletariat and should cooperate with the liberal oppositionist campaign to extend the sphere for political action.[21]

The position of the 'youngsters' was strengthened by the First Congress of the Russian Social Democratic Party. At the beginning of March 1898 on the initiative of the Kievan Social Democrats nine delegates from six organisations met in Minsk to unite all the Social Democratic organisations in Russia into a single Social Democratic party. There was one delegate from the St Petersburg, Moscow, Kiev and Ekaterinoslav Unions of Struggle, two from the group attached to the newspaper *Rabochaya gazeta*, and three from the Bund. There was considerable debate about what the name of the party should be. The name chosen was the Russian Social Democratic Party, the word 'Russian' in the title being '*rossiyskaya*' rather than '*russkaya*' to reflect the multinational character of the organisation.

As regards the way the party was to be organised the congress agreed with the Bund's delegates that this organisation should be allowed to enter the party as an autonomous organisation. It also accepted the autonomy of the local party committees, allowing them to carry out the directives of the Central Committee in the form most appropriate to local conditions. In exceptional circumstances the local committees would be permitted to disregard the Central Committee's decisions entirely if good cause for doing so could be shown.

The congress elected a three-man Central Committee and recognised the Union of Social Democrats Abroad as a constituent institution of the party, designating it as the body to represent the party outside Russia. It was agreed that *Rabochaya gazeta* should be the party's official newspaper. No party programme was drawn up, but Peter Struve was commissioned to write the new party's manifesto. When this appeared Struve inserted the word 'Workers'' into the party's title, which was then accepted without protest. Soon after the congress, however, five of the nine delegates were arrested. This was quickly followed by the arrest of the entire Central Committee. The Kiev Union of Struggle and the editorial board of *Rabochaya gazeta* also fell victim to the tsarist police.[22]

In the spring of 1899 Lenin's sister Anna travelled to St Petersburg to make arrangements for the publication of Lenin's book *The Development of Capitalism in Russia*. To this end she visited the book-shop run by Alexandra Kalmykova, a wealthy patroness of the Union of Struggle, and there acquired a short manuscript document dis-cussing the role of the Social Democrats and the workers' movement drawn up by Prokopovich and Kuskova. Kalmykova explained that although the authors were not themselves active revolutionaries, they enjoyed a certain influence among the 'youngsters'. Anna Elizarova duly transcribed the document into code and sent it on to her brother in Siberia. To avoid lengthy explanations that would have to be laboriously transcribed into code, she simply stated: 'I am sending you some "Credo" of the "youngsters"', though she did not believe that it actually provided guidance for any Social Democrats. Anna was therefore perplexed when her brother on receipt of this laconic message took it literally and assumed that what he had been sent was in fact a programmatic statement of the young activists of the St Petersburg Union of Struggle.[23]

Kuskova's document was a godsend to Lenin, because it was the nearest thing anyone had seen to an explicit statement of Eco-nomism. It had this character because of the accidental circumstance that no care had been taken to arrange the ideas in it in the system-atic and logical sequence needed to address a sceptical or hostile readership. According to his companion in exile Lepeshinskii, when Lenin received the copy of 'Credo' he became as agitated as a hunter in the presence of very big game. He composed a draft protest against it, and, to make the protest a collective one, he called a meet-ing of the local Social Democrats in exile. At the meeting Lenin claimed that the 'Credo' was very symptomatic, that it could not be ignored, and that Economism was in danger of weakening Social Democracy. After some discussion, the text of the protest was finalised and signed by the seventeen Social Democrats present at the meeting.[24]

The Protest contested Kuskova's interpretation of the history of the Western European labour movement and compared her presen-tation of Marxism to Bernstein's revisionism in the German Social

Democratic Party. It was alleged that the policies Kuskova advocated confirmed Akselrod's fears that the workers' movement might be confined to narrow economic channels, while those workers who desired political liberty would have no choice but to look to the liberal intelligentsia for leadership.[25]

The Protest was sent abroad and printed along with the 'Credo' in the newspaper of the Union of Russian Social Democrats Abroad *Rabochee delo* in October. Plekhanov and Akselrod were elated by the appearance of the Protest and referred to it in the circular in which they announced the resumption of the Liberation of Labour's own publications and their declaration of war on the Economist heresy.[26] On the subject of the 'Credo' the editors of *Rabochee delo* added a note saying that they welcomed the robust protest against the views set out in the 'Credo', but were convinced that this 'symbol of faith' was no more than the opinion of individual persons and only reflected the muddle in the heads of its authors.[27]

In order to show that this was not the case, Plekhanov compiled a volume of materials beginning with the 'Credo' and its accompanying Protest and followed by unpublished writings of Prokopovich, Kuskova and Kopelzon, including some of their private correspondence with Akselrod. The collection included Prokopovich's reply to Akselrod's pamphlet which he had not wished to be published.[28] The sequence of documents in the *Vademecum* caused this reasoned argument to be discredited by its summary in Kuskova's 'Credo'. The publication of Plekhanov's *Vademecum* in February 1900 raised the intensity of the conflict between Liberation of Labour and the 'youngsters'.

What Is To Be Done?

Lenin's term of exile ended on 29 January 1900. He settled in Pskov, as he was barred from living in the capital or major university or industrial towns. There he intended to finalise his plans for an all-Russian newspaper to act as the ideological and organisational centre for a political party. In Pskov Lenin met up with Radchenko and A. N. Potresov. He also discovered that he had competition in the attempt to revive the fortunes of the Social Democratic Party. There existed a plan for the immediate convocation of the Second Congress of the party emanating from the Union of Russian Social

Democrats Abroad, supported by the Bund and the *Yuzhnii rabochii* group. Two delegates from the Union, I. F. Teplov and Kopelzon, visited Lenin in Pskov in this connection.

Lenin could have had little sympathy for the preparations for an immediate convocation of the Second Congress. The Second Congress that he envisaged would be one which would undo a great deal of what had been decided by the First Congress and approve his own ideas for party organisation, once the ground for these had been suitably prepared by the circulation of the all-Russian newspaper. Moreover, an immediate Second Congress would have the effect of consolidating the influence of the 'youngsters' in the party, the group whose conception of party organisation was the opposite of his own. Lenin's tactical interests would be best served by backing the Liberation of Labour group against the 'youngsters', or, as the sides were now coming to be designated, the 'orthodox' against the 'Economists'. Lenin, however, was able to gain time, because in April mass arrests throughout the south of Russia and in the area of the Bund took place. Many members of *Yuzhnii rabochii* were arrested. As a result on the appointed day of the Second Congress only three delegates appeared in Smolensk. Having waited for a few days in case more delegates turned up, they dispersed.[29]

In making preparations in Pskov for going abroad Lenin feared that the tsarist authorities might refuse to issue him with a foreign passport. In getting round this potential difficulty he was aided by Krupskaya's friends Sergei Lenin and his sister Olga. Sergei Lenin managed to obtain the passport of his father, Nikolai Egorovich Lenin, who at that time was terminally ill. The passport was altered to conform to the description of its new holder. As it happened, the precaution was unnecessary, because the Governor of Pskov duly issued Lenin with a legitimate passport in his own name. Nevertheless, the acquisition of a false passport provided him with the pseudonym with which he has gone down in history.[30]

At the end of August, Lenin, Martov and Potresov held negotiations at Corsier near Geneva with Plekhanov and other members of the Liberation of Labour group on the publication of the newspaper *Iskra* (The Spark). These talks were extremely difficult because of Plekhanov's arrogant and suspicious character. It was finally decided, however, that the editorial board of *Iskra* should consist of three members from Lenin's group – Lenin, Martov and Potresov – and three from the Liberation of Labour group – Plekhanov, Akselrod and Zasulich. The first number of *Iskra* was published in Munich in December 1900.[31]

On the ideological plane *Iskra* continued the campaign against Economism, Lenin, Martov and Potresov making common cause with the Liberation of Labour group against the 'youngsters'. As a political newspaper it was spectacularly successful, soon overshadowing that of the 'youngsters', *Rabochee delo*, and becoming an authoritative voice in Social Democratic circles inside Russia. The two publications did not differ greatly in the type of items they carried: correspondence from the localities, a chronicle of the workers' movement, reports from non-Russian social democratic groups and developments in the German and other Social Democratic parties abroad. The difference was that *Iskra* was able to give a much fuller coverage of such items and with greater regularity. *Iskra* also carried out its organisational role through a network of agents who distributed the newspaper throughout the country. The intention of its editors was to try as far as possible to make all the local groups supporters of *Iskra*. This objective was not attained because *Iskra* encountered resistance from rivals such as *Yuzhnii rabochii* in the Ukraine, which had a strong local following, and from the Bund with its Yiddish-language newspapers. Nevertheless, *Iskra*'s success in winning over local organisations to its point of view was appreciable, and put the supporters of *Iskra* in a strong position to dominate the forthcoming Second Congress of the Social Democratic Party.

In articles published in *Iskra* Lenin broached the question of how the Social Democratic Party ought to be organised. Although the party had been launched at its First Congress in 1898 it was still only coming into being, and it still did not have a party programme. Drafts of the programme were at that time still being hotly debated by the *Iskra* editorial board. In this state of flux it was possible for Lenin to exercise a profound influence on the future orientation of the party and on the way it would be structured. This was the context in which he wrote his famous pamphlet *What Is To Be Done?* which was published in Stuttgart in March 1902, under his new pseudonym 'N. Lenin'.

Though it claims to have been written in some haste, *What Is To Be Done?* has a sophisticated structure that must have required careful planning on the part of its author. Of its five chapters the first three are devoted to the polemic against Economism. Ostensibly, the fourth continues this polemic at a deeper level, being concerned with combating 'Amateurism' (*kustarnichestvo*) in party organisation, the contention being that Economism was but one manifestation of Amateurism. But in reality the chapter on Amateurism has no necessary connection with what has gone before, and could constitute a separate work. It is in this chapter that Lenin elaborates his characteristic ideas on how a revolutionary party should be constructed. The final chapter discusses the role of a newspaper in the party's organisational structure. *What Is To Be Done?* can be thought of as having two main sections, one against Economism and one against Amateurism. Whereas the section on Economism went over ground that had been well-trodden by Akselrod and Plekhanov before and could be expected to seem uncontroversial to them, the section on Amateurism had some original and rather radical ideas with far-reaching implications. This potentially controversial section was strategically placed after the chapters that were less likely to arouse contention.

On the face of it the first chapter, 'Dogmatism and "Freedom of Criticism"', seems to approach the Economist issue in an indirect way by discussing the question of freedom of criticism. But in the context of the entire work the first chapter is one which subtly foreshadows the conception of the party in Chapter 4 and in this way helps tie the two sections together. In Lenin's view a Social Democratic party cannot countenance the freedom of its members to indulge in questioning the principles on which it is based, as Kuskova had done. That in practice meant 'the freedom to convert social democracy into a democratic party of reform, the freedom to introduce bourgeois ideas and bourgeois elements into socialism'. The example of Bernstein's revisionism in the German Social Democratic Party was held up as the kind of undesirable result of adhering to the principle of 'freedom of criticism'. People joined the party on a purely voluntary basis, and if they disagreed with its basic principles, there was nothing to prevent their leaving it and going elsewhere. This had been Plekhanov's attitude both to Bernstein and to Prokopovich. He believed that both men should have been expelled from their respective organisations. The prime example Lenin had of unacceptable criticism was Kuskova's 'Credo', and this, it was suggested, represented the real views of the entire Economist current. Its content was paraphrased as: 'let the workers have the economic struggle and leave the political struggle to the liberals' – something Kuskova did not say.

By developing the case against 'freedom of criticism' Lenin was able to equate Economism with revisionism, using references to Bernstein to discredit his opponents. He also used the occasion to suggest that the party organisation of the Social Democrats could not be democratic, and that the ideological foundations on which the party was based were all-important. Lenin then went on to stress the importance of theory for the party, laying down the maxim that 'Without revolutionary theory there can be no revolutionary movement'.[32]

The second chapter of Lenin's pamphlet, 'The Spontaneity of the Masses and the Consciousness of the Social-Democrats', contains an account of the workers' movement in St Petersburg remarkable for the effrontery of its distorted presentation. The undisputed facts of the matter were that after the arrest of Lenin and his associates in December 1896 the Union of Struggle had continued to produce agitational leaflets for the workers; that the strike movement had reached unprecedented heights; and that the textile workers had shown extraordinary initiative and independence in the conduct of the strikes. Lenin, however, discounted these strikes as being 'simply trade-union struggles, but not yet Social-Democratic struggles'.[33] The arrest of Lenin and his associates and their replacement by other veterans of Radchenko's group such as Yakubova as well as new recruits was depicted by Lenin as the substitution of orthodox Social Democrats by a young generation of 'Economists'. As Lenin put it: 'The overwhelming of consciousness by spontaneity... occurred because an increasing number of "veteran" revolutionaries were "torn away" by the gendarmes and because increasing numbers of "youngsters" appeared on the scene.' These 'youngsters' then began to collaborate on *Rabochaya mysl*, which set about unconsciously carrying out the programme of the 'Credo'.[34] This stylised version of events was contested by Yakubova and Takhtarev soon after the appearance of *What Is To Be Done?*[35] The function of this version, as well as belittling the significance of the St Petersburg strikes and the activities of the Union of Struggle after 1895, was to create the impression that the opposition of the 'youngsters' to Plekhanov in Geneva and to Lenin in St Petersburg formed part of the same phenomenon – the emergence of revisionism in Russian Social Democracy.

The error of the Economists, Lenin contended, was that they bowed to the spontaneity of the workers' movement; they followed rather than led the workers. But the workers themselves could never attain a Social Democratic consciousness; they could only develop a trade union consciousness and struggle to improve their own economic situation. A socialist consciousness, on the other hand, could only be introduced into the workers' movement from outside, by the intellectuals.[36] This, Lenin asserted, had been shown by the history of all countries. It followed that by bowing to spontaneity the Economists condemned the workers' movement to go no further than trade union activities; the political assault on the autocracy could never be launched. Left to itself the working-class movement would become subordinated to bourgeois ideology, to development according to the programme of the 'Credo'.

Although the idea that a socialist consciousness had to be brought to the workers from outside originated with Akselrod, the source Lenin cited for it was Karl Kautsky's article on the programme of the Austrian Social Democrats.[37] This has given rise to the notion that Lenin derived his conception from Kautsky.[38] The resemblance is, however, superficial. Kautsky did not believe that the workers' class-consciousness was to be equated with their material interests. He stressed that class-consciousness was the consciousness of solidarity of all proletarians, the consciousness of the individual's obligations with regard to the class as a whole. Kautsky saw the class struggle and class-consciousness as ethical entities, and as the proletariat could only achieve its own liberation by eliminating all oppression and exploitation, it would protect all oppressed groups providing the interests of these groups did not collide with social development. In this respect the proletariat accomplished tasks which went beyond its immediate class interests. The function of the Social Democrats was to furnish the workers' movement with an awareness of its general aim and, arising from this, to unite the workers in a single political party. But if socialism was not to remain utterly naive, and consequently politically impotent, it had to understand social relations. Scholarship, however, was still the privilege of the possessing classes, and consequently the proletariat was not capable of elaborating a viable socialism by itself; this would have to be done by people from the bourgeoisie who sided with the proletariat.[39]

In saying that socialist consciousness was something introduced into the proletarian class struggle from outside, Kautsky was doing no more than stating the historical fact that the individuals who had been socialist thinkers had come from the bourgeois intelligentsia. Socialist doctrines consequently required to be communicated to the workers, and this function, Kautsky believed, ought to be performed by the Social Democrats. But of course once the socialist conscious-ness had been communicated to the workers, the workers would then be in possession of that consciousness. Not so with Lenin; in his view the socialist consciousness always remained outside the working class because it could never see beyond its narrow material class interests.

The third chapter, 'Trade-Unionist Politics and Social Democratic Politics', concentrated on showing that the activities of the Russian Social Democrats to date, such as their publication of leaflets expos-ing the injustices and hazards of factory life, were only trade union activities. The true function of Social Democrats, Lenin stressed, was not to represent the working class in relation to a given group of employers, but in relation to all classes in society and to the state. In Lenin's view the role of Social Democrats was to raise the level of working-class consciousness so that the workers were trained to respond to all instances of oppression, tyranny and injustice no matter what class in society was affected.[40] It is interesting to note that this level of working-class consciousness, which for Lenin was only possible through the intervention of the intelligentsia, was for Kautsky something inherent in the class-consciousness of the proletariat.

The fourth chapter, 'The Amateurishness of the Economists and the Organisation of the Revolutionaries', was the one in which Lenin put forward his ideas on what a revolutionary political party ought to be. He began by trying to show what relation these ideas had to the Economist heresy. Lenin's explanation was that the 'economic struggle' did not require an all-Russian centralised organisation capable of concentrating in one general onslaught all and every manifestation of political opposition, an organisation that would consist of professional revolutionaries and would be led by the real political leaders of the whole people. It did not require this and could not create it because the character of any organisation was of necessity determined by the content of its activity; amateurish activ-ity was concomitant with an amateurish organisation; revolutionary activity required a professional organisation.[41] But that meant that even if the Economist heresy had not existed, even if all Russian Social Democrats had been of the same mind as Akselrod and Plekhanov, that would still not, in Lenin's view, have removed the need for a party of professional revolutionaries. There was in fact no real logical progression from the polemic against the Economists to the plea for a professional party organisation.

The rationale for professionalism in revolutionary activity came not from the experience of Economism, but from elsewhere, as emerged from Lenin's explanation of what he meant by 'amateurism'. He did this by giving as an example young radicals who formed Social Democratic groups and launched themselves into propagandist activity among the workers without any kind of preliminary preparation, without contacting existing groups or making a specific plan of action, and without giving a great deal of thought to conspiratorial methods. As a result, the police would have no trouble monitoring the activities of the groups and arresting as many of their members as they chose at times which they deemed appropriate.[42] Lenin stated that the kind of groups he was describing were typical of the period 1894 to 1901, that is, from the time he first joined the Radchenko circle to the time of writing. But Lenin could have cited a much more poignant example of the phenomenon from the previous decade; he himself had lost a brother through the kind of 'amateurism' he described. One must suppose that in the intervening period he had given a great deal of thought to ways of overcoming it, and the fourth chapter of *What Is To Be Done?* to some extent at least must represent the results of these speculations. Symptomatically, the main consideration on which Lenin based his conception of the party was the need to avoid detection by the tsarist police.

The premise of the fourth chapter is that if one is going to engage in revolution, one should not go about it in a haphazard way, but should do it properly with all the necessary preparation and training. What was needed, Lenin believed, was a tightly knit, conspiratorial, organisation of professional revolutionaries capable of maintaining the energy, stability and continuity of the political struggle. Because these people were distinguished by their conspiratorial and organisational skills, it did not matter whether they belonged to the intelligentsia or the working class. Such distinctions, according to Lenin, were irrelevant in this connection.[43]

The clandestine organisation of professional revolutionaries Lenin advocated had little in common with a broad, open and democratic workers' organisation. This he readily admitted, but argued that both types of organisation had their place in the workers' movement. In Lenin's view, the existence of a party of experienced revolutionaries would greatly help the broader workers' organisations by centralising those of their activities, such as the production of leaflets, which required an element of conspiracy. Lenin made no pretence that his revolutionary organisation would be democratic. He believed that in this context democracy would be useless and harmful. It would only facilitate the work of the police in carrying out large-scale arrests, and serve to perpetuate amateurism within the revolutionary movement.[44]

Among the editorial board of *Iskra*, *What Is To Be Done?* was greeted with enthusiasm. Potresov especially thought that the analysis of what constituted trade unionism and Social Democratic politics was written lucidly and convincingly, while the section on Amateurism reached the heights of poetry.[45] Martov also probably was in agreement with *What Is To Be Done?* Plekhanov and Akselrod had suggested that some changes be made to individual passages in the pamphlet, but otherwise expressed no serious objection to Lenin's arguments; it was only in 1904 that Plekhanov made an attempt to refute them. Copies of *What Is To Be Done?* were distributed in Russia by *Iskra* agents and played their part in influencing the local organisations in the run-up to the Second Congress of the party. Nikolay Valentinov, for example, recalls that on reading Lenin's pamphlet he and other young Social Democrats in the Kiev committee were enthralled by the image of the 'professional revolutionary', a kind of St George the dragon-killer who would take up arms against all cases of injustice. For Valentinov and his friends *What Is To Be Done?* struck the right chord, and made them eager to put the message into practice.[46] The impact of Lenin's work is noticeable in the speeches made at the congress itself; there *What Is To Be Done?* was repeatedly referred to, both by supporters and opponents, and provided a ready source of ideas on how a political party should or should not be organised.

The Second Congress of the RSDLP

The Second Party Congress opened on 17 July 1903 in Brussels, but after a few days the attentions of the Belgian police compelled it to transfer to London, where it remained in session until 10 August. Lenin had put a great deal of preparation into the congress in order to ensure that the *Iskra* supporters would be in the majority and would carry all before them. He had, however, to expect resistance from the Economists of *Rabochee delo* and from the Bund. There was also a threat from the smaller groups such as 'Borba' and 'Yuzhnii rabochii', whose support could not be relied upon; these Lenin tried to exclude from the congress.

Initially the Iskraists' 'compact majority' held up well, and voting on procedural questions, the party programme and the endorsement of *Iskra* as the party newspaper went in its favour. But cracks began to appear when, contrary to the previous decision of the *Iskra* group, David Ryazanov of 'Borba' was allowed to attend the congress in a consultative capacity, resulting in a vote of no confidence being passed on the congress's organising committee. Recriminations on this episode served to bring the latent tensions within the *Iskra* camp to the surface.

These tensions erupted when the first paragraph of the party's rules was being discussed. Lenin and Martov submitted competing definitions of what a party member was. Lenin's read: 'A member of the Russian Social Democratic Labour Party is one who accepts its programme and who supports the Party both financially and by personal participation in one of the Party organisations.' Martov's version departed from Lenin's only in its last phrase, which was: 'by personal work under the control and direction of one of the Party organisations'.[47] Martov believed that the more widespread the title of party member the better. He thought it would be desirable if every worker who went on strike or took part in a demonstration could declare himself a party member. For Martov, a conspiratorial organisation only had meaning in the context of a broad working-class party. Lenin, on the other hand, thought that great harm would be done if the party had to bear responsibility for people it could not control. While Plekhanov supported Lenin, other members of the *Iskra* editorial board sided with Martov. The Bundists and adherents of *Rabochee delo* inclined towards Martov's formulation. One of the latter group, Akimov, explained that although both Lenin and Martov aimed at creating a centralised party, Martov's formulation was less likely to achieve this than Lenin's, hence he would give his vote to Martov.[48] With Martov's supporters and the anti-*Iskra* forces against it, Lenin's formulation was defeated by 28 votes to 23.

Because the congress dissolved the Union of Russian Social Democrats Abroad, its two delegates left the congress. The five Bund delegates also left the congress when their demand for organisational autonomy and recognition as the sole representative of the Jewish proletariat was rejected. This left Lenin's supporters in the majority for the remaining part of the congress at which the composition of the *Iskra* editorial board and the party's Central Committee were to be decided. Initially an attempt was made to settle the matter by negotiation, but Martov was prepared to allow only one Leninist among the three members of the Central Committee and insisted on reelecting the old editorial board of *Iskra*, on which his supporters had a two-thirds majority. When the negotiations failed, Lenin used his majority – hence the name 'Bolsheviks' later applied to Lenin's supporters – to reduce the editorial board from six persons to three (Lenin, Plekhanov and Martov) and to place his chosen candidates (Krzhizhanovskii, Lengnik and Noskov) on the Central Committee. Martov, however, declined to take his place on the *Iskra* editorial board, he and his followers – the 'Mensheviks' – refusing to accept the outcome of the vote.

Martov did not accept his defeat and accused Lenin and his followers of having acted in an underhand way, not in the interests of efficiency, but to control the party organisation. He complained that a 'state of seige' had existed in the party against particular persons and groups, and that contrary to his expectations the congress had not put an end to this state of affairs. Lenin did not contest this analysis, but said that such a 'state of seige' was necessary to achieve a united and centralised party organisation.[49]

Following the congress Plekhanov and Lenin jointly edited a few numbers of *Iskra*, but as the Mensheviks gained control of the League of Russian Socialists Abroad, a body created by the Second Congress, Plekhanov insisted on the return of all the old members of the editorial board, thus putting Lenin in a minority. Lenin resigned from the board in November, but was able to get himself coopted on to the Central Committee, from where he waged a campaign against what he considered to be the illegitimately constituted *Iskra* editorial board.

The split of the Social Democratic Party into two fractions had taken even the participants in the congress by surprise, and caused no little bemusement to Russian Social Democrats both inside the country and in emigration. To justify their respective positions both Martov and Lenin produced pamphlets which in their turn served to intensify the polemic. Martov's *Struggle with the State of Seige in the RSDLP* published in 1904 explained that although he had entertained severe doubts about Lenin's plans for party organisation before the congress, he had not opposed them for the sake of

maintaining unity in the *Iskra* camp. He admitted to having overlooked valid criticisms of Lenin's plans emanating from the anti-
Iskra elements of the congress.[50] Lenin, for his part, in *One Step
Forward, Two Steps Back* published in the same year, complained of
Martov's inconsistency and bad faith. He maintained that the measures he had proposed at the congress had been approved before-
hand by the members of the *Iskra* editorial board, and that only on
the floor of the congress had Martov raised objections. It seemed to
Lenin that the position adopted by Martov was akin to that of the
Economists, who had been defeated at the congress, and that the
campaign against Economism by *Iskra* had been in vain.

In *One Step Forward, Two Steps Back* Lenin sought to find some
explanation for the behaviour of Martov and his friends both at the
congress and in its aftermath. This was, he believed, a manifestation
of the intelligentsia's innate individualism, anarchism and abhor-
rence of discipline. The proletariat, by contrast, was trained for
organisation by its whole life, so that it was not the proletariat, but
certain individuals in the party who required training in organisation and discipline.[51] In this contrast between the collectivism of the
proletarian and the individualism of the intellectual Lenin was able
to cite at some length an article by Karl Kautsky.[52]

There was a noticeable difference of emphasis, if not of opinion,
between *What Is To Be Done?* and *One Step Forward, Two Steps Back*. In
the earlier work Lenin had extolled the part played by the intelligentsia in bringing a socialist consciousness to the proletariat; in the
later one he maintained that the intelligentsia had lessons in organisation and discipline to learn from the workers. This contradiction
was noted by Trotsky in his pamphlet *Our Political Tasks* published in
1904. 'Yesterday', he remarked ironically, 'the proletariat was still
crawling in the dust; today it is exalted to unheard of heights!
Yesterday the intelligentsia was still the bearer of socialist consciousness; today it is sentenced to run the gauntlet of factory discipline!'
To Trotsky these contradictions signified that Lenin simply used
Marxist theory for his own political manoeuvring.[53]

Rosa Luxemburg reviewed Lenin's *One Step Forward, Two Steps Back*
in an article printed simultaneously in *Iskra* and *Die Neue Zeit*.
Although agreeing in principle that centralisation in a Social
Democratic party was preferable to a federal conglomeration of
national and provincial subgroups, she was concerned that the kind
of centralism that was fostered should not be of a mechanical,

deadening, type, but should be one that encouraged initiative and creativity. She believed, moreover, that Social Democracy was not something that was connected with the organisation of the working class, but was the movement of the working class itself. It should be the 'self-centralisation' of the leading stratum of the proletariat. In this respect Luxemburg found ominous Lenin's contention that through its training in the factory the proletariat was more amenable to organisation and discipline than the intelligentsia. Factory organisation, Rosa thought, was the mindless and mechanical sort that was out of place in the workers' movement. What was required was the voluntary coordination of the conscious political actions of a social stratum. She herself believed that 'the false steps made by a really revolutionary workers' movement are historically infinitely more fruitful and valuable than the infallibility of the best of all possible Central Committees.'[54]

Lenin wrote a reply to Rosa Luxemburg, but the article was not published. However, Alexander Bogdanov, whom Lenin met in Geneva in May 1904, did reply on Lenin's behalf in an essay entitled 'Rosa Luxemburg contra Karl Marx' which appeared in a pamphlet produced by himself and M. S. Olminsky. Bogdanov began by quoting Marx's *Das Kapital* and the *Communist Manifesto* to demonstrate that Marx had believed that capitalist production had fostered the spirit of cooperation and organisation in the proletariat. He went on to argue that the kind of discipline Lenin had had in mind was not the mechanical discipline inculcated by the fear of starvation but the discipline developed by working together, united by the conditions of highly developed production techniques. On the matter of the intelligentsia's individualism and aversion to collective effort and discipline Bogdanov agreed completely with Lenin. He thought Luxemburg mistaken, however, in her contention that the intelligentsia in Russia was less individualistic than that in the West.

The most significant aspect of Bogdanov's essay was what he had to say about the part played by the workers in the Social Democratic Party. Bogdanov had on the whole a favourable opinion of Lenin's *What Is To Be Done?*, but he regarded the proposition that without the help of the socialist intelligentsia the working class was incapable of rising beyond trade unionism to the socialist ideal as a slip of the pen by the author. It was, he believed, a careless phrase thrown out in the heat of the polemic with the 'Economists'.[55] Although ostensibly defending Lenin's ideas, Bogdanov's essay was hardly a paraphrase of *What Is To Be Done?* Bogdanov was seeking to dispel the impression Luxemburg had gained from Akselrod and Martov that the Russian party consisted mainly of intellectuals. Bogdanov, drawing on his extensive knowledge of the situation inside Russia, denied this, stating that for each intellectual there were dozens of organised workers. These workers, moreover, were by no means passive, unconscious or politically immature, allowing themselves to be led along any old road by the intellectuals. Bogdanov thought it foolish to present the party as being composed of intellectuals precisely when it suffered to such an extent from a shortage of intellectuals to perform those functions which it would be difficult or inconvenient for the 'conscious proletariat' to perform. It was Bogdanov's contention that the Russian party was to a significant degree 'proletarian', and that the emergence of a proletarian avant-garde had already come about, and at that moment formed the basis of the party.[56]

In this essay nothing positive was said about the intellectuals. Their role in the party was presented as being a subsidiary one to that of the workers. And the avant-garde of the workers' movement consisted of advanced workers, who took a critical attitude to leadership by the intellectuals. These conceptions were typical of Bogdanov's thought, and were ones which abounded in his theoretical writings of the time. That Lenin should have endorsed this 'defence' of his *One Step Forward, Two Steps Back* implies that by 1904 his position had moved some way from *What Is To Be Done?* and had come closer to Bogdanov's. This temporary meeting of minds was the preliminary to a fateful alliance between the two men which would restore Lenin's flagging political fortunes.

3

THE 1905 REVOLUTION AND ITS AFTERMATH

Lenin and Bogdanov

Lenin's relationship with Alexander Bogdanov repeats the pattern of his association with Martov. It began with a phase of close friendship and fruitful cooperation, eventually to be replaced by one of alienation and hostility. Lenin, apparently, could not tolerate rivals, but he could not achieve what he wanted without them.

The months following the Second Congress marked a low ebb in Lenin's political career. He did not lead a united and centralised Social Democratic Party, inspired by his theoretical writings on organisation, as doubtless had been his ambition. The party had split; his opponents controlled the highest party organisations, the party newspaper, the Central Committee and the Party Council, which was supposed to coordinate the activities of the other two institutions. His former comrades accused him of Jacobinism, Bonapartism, Blanquism, and now began to express reservations they had apparently always entertained about his book *What Is To Be Done?* Lenin, however, was able to recover from these reverses by forming an alliance with Alexander Bogdanov.

Bogdanov (born Alexander Malinovskii) was three years younger than Lenin and came from a similar family background. He had studied mathematics and physics at Moscow University, then medicine at Kharkov. With his friends V. A. Rudnev (Bazarov) and I. I. Skvortsov-Stepanov he had given lectures on political economy to a workers' circle in Tula. The lectures had been subsequently published as a book, which Lenin had reviewed enthusiastically.[1] The years between

68

1900 and 1903 had been spent in prison and exile. While in exile in Kaluga, along with Anatolii Luncharskii he had debated with Berdyaev on philosophical questions. Berdyaev, Bulgakov, Struve and other 'Legal Marxists' were at that time deserting Marxism in favour of idealism, and Bogdanov and his friends took it upon themselves to defend the Marxist or 'realist' point of view. This campaign was continued in the monthly journal *Pravda*, which first appeared in January 1904.

The articles which Bogdanov published in *Pravda* expressed ideas which were very typical of the general direction of his thought. They concerned the consequences of the division of labour in capitalist society, a problem first raised by nineteenth-century German thinkers. Bogdanov thought that the specialisation into different trades and professions had fragmented human experience and had produced a flawed view of the world that was centred on the individual. The society of specialists was one of individualism, anarchy and disorganisation. The ultimate in fragmentation was the worker who performed operations so limited that they could be carried out by a machine. But the capitalist system also brought workers together in great masses for common effort. Individualist interests were replaced by group and class interests. In this way a step towards the reintegration of humanity had been achieved.[2]

Bogdanov was a highly original thinker who was interested in breaking down the distinctions between the physical, psychical and social areas of investigation to discover a truly 'monist' approach to knowledge. At different times he drew upon different sources of inspiration, but at the turn of the century his attention had been attracted by the philosophers of pure experience Ernst Mach and Richard Avenarius. Lenin, for his part, was very unsympathetic to Bogdanov's ideas. Although he had parted company with Plekhanov politically, he still regarded Plekhanov as the leading authority on questions of Marxist theory. He thought of Plekhanov's interpretation of Marx as being the 'orthodox' one and all others as heresy. As far as interpretations of Marx influenced by Mach and Avenarius were concerned, he followed Plekhanov in regarding these as not only mistaken but reactionary. However, in order to obtain Bogdanov's support for his political ambitions Lenin was constrained to overlook Bogdanov's philosophical views and conclude a pact with him, undertaking not to allow philosophical disagreements to stand in the way of political cooperation.[3]

In an attempt to embarrass Lenin by pointing out the supposedly un-Marxist views of his new ally, Plekhanov encouraged one of his young acolytes, Liubov Akselrod-Ortodoks, to publish an article in *Iskra* in November 1904 showing that Bogdanov's theoretical errors arose from the mistaken ideas of Mach and Avenarius. Lenin, however, at that time did not rise to the bait, and when he referred obliquely to Plekhanov's ruse during the Third Congress it was to ridicule the idea that obscure philosophers, with whom he had no sympathy, could have anything to do with politics.[4]

Bogdanov was a valuable ally for Lenin because of his standing as a theoretician, his literary talents, his personal following and his wide range of contacts within Russia, including the famous writer Maxim Gorky. Bogdanov first came to Geneva while Lenin was in the process of writing his *One Step Forward, Two Steps Back*, and it is significant that it is in the course of this book that Lenin began to contrast the intelligentsia's anarchist and individualist qualities with the workers' propensity for organisation and discipline – quite in the Bogdanov manner. It is also significant that Bogdanov undertook to defend these ideas on Lenin's behalf against Rosa Luxemburg's criticisms.

A plan of action was worked out by Lenin and Bogdanov during August at a retreat in a small village beside the Lac de Brêt near Lausanne. It was decided to convoke a new party congress at which the party's ruling institutions would be reconstituted. This of course would be resisted by the Mensheviks, who now controlled those institutions, but the rules of the party had provided for the convocation of a party congress if a sufficient number of the local committees demanded it. Much depended on the attitude of the local committees, and consequently a great deal of attention had to be devoted to winning these over, both to request a new congress and to support the Bolsheviks at the congress itself.

To prepare the ground in Russia it would be necessary to repeat the technique, so successfully practised with *Iskra*, of using a newspaper and its agents to mobilise opinion. But in 1904 *Iskra* was in Menshevik hands and some of the local party committees at least would sympathise with its new editorial board. The new newspaper which would campaign for the Bolsheviks was *Vpered* (Forward), which first appeared in Geneva in December 1904. A nucleus of contributors to the newspaper would come from among Bogdanov's friends, such as Lunacharskii, Bazarov and Skvortsov-Stepanov.[5]

An important aspect of Bogdanov's activities was to be fund-raising for the newspaper. Somewhat ironically the most likely backers for such an enterprise came from among the Russian business community. Bogdanov's *Pravda*, for example, had been financed by a wealthy Moscow publisher. For *Vpered* Bogdanov approached the writer Gorky for contributions. Gorky not only donated considerable amounts of money on a regular basis, but also successfully approached the Moscow industrialist Savva Morozov for contributions to the funds for *Vpered*.

As part of the campaign to convoke the Third Congress of the RSDLP a conference of 22 supporters of the majority fraction was convened in July–August 1904 outside Geneva. The 22 included practically all of the adherents Lenin could muster at that time and included Krupskaya, Lenin's sister Mariya, Bogdanov, Lunacharskii, V. D. Bonch-Bruevich, Lepeshinskii, S. I. Gusev, V. V. Vorovskii, Olminskii, M. N. Lyadov and R. S. Zemlyachka. The conference approved a declaration, 'To the Party', which explained the split in the party in terms of the individualistic tendencies of the intelligentsia who dominated the *émigré* organisations, and called for a new congress to be summoned. This declaration was followed by the creation of a Bureau of Committees of the Majority (BKB), the Bolshevik centre to work for the convocation of the Third Congress. The Bureau's members were Bogdanov, Zemlyachka, Rumyantsev, Gusev, A. I. Rykov and M. M. Litvinov, who operated within Russia, and Lenin, Lunacharskii, Olminskii and Vorovskii, who worked on the editorial board of *Vpered*. While Lenin remained in Geneva, Bogdanov returned to Russia to work for the BKB in St Petersburg. There he raised funds for *Vpered* and produced leaflets not only on convening the Third Party Congress but also in response to every significant turn of events: the shooting of the demonstrators in January, the conclusion of peace with Japan, the strikes by the workers, peasant disturbances, and the promises of representative assemblies made first by Bulygin and then by Witte on behalf of the tsarist government.[6]

Russia's defeat in its war with Japan brought to the surface social and political tensions throughout the Empire. The catalyst was the shooting of unarmed demonstrators in St Petersburg on 9 January 1905 by government troops. The wave of revulsion precipitated a wave of strikes in Russia's industrial centres. The unrest soon spread to the countryside, the armed forces and the national regions. It was an upsurge that threatened to topple the tsarist regime.

Mass meetings and lectures were organised up and down the country by Bogdanov's associates in the Moscow literary lecturing group, such as M. N. Pokrovskii, A. I. Rozhkov, P. Dauge, D. I. Kurskii and I. I. Skvortsov-Stepanov. These were people who belonged to Bogdanov's personal circle of acquaintances, and when they took on a party affiliation during 1905 they tended to think of themselves as Bolsheviks rather than as Social Democrats, thus giving the Bolshevik fraction in Russia an enhanced sense of identity.[7] The same group of people were involved in publishing the Bolshevik newspapers, *Borba*, *Svetoch* and *Novaya zhizn*, for which Gorky contributed the funds.[8]

When the Third Congress of the RSDLP assembled in London between 12 and 27 April 1905 the Menshevik delegates walked out on the grounds that it was neither legally constituted nor representative. The Mensheviks held a rival meeting in Geneva, but in order not to exacerbate the split, they eschewed any claim to represent the party as a whole, and declared their meeting a party conference rather than a congress.

Considering that much of Lenin's *What Is To Be Done?* had been concerned with the relationship between intellectuals and workers, it is significant that the congress resolution on this subject was introduced by Bogdanov. Little of what he said could have been derived from Lenin's famous pamphlet. Bogdanov said that he believed that relations between workers and intellectuals in the party were on a sound footing, because all members looked on themselves as Social Democrats and no distinctions were made into workers and intellectuals. In the right wing of the party, however, the intellectual element was prone to individualistic and anarchistic forms of action in their opposition to the party majority. Lunacharskii remarked that he believed that the social–psychological way the matter had been formulated by Kautsky, and repeated by Lenin in his 'Steps', was the correct one. He thought it desirable, therefore, that the leadership of the party should be transferred as soon as possible into the hands of the Social Democratic workers. Lenin made it clear that he agreed with this line of argument, observing that: 'Here they said that the bearers of Social Democratic ideas have been mainly the intellectuals. That is untrue. In the era of Economism the bearers of revolutionary ideas were the workers, not the intellectuals.'[9] The congress accepted Lenin's version of the first paragraph of the party rules, the rationale for doing so being the desire to limit scope in the party for 'anarchistic and individualistic tendencies'.[10] There was no suggestion in the congress that the perspectives of the proletariat were limited to trade union objectives. Now it was emphasised that the proletariat by virtue of its social position was the 'most progressive and the only consistently revolutionary class'.[11]

Lenin's main speech at the congress was devoted to the topic that had become the most important one now that the revolution in Russia was gathering momentum: what should the tactics of the party be if the autocracy was overthrown? In that eventuality, Lenin reasoned, the main contenders for power would be the two main classes in the anti-tsarist coalition, the proletariat and the peasantry. These classes would form a democratic dictatorship. A dictatorship was necessary because of the need to overcome the resistance of the privileged classes. The form this dictatorship would take would be a Provisional Revolutionary Government, which would hold power until the convocation of a Constituent Assembly. Lenin believed that the Social Democrats ought to participate in a Provisional Government of this kind.

An important matter to be decided at the congress was what the attitude towards the Mensheviks should be. Although Lenin and Bogdanov had been tempted to break off relations with the Mensheviks completely and form an independent party, the resolution passed by the congress took care to leave the way open to reconciliation in the future. It stated that despite the ideological shortcomings of individuals, they should be permitted to participate in party organisations providing they recognised the party congresses and submitted to party discipline.[12] Lenin was satisfied with the outcome of the congress and in his pamphlet *Two Tactics of Social-Democracy in the Democratic Revolution* contrasted the decisions it had made favourably with those of the conference the Mensheviks had held in Geneva.

While the revolution swept through the Russian Empire in 1905 Lenin remained settled in his Geneva exile. He edited *Proletarii*, as *Vpered* was renamed after the Third Congress, and commented in its pages on the revolutionary events as they unfolded. He showed little inclination to return to Russia and become involved in the events themselves. It was only on Bogdanov's summons that he finally came to St Petersburg in November. On his arrival, Lenin resumed his journalistic activities, by joining Bogdanov and his friends on the editorial board of *Novaya zhizn*. He at once began to purge the newspaper of the broad coalition of literary talent Gorky had assembled and to give it a more pronounced Social Democratic orientation. Lenin set out his ideas on party control over literature in the article 'Party Organisation and Party Literature', which revived some of the themes aired in *What Is To Be Done?* The party, he stated, was a voluntary organisation of people which would inevitably disintegrate if it did not purge itself of people advocating anti-party views.[13]

Despite the massive influx of new members into political parties during the 1905 revolution, most of the workers, peasants and soldiers who took part in the strikes, uprisings and mutinies belonged to no party and were organised by no party organisation. Even the soviets, which sprang up during the revolution in St Petersburg and the provincial cities, did not exercise a great deal of influence over working-class revolutionary action. The revolution in fact demonstrated the inadequacy of any kind of organisation in the face of such large-scale popular mobilisation.

Although the St Petersburg Soviet, chaired by Trotsky, was one of the most popular institutions to be thrown up by the 1905 revolution, Lenin was a very infrequent participant at its meetings. At that time Lenin, like most Social Democrats, was rather dismissive of soviets as a means of mobilising the workers. In this respect he saw them as vastly inferior to the Social Democratic Party. In a conversation with Lyadov Lenin praised the Moscow party organisation for retaining the workers' movement in its hands. In contrast, St Petersburg party organisation, he complained, had been impeded by the soviet, a talking shop with pretensions to being a workers' parliament.[14] On the other hand, Lenin suggested that the soviets might be the form taken by the Provisional Revolutionary Government. But the article in which he elaborated this idea only saw the light of day in 1940.[15]

By 3 December the tide of revolution had ebbed sufficiently for the government to disperse the St Petersburg Soviet and arrest its leaders, including Trotsky and Bogdanov. *Novaya zhizn* was closed down on the same day. Later that month an armed uprising was staged in Moscow, in which various revolutionary groups, including the Bolsheviks, the Mensheviks and the Socialist Revolutionaries (SRs), participated. The insurgents fought valiantly, and despite their efforts to disrupt traffic on the railway line bringing government troops to Moscow, the Semenov regiment was able to enter the city and crush the rebellion with considerable bloodshed.

One casualty of the December uprising was the 23-year-old Nikolai Schmidt, a nephew of Savva Morozov and the owner of a furniture factory in Moscow. Schmidt joined the Bolsheviks in 1905 and provided funds for *Novaya zhizn* and also for arms purchases. His furniture factory, which the police referred to as a 'devil's nest', became a revolutionary stronghold during the December uprising. Schmidt was arrested and while in prison was tortured and finally murdered. Before he died, however, Schmidt succeeded in contacting friends outside prison and arranging to bequeath his considerable fortune to the Bolsheviks.[16] The windfall was to give rise to an additional dimension of political manoeuvring in the years that followed.

Party unity

Soon after Lenin had arrived in Russia negotiations began for the reunification of the Bolshevik and Menshevik wings of the RSDLP. The move was prompted by the awareness of how inadequate the separate fractions were in giving direction to the revolution. In any case Bolsheviks, Mensheviks and social democrats from the national parties had collaborated during the past few months, when party affiliations had become irrelevant. The Bolshevik and Menshevik fractions each held its own conference to approve the merger. The Menshevik conference took place in St Petersburg at the end of November with Lenin and Bogdanov in attendance. It decided on merger with the Bolshevik fraction and accepted Lenin's formulation of Article 1 of the rules defining a party member. It also resolved that the party should be run on the basis of 'democratic centralism' and that the decisions of the leadership should be binding on the local committees.[17] The Bolshevik conference, chaired by Lenin, took place at Tammenfors from 12 to 17 December, during the Moscow uprising. In the light of experience of the past few months, the conference adopted Lenin's motion that the party's agrarian policy of returning the *otrezki*[18] to the peasants should be changed to that of supporting peasant demands for the confiscation of all types of landed estates. The conference accepted the need to reorganise the party on the basis of 'democratic centralism'. This was defined as the introduction of the elective principle on a broad basis, giving those elected the complete freedom of action in both ideological and practical leadership, on the understanding that they could be replaced, that they had to keep the party informed of what they were doing and that they had to give an account of themselves. These were principles that Lenin had insisted were entirely inappropriate in a revolutionary party in *What Is To Be Done?*. The conference resolved to convene a congress to unite formally the two wings of the party, and decided that the party should boycott the Duma, the legislative assembly which the tsarist government had granted under pressure of the revolution.

The Fourth (Unity) Congress of the RSDLP which was held in Stockholm between 10 and 25 April 1906 duly accepted the principle of democratic centralism and party rules incorporating Lenin's formulation of what constituted a party member. Although the congress, which had a Menshevik majority (62 Mensheviks to 46 Bolsheviks), formally united the Bolshevik and Menshevik fractions of the party, differences between them on ideology and policy had not disappeared. There were deep disagreements on the evaluation of the revolution, the agrarian question, and what the attitude should be to the Duma and to the liberals. The resolutions adopted by the conference tended to be those proposed by the Mensheviks, though often with modifications introduced by the Bolsheviks. Lenin, as the advocate of party discipline, was prepared to accept the conference decisions, however much he disliked them. The Menshevik preponderance at the congress was also reflected in the election to the Central Committee of seven Mensheviks to only three Bolsheviks: L. B. Krasin, Desnitskii and Rykov (later replaced by Bogdanov).

Some Bolshevik delegates at the congress were of the opinion that since the fractions had not dissolved, and as the Mensheviks dominated the proceedings, the congress had turned out to be pointless. For Lenin, however, the apparent setback was a price worth paying, because from his point of view there was another dimension to the unity that the congress was intended to bring about that would later pay dividends. An important function of the Fourth Congress was to agree on the conditions by which the national organisations might join the RSDLP. The congress duly accepted the Bund, the SDKPiL and the Latvian Social Democratic Party as territorial organisations (*raiony*) of the RSDLP, the Latvian party accordingly changing its name to Social Democracy of the Latvian Territories (SDLK).

The inclusion of the national organisations created a new kind of politics within the RSDLP. Now that the decisions on key questions depended on the vote of the national groups, it would be essential to ally with them, to cultivate them and try to influence them. Lenin was confident that he would have the Poles and the Latvians on his side, and that at the next party congress the Bolsheviks would be able to win back the party leadership from the Mensheviks.[19]

Although the Unity Congress had demanded that separate fraction meetings should no longer take place, they did so nevertheless. Lenin and his fraction retained a 'Bolshevik Centre' whose membership more or less coincided with the editorial board of the newspaper *Proletarii*, which was also a purely Bolshevik publication. The Mensheviks, for their part, retained a special group to discuss policies in which Akselrod was a leading light. Akselrod at that time was propounding his idea of a 'workers' congress', which would express the interests of the more politically aware stratum of the working class, and would give rise to a broadly based labour party that would embrace Social Democrats, Socialist Revolutionaries and anarchists.[20] The idea, however, did not find a great number of adherents.

In August 1906 Lenin and Krupskaya settled in the Finnish village of Kuokkala, a place relatively safe from the tsarist authorities, but still conveniently close to St Petersburg. They occupied a country house called 'Vasa' belonging to a Bolshevik associate. Bogdanov, who had been released from prison in May, and his wife lived in the upstairs apartment. Meetings of the Bolshevik Centre took place more or less regularly at 'Vasa'. There too the editorial board of *Proletarii* had its sessions. Party workers came from all parts of Russia to report to Krupskaya, who acted as the secretary to the Bolshevik Centre.

It was while living at 'Vasa' that the latent philosophical differences between Lenin and Bogdanov began to come to the surface. Bogdanov had recently published the third volume of his collection of philosophical essays *Empiriomonism*, and during the summer Lenin read this with great concentration and even greater expressions of annoyance. In a discussion with Rozhkov he called it 'nonsense' and 'rubbish'.[21] He sent his comments on the book to Bogdanov, or as Lenin himself described it later to Gorky 'a "declaration of love", a little letter on philosophy running to three notebooks'. Bogdanov found the letter so insulting that he returned it to the sender, saying that if Lenin wanted to maintain personal relations with him, the letter must be treated as 'unwritten, unsent and unread'.[22]

The government had dissolved the First Duma, which had been dominated by the Constitutional Democrat (Kadet) Party, finding it too radical and unruly. But the Duma had shown itself to be an effective platform for revolutionary propaganda, and the Social Democrats decided that for the elections to the Second Duma they would not repeat the boycott tactic. Differences arose between Bolsheviks and Mensheviks, however, on what the attitude towards the liberals ought to be. The Mensheviks advocated alliance with the Kadets to form a united opposition to tsarism, whereas the Bolsheviks believed that the Social Democrats ought to act independently, and only enter into 'technical agreements' in exceptional circumstances, and then only with those parties who recognised the necessity for an armed uprising.[23] When the elections took place in February 1907 a number of Bolshevik deputies were returned to the Duma. Their activities were under the direction of Bogdanov, and the Bolshevik Duma deputies joined the stream of regular visitors to 'Vasa' in Kuokkala.[24] In trying to ensure that the Duma deputies followed party policy, Bogdanov was impeded by the attitude of the mostly Menshevik Central Committee, who tried to come to an accommodation with the liberals. This was a matter raised at the Fifth Congress of the RSDLP which met in London between 30 April and 19 May 1907.

The Fifth Congress was the first which included delegates from the national organisations: the Bund, the SDKPiL and the SDLK. Thus the congress consisted of five independent groupings. There being 89 Bolshevik and 88 Menshevik delegates, the two fractions were more or less evenly balanced, giving the 42 SDKPiL, the 26 SDLK and 55 Bundists a decisive influence on the outcome of the congress. The national groups adopted an intermediate position between the Bolsheviks and the Mensheviks. The SDKPiL agreed with the Bolsheviks on most issues of principle and supported them on the floor of the congress. Although the Bundists ostensibly tried to distance themselves from the Mensheviks, they in fact tended to support Menshevik policies at the congress, though, like the SDKPiL, they tried to ensure that neither fraction would dominate the other. The Latvians were more even-handed than either the SDKPiL or the Bund. Although they largely found themselves in sympathy with the Bolsheviks, they tried wherever possible to reconcile the sides and under no circumstances would they allow the Bolsheviks to win on fractional, organisational or personal issues.[25]

Thus, although the Poles and Latvians joined with the Bolsheviks in condemning the ineffectiveness of the Central Committee, they prevented any motion on the matter being passed. But the Poles and the Latvians were as insistent as the Bolsheviks in their opposition to Menshevik proposals to cooperate with the liberal parties in the Duma, and their support ensured the success of the Bolshevik motion on the subject. In the voting for the Central Committee the impulse to ensure that no fraction had a preponderance reasserted itself.

The Bolsheviks did suffer defeat on one important issue. That was on the dissolution of combat units and special groups formed to carry out 'expropriations' – robberies for the purpose of adding to party funds. It was thought that whereas these might have been appropriate at the height of the revolution, they were no longer permissible in the post-revolutionary era. Most Bolsheviks believed, however, that the revolution had not really ended and that a new upsurge would soon begin. At the end of the congress elections took place to the Bolshevik Centre. Those elected were: Lenin, Bogdanov, I. P. Goldenberg, I. F. Dubrovinskii, G. E. Zinoviev, L. B. Kamenev, L. B. Krasin, V. P. Nogin, A. I. Rykov, M. N. Pokrovskii, I. A. Teodorovich, V. K. Taratuta, G. A. Leiteizen, N. A. Rozhkov and V. L. Shantser.[26]

The Fifth Congress had shown that Polish and Latvian support for the Bolsheviks could be extremely effective, but that it could not be taken for granted. The Bolshevik–Menshevik split was a peculiarity of the Russian party, and both the SDKPiL and the SDLK were rather bemused by it. They did not wish to be involved in the fractional fights, and though they might sympathise with Bolshevik policies, they regarded themselves as belonging to neither of the two RSDLP fractions. In this non-fractional stance they found that the grouping within the RSDLP with which they had most in common was Trotsky's, because Trotsky too held aloof from both Bolsheviks and Mensheviks. Trotsky had discovered this common ground with the SDKPiL and the SDLK at the Fifth Congress, which he had attended following his escape from Siberian exile. Even then there had been speculation that Trotsky might form a central grouping and take the whole party with him.[27] Although, fortunately for Lenin, this was not to happen, after the congress Trotsky made the most of his non-fractional position to cultivate the Poles and the Latvians.

Trotsky's newspaper *Pravda*, which began to appear in Geneva in 1908, tried to appeal to the national organisations. The paper in fact described itself as the organ of the Ukrainian Union (*Spilka*) of the RSDLP.[28] It published items on the SDKPiL and the SDLK, and emphasised to these groups its non-fractional stance. The Latvians in their turn complimented Trotsky for his struggle against fractions and, in recognition of this, contributed to *Pravda*'s funds.[29]

Despite the blandishments of Trotsky, the fact remained that on the cardinal tactical questions of the day the SDKPiL found themselves in general agreement with Lenin. They concurred with him in condemning the current in Menshevik thought which advocated the liquidation of the underground party, believing that it was essential to retain the clandestine party organisation. They also agreed with Lenin in opposing a boycott of the Duma, because they believed this would be to neglect a valuable legal platform for Social Democratic propaganda. However, the SDKPiL rejected entirely the course advocated by the Mensheviks of an alliance with the liberals within the Duma.[30] This meeting of minds between the SDKPiL and Lenin was to leave Bogdanov and much of the Bolshevik party on the sidelines.

'Recallers' and 'Ultimatists'

Soon after the Fifth Congress came to an end the Second Duma was dissolved. Most Bolsheviks shared Bogdanov's belief that this would be followed by a new revolutionary upsurge and thought that a boycott of the elections to the Third Duma would send an appropriate signal throughout the country. Lenin, however, parted company with the Bolshevik fraction on this issue and strenuously opposed the boycott. In his view a boycott would have been appropriate only if the revolutionary upsurge was on the point of overthrowing the tsarist regime.[31] He was able to carry the day, however, because in the united party he was able to command a majority.

The tactic to be adopted on the elections to the Duma was debated at a conference at Kotka in Finland held from 21 to 23 July 1907. It was attended by 26 delegates with full voting rights consisting of nine Bolsheviks, five Mensheviks, five Bundists, five SDKPiL and two Latvian Social Democrats. Three points of view could be identified among the delegates. The Mensheviks were in favour of the Social Democrats being represented in the Duma and cooperating with the Kadets. The Bolsheviks with the exception of Lenin wanted to boycott the Duma. Lenin's position represented a mixture of the other two points of view. Like the Mensheviks he wanted the Social Democrats to be represented in the Duma, but unlike them, he did not want to enter an alliance with the Kadets. Lenin's point of view had the support of the Polish and one of the Latvian delegates; the Bundists were all on the side of the Mensheviks.

Bogdanov put the case for the boycott, and when this motion was voted on it was defeated by 15 votes to 9. All the Bolsheviks except Lenin plus one of the Latvians had voted for it, there being two abstentions. It was clear that any boycottist motion would be lost, in face of the combined strength of the Mensheviks, the Bundists and Lenin and his supporters. Moreover, the kind of resolution that would be adopted would be one dictated by Menshevik thinking and would recommend not just participation in the Duma, but also coop-eration with the Kadets. The Bolsheviks would be able to avoid this outcome, however, if they joined forces with Lenin. Accordingly, a compromise motion was drawn up, based for the most part on Lenin's formulation, and this was carried by 15 votes to 11.

This was a remarkable outcome, because it meant that Lenin, in a minority of one on the boycott issue, had managed to impose his point of view on the rest of the Bolshevik fraction. It also meant that Bogdanov and the Bolshevik majority were committed to a course of action in which they did not believe, and which to them had no real legitimacy in a Bolshevik context. The majority of the Bolshevik del-egation made it clear that the course they had adopted was to pass the anti-boycottist resolution that seemed to them the lesser evil. Bogdanov was later to remind Lenin of his tactics at Kotka as an instance of his unscrupulous behaviour.[32]

The controversy over the boycott of the Third Duma was the pre-lude to the schism in the Bolshevik ranks that would result in the emergence of the *Vpered* (Forward) group. In terms of the personal-ities involved one can observe that the anti-Leninists consisted of Bogdanov and the friends he had brought into the Bolshevik party in 1904: Lunacharskii, Bazarov, Pokrovskii and so on. The people who had joined the Bolsheviks as a group left as a group. The mat-ters around which contention raged – Duma tactics, philosophy and party funding – were not in themselves necessarily serious and might have been resolved given the necessary goodwill. It is symptomatic that the members of the SDKPiL and the SDLK who observed the developments from the sidelines were bemused that matters of such secondary importance should be so bitterly contested.

The boycott of the Third Duma had been defeated at the Kotka conference, but the question of the RSDLP's representation in the Duma was by no means solved. Whereas the Central Committee elected at the Fifth Congress had a Bolshevik majority, most of the 19 Social Democrat Duma deputies were Menshevik. The deputies regarded themselves as an autonomous group, and collaborated with other opposition parties in a manner prohibited by the Fifth Congress. Lenin's reaction was to try to bring the deputies more under party control, but the response of the Bolsheviks who had supported the boycott of the Duma was to propose that the Central Committee should serve an ultimatum on the Duma deputies demanding that they submit to party directives (Ultimatism). Should they fail to comply with this demand, they should be recalled from the Duma (Otzovism). The Recallist mood was widespread in local party organisations, especially those in the Central Industrial region.[33]

In the summer of 1907 the controversy raged on the pages of *Proletarii*. In his article 'Boycottists and Recallers', Bogdanov upheld the party decision in favour of participating in the Duma, but he thought that the behaviour of the Social Democrat Duma fraction had justified the fears of those who had previously advocated a boycott. Bogdanov favoured delivering the ultimatum, but he did not think that it was desirable that the deputies should be removed from the Duma. Other members of the Bolshevik Centre, G. A. Aleksinskii and V. L. Shantser, were quite prepared to see the deputies recalled from the Duma.[34] The issue was discussed at the Fourth Conference of the RSDLP held in Helsingfors in November 1907, which laid down policy guidelines for the Social Democrat Duma deputies to follow, to ensure that they did not support or appear to be supporting the bourgeois parties. The conference also reaffirmed the party's determination to eliminate all fractions within its midst and achieve unity throughout all its local organisations.[35]

In December the Bolshevik Centre decided to transfer the publication of *Proletarii* abroad, and Lenin moved from Finland to Geneva. There the dispute between Lenin and Bogdanov on philosophical questions was resumed with increased intensity. Early in the new year Lenin read the collection of articles by Bogdanov, Bazarov, Lunacharskii and others entitled *Studies in the Philosophy of Marxism* which had just been published. Every article evoked his indignation as the authors seemed to have nothing in common with Marxism as he understood the term. He lost no time in communicating this impression to Bogdanov.

The situation was inflamed by the article 'The Disintegration of the Individual' which Gorky had submitted to *Proletarii* for publication.

As the article had been influenced by Bogdanov's philosophical ideas, Lenin opposed its publication. He wrote Gorky a long letter explaining his position and detailing his increasing irritation with what he saw as Bogdanov's attacks on Marxism. He said he believed that a conflict among the Bolsheviks on the question of philosophy was now unavoidable. He added, however, that to cause a split on this matter would be the height of folly, because cooperation with Bogdanov and his friends had gone relatively smoothly. The only disagreement had been on the boycott of the Third Duma. But that disagreement had not been serious enough to cause a split, and in any case not all who agreed with Bogdanov in philosophy agreed with him on Duma tactics. His close friend Bazarov, for example, had sided with Lenin in opposing the boycott and had written an article on the subject in *Proletarii*. In order not to exacerbate a delicate situation, Lenin requested Gorky to rewrite his article removing those elements which had a bearing on Bogdanov's philosophy. These, Lenin suggested, might be published elsewhere. In the light of subsequent developments, it is significant to note that at this juncture, in common with most contemporary observers, Lenin believed that neither philosophical questions nor questions of Duma tactics were matters which could justify splitting the Bolshevik fraction. He thought that it ought to be possible to have a philosophical debate in such a way that the Bolsheviks 'as a fraction of the Social-Democratic party would not be affected by it'.[36] Doubtless it was in this connection that he sent a note to Bogdanov in April stressing that for 'the success of our cause in the Central Committee' it was important not to mention to Jogiches the intensification of philosophical differences.[37]

Gorky, for his part, was anxious that Lenin and Bogdanov should be reconciled, and to this end invited Lenin to visit him at his home on the island of Capri where Bogdanov, Lunacharskii and Bazarov were then staying. Lenin, however, warned Gorky that any efforts to reconcile him with the 'Machists' would be in vain, that he would not talk to people who were preaching the 'union of scientific socialism with religion'. This was a reference to Lunacharskii's major work *Religion and Socialism* which had just been published in St Petersburg.

In fact the book did not advocate the union of socialism and religion. Lunacharskii's approach to religion had grown out of his interest in aesthetics, which he had come to view as a particular manifestation of the more general impulse of evaluation. It was evaluation together with cognition, Lunacharskii believed, which made

action possible. Through evaluation one became aware of the difference between what the world was and what it ought to be, between
reality and ideals. According to Lunacharskii the elemental approach
to resolving this contrast was religious, and this provided him with
his definition of religion: 'Religion is that thinking about the world
and that world-sensation which psychologically tries to resolve the
contrast between the laws of life and the laws of nature.'[38]

Religion, however, in Lunacharskii's view was not capable of satisfactorily resolving the contradiction. This would only be accomplished by scientific socialism, by means of knowledge and labour,
science and technology. In sum, what Lunacharskii's book set out to
do was to place modern socialism in the context of earlier systems
which were concerned with human ethical ideals, and to demonstrate that socialism was the answer to mankind's earliest and most
fundamental aspirations.

Lunacharskii's book was a serious and stimulating investigation
into the relationship between religion and modern socialism. Its
argument advocated the rejection of religion in favour of socialism.
Lenin's impression of the book was clearly not derived from actually
reading it. More likely what he had read was Plekhanov's review of it,
which distorted Lunacharskii's meaning to give the impression that
Lunacharskii was propounding a new socialist religion without God.
In the second volume of his book, Lunacharskii drew the attention of
his readers to the way Plekhanov had read into the book only what he
wished to find.[39] These protests were to be of no avail; Lunacharskii's
'religious seekings' were to be held up by both Plekhanov and Lenin
as an indication of where Machist philosophy might lead.

In the event, when Lenin went to Capri for a few days in April no
reconciliation with the 'Machists' took place. According to Gorky, on
that occasion Lenin was frosty and mocking, studiously avoiding
involvement in serious philosophical discussions, but making some
acerbic remarks about Bogdanov's ideas. He played a game of chess
with Bogdanov and surprised Gorky by the childish way he sulked
when he lost.[40] After leaving Capri Lenin made for London where
he worked in the library of the British Museum on his anti-Machist
book *Materialism and Empiriocriticism*.

Despite attempts at reconciliation, Bogdanov was becoming increasingly aggrieved at the way Lenin condoned Plekhanov's behaviour.
Plekhanov had misrepresented not only Lunacharskii's ideas in
order to discredit them; for polemical purposes he had distorted

Bogdanov's as well. Moreover, Plekhanov had no compunction about doctoring quotations from Marx and Engels in order to align them with his own point of view. This unethical conduct had caused Bogdanov to write an open letter of complaint to Plekhanov in the journal *Vestnik zhizni* in July 1907. To this letter Plekhanov wrote a long blustering response entitled 'Materialismus Militans' over two issues of the Menshevik journal *Golos sotsial-demokrata* in the following year. More would have followed if Plekhanov had not broken off relations with his colleagues on the journal at that time.

In May Bogdanov delivered a lecture in Geneva entitled 'The Adventures of One Philosophical School'. Its purpose was to demonstrate the falsity of the claim made by Plekhanov and his followers, A. M. Deborin and Akselrod-Ortodoks, that they propounded the authentic philosophy of Marx. It also was intended to expose the illegitimate and dishonest methods which they employed to discredit their opponents.[41] Lenin tried to disrupt Bogdanov's efforts by sending from London a set of 'Ten Questions to the Lecturer' for the Bolshevik Centre member Dubrovinskii to put at the session. That Lenin should have acted in this underhand way must have seemed to Bogdanov deeply offensive. But even more substantial grounds for complaint was that Dubrovinskii's intervention at the lecture violated the agreement that philosophical matters were to be regarded as a neutral area. One of the questions put to Bogdanov at the lecture asked him to confirm that 'Machism had nothing in common with Bolshevism', and Dubrovinskii had gone on to state in his intervention that in his own and Lenin's opinion Bolshevism had nothing in common with Bogdanov's philosophical doctrines.[42] Following this incident Aleksinskii and Mikha Tskhakaya wrote in protest to Lenin. Bogdanov brought before the editorial board of *Proletarii* a resolution that the philosophy of empiriocriticism did not conflict with the interests of the Bolshevik fraction and when Lenin and Dubrovinskii rejected this resolution Bogdanov resigned from the editorial board.[43]

Materialism and Empiriocriticism

In 1908 Lenin found that he had more in common with Plekhanov than with Bogdanov not only in philosophy but in politics as well. After the 1905 revolution, as among the Bolsheviks, so among the Mensheviks divisions in the fraction began to appear. Some thought that a reform of the party was necessary, to get rid of the old underground hierarchy of committees and instead to have the workers send delegates from their unions and educational clubs to a more representative organisation. The idea did not enjoy much support, but the existence of the trend allowed Plekhanov and Lenin, with their passion for attaching labels, to speak of 'Liquidationism' as a new heresy to be combated.[44] Both in their respective theoretical journals took up the campaign in defence of the underground revolutionary organisation.

Plekhanov was dismayed to find that the cause of the revolutionary underground was being betrayed within his own camp. Some of his colleagues including Martov, Potresov and Maslov had been commissioned by the publishing house Mir to compile a multivolume history of the 1905 revolution under the title of *The Social Movement in Russia at the Beginning of the XX Century*. The authors' historical interpretation of the events in question naturally reflected Menshevik political thinking of the time. This was that national revolution against the autocracy had been unsuccessful because of the weakness of the forces representing liberal democracy, which had been prominent in revolutions in the West. The continued evolution of Russia in the direction of bourgeois democracy was consequently held to depend on the leftward shift of the Russian bourgeoisie as it came into increasing conflict with the tsarist regime. As it was essential that the bourgeois liberals should not be frightened off by revolutionary radicalism, the authors implied that the underground party would not be playing a prominent part in the process. Plekhanov was especially aggrieved by Potresov's chapter on the evolution of social–political thought in the period before the 1905 revolution. Little attention was paid to the 'underground' Marxism to which Plekhanov had made a notable contribution. Instead Potresov chose to emphasise the writings of the 'legal' Marxists, especially Peter Struve. Deeply offended, Plekhanov resigned from the editorial board of the Menshevik journal *Golos sotsial-demokrata* in the midst of his polemic with Bogdanov.[45]

Plekhanov could now see an opportunity for a new alignment within the Social Democratic Party. If the Mensheviks could rid themselves of their 'Liquidationist' wing and if the Bolsheviks managed to dissociate themselves from the 'Recallers' and 'Ultimatists', then the 'Party Mensheviks' and the Leninist Bolsheviks might come together as truly Social Democratic elements who regarded the underground organisation as the core of the party. Lenin was also much attracted by this idea, and he understood that the more resolutely he opposed Bogdanov and his philosophy the greater were the chances of a *rapprochement* with Plekhanov.[46] But to bring about that kind of realignment – or any other for that matter – the party as a whole, including the national groups, would require to be convinced of its desirability. That promised to be difficult, as the national groups believed that party fractions ought to be eliminated, whereas the kind of purges that Plekhanov and Lenin had in mind were designed to consolidate and strengthen their respective fractions.[47] Nor were there many in the national groups who shared Lenin's conviction that Machist philosophy was incompatible with Marxism and Social Democracy. The objective of his book *Materialism and Empiriocriticism* was to prove to them and the world at large that far from complementing Marx's ideas, the philosophy of Mach and Avenarius was anathema to the socialist standpoint.

At first sight Lenin's book is an impressive work of scholarship and erudition. The text abounds in references to many philosophers and in quotations from their writings. The opinions of numerous commentators are cited drawing upon the philosophical journals of the day. From the sources Lenin utilised it is clear that he had made an extensive study of the empiriocriticist school. He knew his way around the subject to such an extent that he was able to say which writers had been influenced by whom and who had been recommended by whom.

Despite this expertise, *Materialism and Empiriocriticism* is on the whole an uninformative book. The reader is not told what the ideas of the empiriocritics are. The quotations from their works are taken in isolation from their systems of thought as a whole, and are reproduced only because they contain something which, to Lenin's mind, discredits them. The method used is the same as that employed in the polemics against the Narodniks in the 1890s. The tone is abusive; at every stage words like 'nonsense' and 'gibberish' are used, leaving the reader in no doubt about what conclusions Lenin wishes to be drawn from the material he presents. The book does not say to the reader: 'Here are the ideas of Mach, Avenarius and so on. Here is what is wrong with them.' Lenin expects the reader to reject the philosophy of the empiriocritics without getting to know what it is.

Lenin's tactic in *Materialism and Empiriocriticism* was not to mount a frontal attack on the empiriocritics, but to establish guilt by association. Taking his cue from Plekhanov's 'Materialismus Militans', he began by outlining the ideas of Bishop Berkeley, who argued that there were no grounds for positing the existence of something one did not directly perceive. He then went on to show that the conceptions of Mach, Avenarius and related philosophical schools were simply restatements of Berkeley. Since Berkeley belonged to the idealist school, and since idealism was considered to be reactionary, it followed that the empiriocriticist school served the interests of reaction.

Lenin regarded as the acid test of all philosophical ideas whether they could be classed as materialist or idealist. He thought it highly significant that Marx and Engels had (allegedly) called their philosophy 'dialectical materialism'. But beyond definitions and classifications, Lenin's book did not venture to expound or elaborate Marx's philosophical system. Lenin's implication was that this had already been done quite satisfactorily in Engels's work *Anti-Dühring*. In fact Lenin reproached Bogdanov with having tried to reformulate Marx's ideas in different terms from Engels.

Bogdanov was unimpressed by *Materialism and Empiriocriticism*, finding in it 'nothing but arrogance and ignorance'.[48] His reply was a volume containing a survey of his own philosophical ideas entitled 'The Fall of the Great Fetishism' and a shorter section specifically on Lenin's *Materialism and Empiriocriticism* called 'Faith and Science'. Due to the delay in finding a publisher, the volume only appeared in 1910. In contrast to Lenin's book, Bogdanov's reply was concise, restrained and to the point. Bogdanov not only exposed Lenin's individual errors and misapprehensions, but went beyond these to point out the attitudes which characterised Lenin's approach to the polemic.

For Bogdanov the most characteristic feature of Lenin's attitude in *Materialism and Empiriocriticism* was its authoritarian quality. Lenin held that the ideas expressed somewhere and at some time by Marx and Engels embodied the absolute truth. He treated the writings of Marx and Engels like holy writ, something which should not be questioned but believed in, rather as one should believe in a religious dogma.

Another aspect of Lenin's authoritarianism was embodied in the way he tried to parade his philosophical erudition to impress his readers, and to persuade them of their own ignorance in philosophical matters in order that they would believe him, that they would regard him as an authority. In Bogdanov's view, Lenin's book was constructed in a way that taught the reader to *believe* in the professional erudition of the specialist, and taught the reader to *believe* in Marx.

In a few well-chosen examples Bogdanov was able to show that Lenin's philosophical erudition was quite specious. He pointed out that Lenin's method of equating the ideas of the empiriocritics with Bishop Berkeley depended on confusing and misapplying the concepts and terminology involved. He exposed Lenin's method of assigning guilt by association and finding soft targets to attack, by ridiculing the idea that 'if A recommends B, then why criticise A when you can criticise B'.

Bogdanov devoted considerable attention to criticising the ideas of Plekhanov, Lenin's teacher in philosophical matters. He pointed out that many of Plekhanov's misconceptions derived from his adoption of a Kantian standpoint. Both he and Lenin spoke in Kantian terms of 'things-in-themselves', representing the material world. Plekhanov, moreover, followed Kant in thinking that 'things-in-themselves' were unknowable, and that what appeared to human perception were only symbols or 'hieroglyphs' of the underlying reality. Lenin, however, insisted that what was perceived were 'copies' or 'reflections' of the original. To Bogdanov both conceptions were derived from erroneous – and idealist – premises.

As in *The Adventures of One Philosophical School*, an important element in Bogdanov's critique of Plekhanov was the demonstration that Plekhanov was unethical as a writer, and manipulated his evidence to suit his purposes. Thus, in order to make it appear that Marx had subscribed to the kind of epistemology that he himself propounded, Plekhanov had deliberately mistranslated one of Marx's 'Theses on Feuerbach'. This incorrect translation had then been used by Plekhanov's followers as an argument against their opponents in the 'Machist' camp.[49]

There are indications that Lenin was not entirely satisfied with *Materialism and Empiriocriticism* either. In 1914, when Lenin moved to Berne, which had a good library, he took the opportunity to read Hegel and deepen his knowledge of 'dialectical materialism' and to produce notes that were published in 1929 under the title of 'Philosophical Notebooks'. The purpose Lenin had in mind was probably to produce a book, which would have been a sequel to *Materialism and Empiriocriticism* and a continuation of his polemic against Bogdanov and the 'Machists'. That Lenin had the Machists in mind when reading Hegel is shown by the repeated references to them in the manuscript. In one place he notes that to date Marxists have been prone to criticise their philosophical opponents from a vulgar–materialist point of view more akin to that of Feuerbach and Büchner rather than from a dialectic materialist standpoint. Lenin's purpose was obviously to attempt a dialectical–materialist critique of Bogdanov and Mach, which would not just be a rejection of their views, but one which would correct them, 'deepening, generalising and extending them, showing the connection and transitions of each and every concept'.[50] For that he needed to understand the dynamics of Marx's philosophical system, and he thought that a familiarity with Hegel would enable him to do this.

In the endeavour of reading through Hegel's works Lenin was to some extent guided by the writings of Engels and Plekhanov, his two main philosophical teachers. Influenced by Plekhanov, he professed to find everywhere in Hegel's philosophy the 'leaps' that according to Plekhanov characterised Hegel's dialectical method. Nevertheless Lenin's perseverance in wading through Hegel's *Logic* was eventually rewarded. Just as he was complaining that Hegel's analysis of Syllogisms in terms of 'Universality', 'Particularity' and 'Individuality' was 'in the highest degree abstract and abstruse' and 'the best means of getting a headache', he thought he recalled seeing Marx emulate Hegel by using the same terms in the first chapter of Volume I of *Das Kapital*.[51] This led Lenin to conclude that: 'It is impossible to understand Marx's *Das Kapital*, and especially its first chapter, without having thoroughly studied and understood the whole of Hegel's *Logic*. Consequently, half a century later none of the Marxists understood Marx.'[52]

In fact the work in which Marx referred to Hegel's treatment of the Syllogism with its component elements 'Universality', 'Particularity' and 'Individuality' was not *Das Kapital*, but *A Contribution to the Critique of Political Economy*. But in essence Lenin was right; Marx's approach to the economic categories of capitalism in the first edition of *Das Kapital* did emulate Hegel's treatment of the logical categories in his *Science of Logic*. As Lenin's note 'On the Question of Dialectics' shows, he had got as far as an awareness that 'Universality', 'Particularity' and 'Individuality' were central elements in the respective systems of Hegel and Marx, but he was not able to establish what the significance of this terminology was. To have done so would have required an acquaintance with Marx's early manuscripts, and these only began to be published after Lenin's death.

The 'Philosophical Notebooks' did not result in any published work embodying the results of Lenin's study of Hegel. Considering that the purpose of such a work would have been to make a deeper and more thorough critique of the empiriocriticist school and of Bogdanov's philosophy in particular, what would have prompted Lenin to write it would have been a new book by Bogdanov or another collection of articles by Bogdanov and his friends. That kind of book, however, never appeared, because by that time the direction of Bogdanov's thought had changed – from philosophical matters to what one would now call 'systems thinking' or, in Bogdanov's term, 'Tektology', the 'science of universal organisation'.

The Tenth Plenum of the Central Committee

Soon after the publication of *Materialism and Empiriocriticism* a meeting of the Bolshevik Centre was held in Paris in June 1909, ostensibly as an expanded meeting of the *Proletarii* editorial board. Lenin had managed to secure a majority and succeeded in passing a series of resolutions condemning Recallism and Ultimatism as well as Lunacharskii's 'God-building'. He also succeeded in having Bogdanov expelled from the Bolshevik fraction.[53] Lenin of course had no power to expel Bogdanov from the RSDLP, and indeed from the point of view of the party as a whole Bogdanov's expulsion from the Bolshevik fraction was entirely irregular, since officially no such fraction existed. Bogdanov was therefore able to go ahead, despite opposition from Lenin, with organising the party schools for workers he and his friends had planned to hold on Capri. However, since Bogdanov was no longer a member of the Bolshevik Centre, he had to relinquish control of the considerable funds that the Bolshevik fraction had at its disposal from the Schmidt inheritance and from bank robberies. Control of these funds now passed to Lenin.

How Lenin might follow up his victory in the Bolshevik Centre would depend on how the RSDLP at large would react to Bogdanov's expulsion from the Bolshevik fraction, and to how they would receive *Materialism and Empiriocriticism*, which sought to justify the campaign against Machist philosophy. Lenin was soon to discover that although the Poles and Latvians had sided with him against Recallers and Liquidationists, they agreed with him on little else and would frustrate his attempts to divest the party of its troublesome right and left wings.

To canvass the support of the SDKPiL Bogdanov lost no time in giving his account of the *Proletarii* editorial meeting to Rosa Luxemburg and Jogiches. He said that he objected to Lenin's consolidating the Bolshevik Centre for ideological purposes, and considered it necessary to have a congress or a conference of the RSDLP to resolve matters. He declared that he had nothing against closer cooperation with Plekhanov, but not if this implied the coming together of a Leninist and a Plekhanovite fraction. He told Jogiches that he found it repugnant that the money bequeathed to the *Bolsheviks* by Schmidt, who had perished in the Moscow uprising, should 'be allocated and utilised in the struggle against Bolshevism by the very same Plekhanov who at the graveside of the Moscow fighters had declared "We should not have recourse to arms"'.[54]

Luxemburg reacted to Lenin's behaviour with revulsion, describing it in a letter to Jogiches as 'Tatar–Mongol savagery'. She and Jogiches found Bogdanov's expulsion from the Bolshevik fraction objectionable on two counts. One was that it seemed to them ridiculous that an organisation should split on philosophical questions. They regarded philosophy as a private matter, and in this opinion they were supported by Karl Kautsky, who said as much in an open letter published in *Der Kampf* in July 1909. The other ground for objection was that the incident demonstrated the existence of a Bolshevik fraction within what was supposed to be a united party. As Jogiches made clear to Bogdanov, the existence of this 'party within a party' was unacceptable. The SDKPiL would have published an immediate open condemnation of Lenin and his supporters but for the fact that this might strengthen the Mensheviks, who were allies of the rival Polish group the PPS. Luxemburg and Jogiches resolved instead to oppose the Bolsheviks on the Central Committee when the opportunity presented itself. In the meantime Jogiches communicated the displeasure of the SDKPiL to the *Proletarii* editorial board.[55]

Just as the Poles in the past had maintained equidistance from the Bolsheviks and Mensheviks for the sake of party unity, they now acted with impartiality between Lenin and Bogdanov. Thus, although Lenin sent Rosa Luxemburg *Materialism and Empiriocriticism* for review in *Die Neue Zeit*, she refrained from doing this and Kautsky only gave it a short book-note. Nor was the book reviewed in the SDKPiL's own journal *Przegląd Socjaldemokratyczny*. On the other hand, when Bogdanov invited Luxemburg to lecture at the party school on Capri she refused in order not to appear to be taking sides.[56]

After his expulsion from the Bolshevik fraction Bogdanov and his group had constituted themselves into a literary group within the RSDLP called '*Vpered*' (Forward). It immediately set about organising a party school on Capri to train workers from local party organisations in Russia to take over the functions formerly carried out by those members of the intelligentsia who had left the party after the revolution. Lenin was firmly of the opinion that the school would be used to promote Machist and 'God-building' ideas, and refused the invitation to lecture to its students, writing to them instead to denounce the content of the school's curriculum.[57]

Bogdanov's efforts to canvass the support of the SDKPiL against Lenin and his supporters paid off, when in January 1910 a Plenum of the Central Committee was held in Paris at the insistence of Jogiches and Adolf Warski.[58] It lasted from 2 to 23 January, and from Lenin's point of view it was 'three weeks of hell'. Present were the fourteen voting members of the Central Committee (four Bolsheviks: Dubrovinskii, I. P. Goldenberg, Zinoviev, V. P. Nogin; four Mensheviks: A. S. Martynov, B. I. Goldman, N. Zhordania, N. Ramishvili; two SDKPiL: Jogiches, Warski; two Bundists: F. M. Koigen, I. L. Aizenshtadt; one SDLK: M. Ozolins; and one Vperedist: Shantser) plus representatives of the various socialist publications: Lenin, Kamenev, Martov and Trotsky. Bogdanov attended as a candidate member of the Central Committee.[59]

On the main topic for discussion, the state of affairs in the party, there was a collision of two points of view. Jogiches and Adolf Warski for the SDKPiL – supported by the Bolshevik members of the Central Committee, including Lenin's hitherto faithful supporter Dubrovinskii[60] – proposed that all fractions in the party be dissolved forthwith, while Lenin demanded that the meeting endorse his call for a struggle on two fronts, against the Liquidators on the right and against the Recallers and Ultimatists on the left. The resolution that was finally adopted gave a small concession to Lenin by outlining the two extreme viewpoints and suggesting that both should be overcome by broadening and deepening Social Democratic work in all spheres of the class struggle. But the main import of the resolution was the requirement that all fractionalism be eliminated and that all fractions be dissolved and transformed into currents which would not prejudice unity of party action.

Other resolutions spelt out in detail the implications of this requirement. Lenin had to undertake to dissolve the Bolshevik Centre and close down *Proletarii*. The Mensheviks for their part were expected to discontinue their *Golos sotsial-demokrata*. The funds which the Bolshevik Centre disposed of had to be handed over to the trustees Karl Kautsky, Franz Mehring and Klara Zetkin. *Vpered* was recognised as a literary and publishing group within the party, though its members were not permitted to organise separate party schools. In recognition of its non-fractional stance, Trotsky's paper *Pravda* was allocated a subsidy and a representative of the Central Committee (Kamenev) was delegated to serve on its editorial board. Infringements of party discipline which had occurred, particularly those arising from the existence of fractions, were condemned.[61]

Precise stipulations were made on how the various currents of opinion in the party would be represented on the various party institutions so that none would have preponderance. This applied to the Central Committee itself and its Foreign Bureau, the party newspaper *Sotsial-demokrat* and the committee for organising party schools. One of the few resolutions passed which was not concerned with the elimination of fractionalism was that dealing with the convocation of a party conference to discuss the direction of future social democratic activities inside Russia.

Following the plenum Jogiches remarked with some satisfaction that 'The Bolsheviks as a party within a party (as a separate organisation) have suffered outright defeat, as has Lenin's very narrow conception of intra-party objectives.'[62] Rosa Luxemburg was convinced that finally the unification of the Russian fractions had been achieved, but other observers, like Feliks Dzierżyński and Karl Kautsky, were more sceptical, believing that the compromise would be of short duration. In the event the pessimists proved right; Lenin was soon able to extricate himself from the stipulations of the January plenum and indeed to utilise them to reconstruct the RSDLP in such a way that the Bolsheviks were the dominant fraction.

Lenin was able to justify his refusal to adhere to the compromise by the behaviour of other parties to the agreement. The Mensheviks did not discontinue the publication of their *Golos sotsial-demokrata*; Trotsky dismissed Kamenev, the Central Committee's representative from the editorial board of *Pravda*, and Martov would not work with Lenin on the editorial board of the party paper *Sotsial-demokrat*; the two *Vpered* representatives left the party school organising committee when they discovered that the Central Committee had allocated insufficient funds for the purpose, and *Vpered* went ahead and organised on its own a second party school, this time in Bologna.[63]

Lenin spared no effort in pointing out the various breaches of the January plenum's resolutions, and to emphasise the point demanded the return of the Bolshevik funds which had been deposited with the trustees. He tried to ensure that the balance of representation would not be maintained on the various party bodies, recalling Semashko, the Bolshevik representative from the Central Committee's Foreign Bureau, in pursuit of that end. Lenin's main aim in the wake of the January plenum, however, was to gain control of the arrangements for calling the projected party conference so that it would be an overwhelmingly Bolshevik one.

In May 1911 Lenin did what he had accused Bogdanov and his friends of doing – organising a party school for fractional purposes. The school was held in the village of Longjumeau near Paris and had eighteen students from party organisations in Russia. Among the students were not only Bolsheviks but also Party Mensheviks, Vperedists and SDKPiL. Among the Bolshevik students were Sergo Orjonikidze and R. V. Malinovskii, who was later to be exposed as a police spy. Lenin was able to send three of the students at the Longjumeau school back to Russia and organise elections for the forthcoming party conference. Indeed, some of the students themselves would become conference delegates.[64]

The Prague Conference and the 'August Bloc'

Helped by the tardiness of the Central Committee and its subsidiary bodies in summoning a party conference, Lenin was able to take the initiative in doing so. The requisite resolution was passed at a meeting of members of the Central Committee living abroad in Paris in May–June 1911. Lenin was able to command a majority of votes at this meeting because most of his opponents on the Central Committee, such as Martov, Bogdanov and Trotsky, were absent, and because he had the backing of the Poles Jogiches and Dzierżyński. The support of the SDKPiL, however, was not to last. While the Poles might agree with Lenin that it was desirable to rid the RSDLP of its right wing, the 'Liquidators', they were adamant that the left wing of the party, the *Vpered* group and Trotsky and his circle, should not be purged. Moreover, Jogiches had the impression that Lenin and his associates used the term 'Liquidator' rather loosely, so that it seemed to apply to everyone in the party except the Bolsheviks and the SDKPiL.[65] By the end of 1911 the friction between the SDKPiL and Lenin's little band of followers had become so severe that organisational ties between the two groups were broken off completely.

The Sixth Party Conference of the RSDLP met conspiratorially in Prague in January 1912, with delegates claiming to represent the major party organisations in Russia. In reality the conference consisted largely of Lenin's supporters. Of the 18 delegates sixteen were Bolsheviks and two were Party Mensheviks. Former students of the Longjumeau school were well-represented (four), as were police spies (three). In the case of Malinovskii these two categories coincided. Although invitations had been sent to the national organisations, to the *Vpered* group, to Trotsky and to Plekhanov, these declined to attend as they did not recognise the legitimacy of the gathering. Thus Lenin was left free to pass what measures he thought fit.

One important function of the Prague Conference was to bring to an end the alliance with the national parties that had been initiated at the Unity Congress in 1906. The discussion on the absence of the national parties at the Prague Conference gave vent to the fury the Bolsheviks felt at the obstructive way the national groups had acted in their determination to preserve party unity. It was decided that this situation, which seemed to have been created by 'a federation of the worst sort', could not be allowed to continue. Henceforth the party would not tolerate separate national organisations.[66]

Although Lenin did not in so many words expel the Menshevik Liquidators and the *Vpered* group from the party, resolutions were passed which were designed to achieve this result. The Menshevik Liquidators grouped around the periodicals *Nasha zaria* and *Delo zhizni* were declared to have 'placed themselves once and for all outside the party'. The *Vpered* group was put in the same position by the requirement that all political groups abroad subordinate themselves to the Central Committee or forfeit the right to call themselves 'Social Democratic'. Groups were also obliged to communicate with organisations in Russia only through the Central Committee.[67]

The discussions at the conference show that the delegates had an impatience with fractions and groups in the RSDLP and envisaged a party organisation which would be completely united and subject to an iron discipline. Lenin had to explain that a long struggle against the Liquidators in the party as a whole lay ahead before the organisation could be united and the requisite discipline imposed. He stressed that whereas one should condemn fractionalism one should not condemn the struggle between groups, as this was an essential element in the life of the party.[68] In these discussions Lenin's attitude towards the delegates was as a teacher to his pupils – as indeed he had recently been in the case of some of them.

A new Central Committee was elected consisting of six Bolsheviks (Lenin, Zinoviev, Orjonikidze, Malinovskii, S. S. Spandarian and F. I. Goloshchekin) and one Party Menshevik (D. M. Shvartsman). Within a year Lenin had coopted six more Bolshevik members to the Central Committee including Sverdlov and Stalin. *Sotsial-Demokrat* was confirmed as the party's official publication, and it was decided to launch a new daily newspaper for workers to be distributed legally in Russia. The subsidy to Trotsky's *Pravda* was discontinued and, to add insult to injury, the title *Pravda* was appropriated for Lenin's new workers' newspaper.

The reaction of other groups in the RSDLP was predictable. At a gathering held in Paris in February 1912 cautiously calling itself a 'meeting of representative currents' adherents of the Mensheviks, *Vpered*, the Bund and Trotsky's *Pravda* group denounced Lenin's conference as unconstitutional and derided its claim to be 'All-Russian'. The meeting decided to convoke a conference which would be genuinely representative and which would restore party unity. The conference was held in Vienna in August 1912 and attended by the Mensheviks, the Bund, the SDLK, Trotsky's *Pravda* group and the *Vpered* group. Representatives of the PPS–Lewica and the Lithuanian Social Democratic Party attended as guests. The SDKPiL, however, declined the invitation to attend, as did Lenin and the Party Mensheviks.

On the face of it this could have been the ideal opportunity for Trotsky to unite the non-Leninist currents in the party under his banner of non-fractionalism. Trotsky in fact was one of the moving forces behind the conference and was a leading figure in the 'August Bloc' which emerged from the conference. Moreover, the national parties which had been so conspicuously absent at Lenin's Prague Conference had all supported him in his non-fractional stance, and might be counted upon to rally round him now as the champion of party unity.

In reality the groups attending the Vienna Conference were so disparate that they found little in common beyond their hostility to

Lenin. Political differences were compounded by national ones, and by the time of the Vienna Conference there were five national parties associated with the RSDLP, according to an Okhrana survey. These were the SDKPiL, the Bund, the SDLK, the Lithuanian Social Democratic Party and the Ukrainian Union 'Spilka', with which Trotsky was connected.[69] While the August conference's concession to national cultural autonomy might be attractive to the Bund it would just as surely alienate the ultra-internationalist SDKPiL, which stayed away from the gathering. No united Social Democratic organisation was to emerge from the August conference, and Trotsky himself soon became disillusioned with the 'August Bloc', which disintegrated within a year and a half.

The August conference did however establish an Organising Committee which acted as the equivalent of Lenin's Central Committee. And, like Lenin's group, the 'August Bloc' decided to publish a daily legal newspaper for workers in Russia. The newspaper *Luch* (Beam), commenced publication in September 1912 in St Peters-burg. Initially Trotsky contributed articles to *Luch*, but since the tenor of the paper was dictated by the more right-wing of the *émigré* Mensheviks, and displayed hostility towards the underground party, Trotsky gradually distanced himself from the newspaper. From March 1914 he began to publish the paper *Borba* in St Petersburg, drawing contributors from the various groups in the RSDLP and once again promoting the idea of party unity.[70] In St Petersburg itself non-Leninist Social Democrats, who considered Trotsky's conception of party membership too all-inclusive, formed their own organisation known as the 'Mezhraionka' (Inter-District group), which published the journal *Vpered*.[71] Subsequently the Mezhraionka was to become the main organisation which embraced former members of *Vpered* such as Lunacharskii and Pokrovskii, Latvian and Lithuanian Social Democrats, and Trotsky and his circle.

In its early days Lenin's *Pravda* published contributions from a variety of social democratic currents, but on Lenin's insistence turned increasingly to the unremitting campaign against 'Liquidationism'. Its popularity declined as a result. A similar unpopular move on Lenin's part was to divide the Social Democratic fraction in the Duma. The election campaign for the Fourth Duma in 1912 had returned seven Mensheviks and six Bolsheviks, including the police spy Malinovskii. When the deputies resolved to provide an example of party unity by contributing articles both to *Pravda* and to *Luch*, Lenin was aghast and a split in the Social Democratic fraction in the Duma was engineered, much to the dismay of Social Democrats of all fractions in Russia.[72]

The justification Lenin had used for his actions from the 1910 January plenum onwards was that the workers' movement, which had been subdued after the 1905 revolution, had become revitalised. The shooting of unarmed workers on the Lena goldfields in April 1912 had an effect comparable to the shooting of unarmed demonstrators on Bloody Sunday in 1905. A wave of strikes swept the country and showed the renewed force of workers' militancy. However, neither the Bolsheviks nor any other of the revolutionary parties in Russia played any noticeable part in leading the workers in this period. Links between the political emigration and party organisations within Russia in the period were tenuous and sporadic. Lenin's political manoeuvres in emigration had served only to confuse the local Bolshevik activists, and to render them less able to give the kind of leadership the situation demanded.[73]

4

THE FIRST WORLD WAR

The national question

In June 1912 Lenin and Krupskaya had moved from Paris to Cracow in the Austrian part of Poland to be nearer to the Russian frontier. This location afforded better opportunities for sending articles to *Pravda* and maintaining contact with organisations inside Russia, particularly as the elections to the Fourth Duma were in the offing. In fact the election campaign was successful from Lenin's point of view, as six Bolshevik deputies were elected. Unfortunately one of these deputies was Malinovskii, who was soon to be exposed as a police spy. It was in Cracow that Lenin first made the acquaintance of the young Marxist Nikolai Bukharin, who was then living in Vienna. Another visitor to Cracow was Stalin, whom Lenin had met previously at party congresses, and whom he encouraged to write a book on the national question.

In Cracow Lenin himself became absorbed with the national question. While an opponent of nationalism and a firm believer in internationalism, he had always been a supporter of Clause 9 of the party programme which recognised the right of all nations in the state to self-determination. The August conference in 1912 had raised the question of interpreting this right to self-determination in the sense of 'national–cultural autonomy'.[1] Lenin, however, argued that 'national culture' served as the pretext for everything that was most obscurantist, divisive and reactionary in nationalism. The programme of 'national–cultural autonomy' was based on the idea of 'national culture' and consequently fostered nationalism of the worst and most extreme sort.[2] Lenin was insistent that 'national–cultural autonomy'

100

was incompatible with the party programme, and in his view the 'self-determination of nations' could mean nothing but political self-determination, state independence and the formation of national states.

Because their main political opponents had been the nationalist parties, the SDKPiL had always condemned the demand for national self-determination, as they thought it encouraged nationalism. Rosa Luxemburg had argued this point on economic grounds, showing that Polish independence would be advantageous to no one since Polish capitalism benefited from Russian markets. She subsequently developed this argument, asserting that the right to self-determination of small nations is rendered illusory by the development of the great capitalist powers and by imperialism. Lenin, however, countered this by pointing out that Luxemburg had substituted the question of economic independence for the question of the political self-determination of nations and their independence as states. In her anxiety not to give aid and comfort to the Polish nationalists, Luxemburg was instead assisting the most reactionary currents of opinion in Russia.[3]

Despite Lenin's condemnation of the national parties at the Prague Conference, he continued to court the support of their members. He hoped to revise the terms on which the national parties had been admitted at the Unity Congress in 1906 in such a way as to incorporate them into a single centralised party covering the entire Russian Empire. But neither of the parties with which Lenin had been in closest alliance, the SDKPiL and the SDLK, had the slightest intention of giving up their autonomy.[4]

At the end of 1911 discontent with the party leadership caused the SDKPiL to split into two wings, the supporters of Rosa Luxemburg and Leo Jogiches and the dissidents, the '*Rozłamowcy*', who included Jakub Hanecki and Karl Radek. Lenin assiduously cultivated the dissidents, who were in general sympathetic to the Bolsheviks, but who defended SDKPiL autonomy no less staunchly than the old leadership had.

In January 1914, along with Malinovskii, Lenin attended the Fourth Congress of the SDLK held in Brussels in the hope of inducing the Latvians to affiliate to the Bolshevik Central Committee. At the congress Lenin spoke on the attitude of the SDLK to the RSDLP and denounced the SDLK leadership for its conciliatory attitude towards the Liquidators. But the congress did not go entirely Lenin's way – partly at least through the manoeuvrings of Malinovskii.

Although the decision was taken to dissociate the SDLK from the Organising Committee of the 'August Bloc', it was also resolved to remain independent of Lenin's Central Committee. The congress, moreover, deplored the split in the Duma Social Democratic fraction and expressed the hope that it would be reunited as soon as possible. Nevertheless, Lenin presented the outcome of the congress as a success, particularly as the new Central Committee elected at the congress was overwhelmingly pro-Bolshevik.[5]

A setback for Lenin was that at the session of the International Socialist Bureau held in London in December 1913, Karl Kautsky, appalled at the division of the Duma Social Democratic fraction, had called for an investigation into the causes of friction in the Russian party and ways by which unity might be restored. A conference was to be held on the question with the participation of all sections of the RSDLP as well as all Social Democratic parties active on Russian territory. Lenin did not attend this conference which took place in Brussels on 20 June (3 July 1914), sending instead Inessa Armand to read a prepared report which he had written. The report stressed the success of the Bolshevik fraction in attracting the support of the workers in Russia. It argued that experience had shown that it was impossible to unite with the Liquidators. Here the report pointed to the fact that Trotsky had ceased to collaborate with *Luch* and was now publishing *Borba*. It also referred to the withdrawal of the SDLK from the August Bloc. The report then laid down the conditions on which the Bolshevik Central Committee thought party unity possible. This in practice amounted to constituting the entire RSDLP according to Bolshevik principles, something entirely unacceptable to most delegates at the conference.[6]

Ironically, one of the accusations that Lenin had levelled against the Liquidators in his report to the conference was that they had been publishing anonymous rumours that Malinovskii was a police spy. Lenin had assured the conference that his Central Committee had investigated these rumours and had not found any truth in them. He personally had complete confidence in Malinovskii and thought it deplorable that the Liquidators should continue to slander him in their newspapers. Despite the suspicion surrounding him, however, it would only be after the February revolution in 1917 that Malinovskii's guilt was fully established.[7]

Kautsky proposed a motion that since there were no tactical disagreements between the various groups which were sufficiently important to justify the split, all groups should declare that they agreed to participate in a general party congress, which must resolve all the questions now under dispute.[8] The motion was supported by a majority of the groups represented at the conference, even by the SDKPiL dissident wing whom Lenin had counted on as allies. Only Janis Berzins for the SDLK sided with the Bolsheviks. On Rosa Luxemburg's suggestion, it was decided to bring the materials from the Brussels Conference to the next congress of the International, which was scheduled to be held in Vienna in August of that year.[9]

The reversal for Lenin revived the hopes of the anti-Bolshevik forces, and a reincarnation of the August Bloc met in Brussels on 3 July. A meeting took place of the Organising Committee, Trotsky, Rosa Luxemburg, Aleksinskii, the Bundists, the Caucasian Organisation, the Lithuanian Social Democratic Party, the PPS and the 'Rozłamowcy'. Only the SDLK and the Bolshevik Central Committee were absent from this 'Third of July Bloc'.[10] For Lenin the forthcoming Vienna Congress of the International took on a grim prospect. His answer would have been to send a strong delegation of authentic Russian workers to the congress to show by their numbers that the RSDLP was overwhelmingly Bolshevik.[11] But the Vienna Congress of the International was never to meet, as it was overtaken by the onset of war.

The war and the International

For the sake of Krupskaya's health Lenin rented a lodge in the village of Poronin in the Tatra mountains, where he and Krupskaya lived along with the Zinovievs and the Polish couple Sergiusz and Natalia Bagocki, both members of the dissident wing of the SDKPiL. It was in Poronin that Lenin learnt of the outbreak of war in the summer of 1914. On 23 July (5 August) Sergiusz Bagocki brought Lenin the Cracow newspapers with the information that the Reichstag had approved the war credits unanimously. Unable to believe the statement, Lenin at first thought that Bagocki had mistranslated the Polish text. It was only when Krupskaya confirmed Bagocki's translation that Lenin was able to take in the awful truth that despite repeated anti-war resolutions of the Second International the German Social Democratic Party (SPD) had voted for the war credits. He was appalled at what seemed to him an act of treachery on the part of the German socialists. According to Bagocki, Lenin declared: 'This is the end of the Second International.'[12]

Being at war with the Entente, Austrians now regarded Russians living in their midst with distrust and hostility, and on 25 July (7 August) Lenin was arrested on suspicion of being a Russian spy. By assuring the authorities that Lenin was in fact an implacable enemy of the tsarist government, the Austrian socialist leader Victor Adler was able to obtain his release almost two weeks later. As it was no longer safe to remain on Austrian soil, Lenin moved to the neutral Switzerland and took up residence in Berne. There in the company of the local Bolshevik group he was able to take stock of the new political landscape that had emerged since the outbreak of the war, and in which he would have to operate.

Over the previous decade there had been repeated threats of war, and the International had discussed what action it would take in the eventuality of war at its congress in Stuttgart in 1907. Lenin and Rosa Luxemburg had both taken part in this congress, and through their efforts the resolution had been passed calling on the parties of the International to do everything in their power to prevent the outbreak of war. If war nevertheless broke out, the socialist parties of the International ought to strive to bring it to a speedy end and exploit the economic and political crisis created by the war to hasten the downfall of the capitalist system.[13] The Stuttgart resolution had been confirmed by the Copenhagen Congress in 1910 and by the Basel Congress in 1912. Since the International had been so definite about the matter, it was all the more traumatic that when the decisive moment came the European socialist parties were overwhelmed by the reality of mobilisation and the pressure of events.

How the International reacted to the crisis was determined to a great extent by the attitude of the SPD, the strongest and most influential party in the International. When the Austrian ultimatum was delivered to Serbia, the German Social Democrats could still hope that the conflict would be localised and had decided that the party's Reichstag fraction would not vote for the war credits. But when the Russian army mobilised and the danger had appeared that the country might be invaded, the war appeared as one of national defence. In the words of Friedrich Stampfler: 'We must not let our women and children be sacrificed to Cossack atrocities.' In these circumstances a majority of the Reichstag fraction favoured voting for the war credits, and in order to maintain party unity, even those who were against this course of action, like Karl Liebknecht and Hugo Haase, voted with the rest. The vote of the SPD Reichstag delegates on 4 August 1914 was a defining moment in the history of European socialism, and was interpreted by the left wing as marking the end of the Second International.

Karl Kautsky had attended the session of the SPD Reichstag fraction on 3 August at which the vote on the war credits was discussed. Despite the fact that in his writings he had predicted the coming of war and the tactics that would be adopted by belligerent governments to make it appear as one of national defence, Kautsky was swayed by the patriotic fervour which swept the country and felt it impossible to counsel opposition to the war credits. As abstention was also considered out of the question, Kautsky recommended that the SPD's approval of war credits should be conditional on Germany's renunciation of any territory gained as a result of military action. On the insistence of the Chancellor Bethmann-Hollweg, however, this condition was removed, and consequently the SPD declaration to the Reichstag gave its unreserved endorsement to the war effort. Kautsky had long been a revered figure for Lenin, but Kautsky's behaviour in August 1914 diminished him in Lenin's eyes. Henceforth for Kautsky Lenin would have nothing but condemnation and disdain.[14]

After the capitulation of the SPD to the government, there was little the other socialist parties could do but to follow the SPD's example and vote for war credits. The Austrian Social Democrats, who closely identified themselves with the SPD, voted with the same misgivings and soul-searchings as their German comrades had done. The Hungarians, on the other hand, had no such qualms and gave unqualified approval to the war effort. The French socialists showed little reluctance. Jean Jaurès, who had been a vociferous opponent of war, fell victim to an assassin's bullet shortly before it broke out. But despite their regard for their fallen leader, the parliamentary group unreservedly voted through the war credits, convinced that their country was the victim of German aggression. They even sanctioned two of their number, Jules Guesde and Marcel Sembat, to join the Ministry of National Defence, then being formed. The Belgians, whose neutrality had been infringed by the German armies, also rallied round their government. Emile Vandervelde, the Belgian socialist leader, who was also chairman of the International Socialist Bureau (ISB) of the Second International, joined the Ministry of National Defence. In Britain the labour movement as a whole responded positively to the Liberal government's appeal to support the Allied cause, the trade unions promising an industrial truce for the duration of the war.

In only two of the belligerent countries did the socialist parties vote against granting war credits to their respective governments: in Serbia and Russia. Though belonging to the country which was under attack, two Social Democrat deputies in the Serb parliament spoke against the war and refused to approve the war credits. On 26 July (9 August) the tsarist government called an extraordinary session of the Duma to approve the war credits. Despite the encouragement of Vandervelde to rally round their government, both Duma fractions of the RSDLP condemned the war, refused to vote for the war credits and walked demonstratively out of the debating chamber. The five Bolshevik deputies paid dearly for their bravado. They were arrested in November 1914, put on trial and sentenced to permanent exile in Eastern Siberia.[15]

Although attitudes to the war in the RSDLP tended to follow the existing political spectrum with greatest support for the war on the right and least on the left, the new situation did create some new and somewhat surprising alignments. Akselrod and Martov, whom Lenin despised for their toleration of Liquidators, were prominent among the opponents of the war. Plekhanov, on the other hand, whom Lenin had regarded as a possible ally and who as recently as 1912 had declared that 'only a war between classes could stand in the way of a war between nations', became an ardent Francophile and an advocate of the Allied cause. He considered the war to be a struggle for democracy against Austro-German tyranny and encouraged the Russian socialist exiles in France to enlist in the French army, and delivered rousing speeches to them as they departed for the front.[16] The ultra-leftist and 'Vperedist' Gregory Aleksinskii also became convinced of the justice of the Allied cause and joined with Plekhanov in supporting the war effort. Along with like-minded Socialist Revolutionaries, they published the Paris-based weekly journal *Prizyv* (Clarion Call), which argued that an Entente victory would bring freedom, whereas a German victory would preserve the autocratic regime in Russia.[17]

Within Russia the pro-Entente views were propounded by the group associated with the journal *Nasha zaria*, which Lenin had castigated as 'Liquidator'. The journal was closed down along with other Russian socialist publications in July 1914, but was replaced by

Samozashchita (Self-Defence). This group, which included A. Potresov, P. Maslov, Vera Zasulich and Noi Zhordaniia, believed that the war was being fought to defend the country against Prussian militarism. They were aware that it might lead to annexations, but thought that these ought to be carried out with the consent of the populations involved.[18]

The Organising Committee of the August Bloc had a distinctly anti-war orientation. The leaflet it issued in October 1914, 'The War and the Proletariat', traced the origins of the war back to the imperialist rivalries of the great European powers, and refrained from taking sides in the conflict. The leaflet indicated that the conditions created by the war provided fertile soil for revolution. It predicted that the present war would be brought to an end by the proletarians of all countries acting in solidarity.

The Organising Committee had a Foreign Secretariat whose most prominent members were Semkovskii and Akselrod. The policies advocated by the Secretariat were intended to reflect a consensus of Russian socialist opinion in order to preserve what unity remained in the Social Democratic camp. In the Secretariat's journal Akselrod advocated the convocation of an international conference by social-ists in the neutral countries to agree on conditions for a democratic peace to bring the war to a speedy end.[19]

Further to the left were the Menshevik Internationalists grouped around the newspaper *Golos* (Voice) founded by V. A. Antonov-Ovseenko and Dmitrii Manuilskii in Paris in September 1914. Martov joined its editorial board in November. *Golos* condemned the war as resulting from the imperialist aspirations of the ruling classes of Europe and of certain dynastic interests. It held that those social-ists in belligerent countries who supported their governments were betraying the interests of the workers' movement. It believed that the efforts of these socialists to present this predatory war as one of national liberation was to foster illusions. *Golos* called for an imme-diate end to the war and an assault on capitalism by the masses. Lenin thought that *Golos* was the best socialist newspaper at the time, and he applauded Martov for his principled stand on the war.[20]

After he was forced to leave Zurich in November 1914 Trotsky joined the editorial board of *Golos*. He had just written the pamphlet *The War and the International*, which was serialised in the newspaper. In *The War and the International* Trotsky argued that the present war had been brought about because the economic systems of the advanced European states had outgrown their national boundaries. The entire world had now become a single economic unit in which the various parts were inseparably connected with one another. In the process of world economic integration the capitalist states had been driven to struggle for the subjection of the world economic system to the profit interests of each national bourgeoisie. In these circumstances it made no sense for the proletariat to 'defend the fatherland', since national boundaries had become the main obstacle to economic progress. Now the task of the proletariat was to create a republican United States of Europe, which would be the foundation of a United States of the World.[21]

Golos ceased publication on 26 January 1915 but was succeeded by *Nashe slovo* (Our Word) two days later, which continued to appear until September 1916. (*Nashe slovo* in its turn was replaced by *Nachalo* (Beginning) in September 1916 and the newspaper continued under this title until March 1917.) After Trotsky's arrival, editorial meetings of *Golos* became acrimonious as Trotsky's radical internationalism conflicted with Martov's more cautious brand and his unwillingness to disown the more right-wing elements of the August Bloc in the interests of party unity. Martov finally resigned from the editorial board of *Nashe slovo* in April 1916.

Nashe slovo provided an important platform for Russian internationalist opinion. It also acted as a rallying-point for those Social Democrat internationalists who wished to escape from the amorphous August Bloc, but who did not want to join the Bolshevik party. The contributors to *Nashe slovo* included people later to become prominent in the Bolshevik party. Among them were: Antonov-Ovseenko, Angelica Balabanova, G. I. Chudnovskii, G. V. Chicherin, Alexandra Kollontai, L. I. Lozovskii, Lunacharskii, Pokrovskii, Karl Radek, Christian Rakovskii, Theodore Rothstein and M. Uritskii. Some, like Lunacharskii, Manuilskii, Uritskii and Trotsky himself, were to join the Bolsheviks in 1917 via the Mezhraionka organisation.[22]

Lenin's initial response to the war was contained in the document drawn up in consultation with the Bolshevik group in Berne and entitled 'The Tasks of Revolutionary Social-Democracy in the European War'. The document characterised the war as bourgeois, imperialist and dynastic, a struggle for markets and the freedom to loot foreign countries. It considered the actions of the German Social Democrats in voting for the war credits as unpardonable and a betrayal of socialism. Just as reprehensible was the conduct of the

Belgian and French Social Democratic leaders who had entered bourgeois governments to help the war effort. The document stressed that the betrayal by the socialist leaders signified the ideological and political bankruptcy of the Second International. Considerably more attention was paid in the document to analysing the roots of this betrayal than to discussing the nature of the war itself. Lenin believed that the capitulation to their governments by the socialist leaders when war came was not from momentary faint-heartedness, but was the culmination of opportunist and reformist trends that had been observable for some time. The document rejected the argument by European socialist leaders that they had to support the war effort for the sake of defending the country against external attack. These claims, it declared, were completely spurious; both sides were intent on making territorial acquisitions. In respect of aggression there was nothing to choose between the belligerent countries.

The most characteristic and the most controversial section of the document was that which spoke of the tasks of Russian Social Democrats. In Lenin's view it was necessary for them to combat Great Russian and tsarist monarchist chauvinism and to counter the arguments of those who maintained that a Russian victory would be in the interests of progress. On the contrary: because of the oppressive nature of the tsarist regime Lenin considered that in the interests of the common people and the nationalities which composed the Russian Empire the lesser evil would be the defeat of tsarist Russia in the war. It was the advocacy of a Russian defeat which caused his political opponents to refer to his views as 'defeatism'. Like Trotsky and Martov, Lenin thought that Russian Social Democrats should agitate for the transformation of the separate countries in Europe into a republican United States of Europe.[23]

In October Lenin expanded the ideas set out in 'The Tasks of Revolutionary Social-Democracy' into a manifesto of the Central Committee entitled '*The War and Russian Social Democracy*'. In the intervening period an article by Kautsky had appeared defending the actions of the Social Democrats at the beginning of the war. This caused Lenin to conclude that Kautsky was the 'most harmful of all', and to strengthen in the manifesto those passages critical of 'centrism', the current which vacillated between opportunism and revolutionary Social Democracy, trying to conceal the collapse of the Second International behind hypocritical phraseology. The manifesto did not overtly advocate a Russian defeat, but stated that the only correct proletarian slogan was turning the present imperialist war into a civil war.[24]

Lenin's conception of the character of the war did not differ greatly from Martov's or Trotsky's. He too believed that capitalism had outgrown the confines of the nation state and that the present conflict had been brought about by competition among the capitalist powers to divide up the world amongst themselves. Trotsky, however, did not agree with Lenin that for socialists the defeat of one's own country was a lesser evil. A defeat for one country, in his opinion, would only strengthen the opposing powers. And although it would undermine the ruling classes, it would also disorganise the workers and create conditions unfavourable for a socialist revolution. Trotsky preferred the slogan 'the struggle for peace', but Lenin rejected this, thinking that it encouraged pacifist tendencies, which would stand in the way of a civil war.[25]

Zimmerwald

Being convinced that the Second International was defunct and incapable of ever again providing leadership for the European socialist parties, Lenin directed most of his efforts during the war towards creating an anti-war international socialist movement. He wished to bring together all the socialist groups which unreservedly subscribed to the slogan of turning the imperialist war into a civil war. Conversely, he was determined that those socialists who had betrayed the cause of internationalism by supporting the war effort should play no part in future international socialist organisations. Lenin was also deeply suspicious of the 'centrists', those who were prepared to tolerate the 'social-chauvinists' and who still believed that something of the Second International might be salvaged. The means Lenin employed to consolidate and foster the forces of internationalism during the war was a series of conferences, which he either attended in person or at which he contrived to make his influence felt.

At the end of 1914 the anti-war elements began to rally. A left opposition developed within the SPD as Karl Liebknecht, Rosa Luxemburg, Klara Zetkin, Leo Jogiches and Julian Marchlewski declared themselves against the war. On 3 December Karl Liebknecht voted against the war credits, but in February 1915 he was drafted into the army as a construction worker. Rosa Luxemburg was imprisoned for her anti-war agitation in the same month, but in prison under the pseudonym of Junius she wrote a pamphlet entitled *The Crisis in German Social Democracy*, which was smuggled to the outside world. In the pamphlet Luxemburg characterised the war as an imperialist conflict and castigated the German Social Democrats for their failure to oppose it. She thought that the Social Democrats' betrayal signified the collapse of the Second International, but believed that the organisation of the proletariat on an international scale was necessary for the defeat of imperialism. She advocated the creation of a new International whose decisions would take precedence over those of the constituent national parties, an idea which Lenin was to adopt when the Comintern was created some years later.[26]

In September 1914 Swiss and Italian socialists met at Lugano in an effort to revive the ties among socialist parties which had been broken by the onset of war. Lenin sent the meeting a copy of his first document on the war and asked those present to discuss it, and some of the ideas in the document were incorporated in the Lugano resolution. Following this meeting the Italian socialist leader Oddino Morgari approached the head of the ISB, Emile Vandervelde, to call an international socialist conference. In face of the French socialists' refusal to meet with their German counterparts, Vandervelde declined to convoke a conference even of the socialist parties of neutral countries. The Italians then felt free to take upon themselves the organisation of a conference of socialist parties which remained faithful to the principles of the class struggle and international solidarity. In discussing the Italians' proposal, the Swiss party resolved not to take part in the conference officially, but gave its individual members complete freedom to do so.[27]

Together with the representatives of the Italian party, Morgari and Angelica Balabanova, the Swiss Social Democrat Robert Grimm made preparations for the projected international socialist conference. But while the resolution of the Italian party's Central Committee had envisaged a conference limited to those socialists who adhered to certain socialist principles, Grimm set out to widen the circle of participants.

In the intervening period two other international conferences took place in the spring of 1915. The first of these was an international women's conference held in Berne in March. The initiative for holding the conference came from the editorial board of *Rabotnitsa* (The Woman Worker), a journal founded in St Petersburg by Inessa Armand and Anna Ulyanova-Elizarova, and Clara Zetkin, the Secretary of the International Women's Organisation. Because mainly pacifist opinions were represented at the conference, the RSDLP delegation, consisting of Krupskaya, Inessa Armand, E. Rozmirovich and Olga Ravich, did not succeed in having accepted a resolution drafted by Lenin. There was a similar outcome at the International Youth Conference held at the beginning of April. Although this conference had more of a left-wing internationalist presence, and although a resolution was passed condemning the war and the policy of 'civil peace', the gathering still fell short of Bolshevik expectations, as it did not call for civil war and it did not demand a break with the social-chauvinists. The conference did, however, found a journal, *Die Jugend-Internationale*, which Lenin was able to utilise as a platform for his ideas.

In order to muster the anti-war forces, Lenin tried to launch a new periodical, *Kommunist*, to act as a forum for internationalist opinion. Trotsky was invited to contribute, but he declined in an open letter to Lenin published in *Nashe slovo*. Trotsky said that he had theoretical disagreements with Lenin, one being that he attached a great deal of importance to the slogan calling for a struggle for peace whereas Lenin did not. Another disagreement was with Lenin's idea that a Russian defeat would be the lesser evil, Trotsky believing that this eventuality would not provide suitable conditions for a socialist revolution. Such differences might be overcome, but he could not condone the fact that Lenin refused to regard certain groups as his allies for purely fractional reasons. For Trotsky this attitude made cooperation with Lenin impossible.

Only one issue of *Kommunist* was published, but it was an important one. As well as containing Lenin's article 'The Collapse of the Second International', it included Bukharin's article 'The World Economy and Imperialism', which would later be expanded into a pamphlet. It was a work which Lenin drew upon in writing his own study of imperialism. The issue, however, also contained an article on the national question by Karl Radek, whose ideas on the subject were similar to Rosa Luxemburg's, and had been espoused by Bukharin and his friends, Yuri Pyatakov and Evgenia Bosh. Lenin objected violently to the article and demanded the discontinuation of the journal.[28]

In order to mobilise anti-war opinion Lenin and Zinoviev wrote the pamphlet *Socialism and the War* for distribution at the forthcoming international conference. Lenin suspected that as Robert Grimm was organising the conference it would be an assembly of mainly centrists, which would pass anodyne resolutions deploring the war, but not setting out any concrete plan of action for bringing it to a revolutionary conclusion. At the preparatory meeting which preceded the conference in June, Lenin and Zinoviev accordingly directed all their efforts at trying to ensure that the internationalist opponents of the war were well-represented. In this endeavour they were not greatly successful and the political complexion of the conference itself was overwhelmingly centrist.

The conference was held in the Swiss village of Zimmerwald between 23 and 26 August 1915 with 38 participants from eleven countries. The centrist majority was composed of most of the German delegation and part of the Italian, Swiss, Polish and Russian delegations. The Zimmerwald left was in a small minority, with Lenin and Zinoviev from the RSDLP, the SDLK representative Berziņš, the SDKPiL delegate Karl Radek, the German delegate Julian Borchardt, the Swiss Fritz Platten, the Swede Höglund and the Norwegian Nerman. The main ideological conflicts at the conference were between the centrists and the left. Trotsky, representing *Nashe slovo*, characteristically took upon himself the role of trying to reconcile the two sides.

Prior to the conference Lenin and Karl Radek had worked on drawing up draft manifestos which the left wing would try to have accepted. The left agreed on a manifesto which took Radek's draft as a basis and incorporated modifications in keeping with Lenin's version. When Radek introduced this draft at the conference, it was clear that it would be unacceptable to the centrist majority in the conference, whose main spokesman was Ledebour. In conjunction with the French socialists Ledebour had drafted a manifesto representing centrist opinion for the consideration of the conference. Trotsky, who said that he agreed in general with Radek's draft, had composed a draft of his own designed to bring together the conflicting points of view. A commission was elected consisting of Grimm, Ledebour, Lenin, Trotsky, Rakovsky and Merrheim and Modigliani to consider the three versions of the manifesto. The result was a compromise which Lenin found not entirely unsatisfactory.

The Zimmerwald manifesto painted a grim picture of the slaughter, cultural devastation, economic decline and political reaction the war had brought about. It declared that the war was beyond dispute an imperialist conflict caused by capitalist greed for profit, and rejected any idea that it was being fought for defensive ends or that it was one of national liberation. It went on to say that the calamity had been foreseen and at 'Stuttgart, at Copenhagen, at Basel, the International Socialist congresses had indicated the course that the proletariat must follow'. What this course was the manifesto did not make explicit.

It did, however, make plain that the socialist parties had not lived up to their obligations since the outbreak of war. They had failed in various ways: they had called on the working class to renounce the class struggle; they had agreed to war credits; they had placed themselves at the disposal of their governments; they had delivered up to their governments socialist ministers as hostages for the preservation of 'civil peace'. Not only individual national parties, but also the International Socialist Bureau had been found wanting. The manifesto urged the proletariat to withdraw their support for the ruling classes and to stand up instead for the cause of socialism, 'for the emancipation of the oppressed nations as well as the oppressed classes, by means of the irreconcilable class struggle'.[29]

Imperialism

For socialists the question of the character of the war became a crucial one. On this depended whether the war was simply a humanitarian disaster or whether out of the devastation a new socialist order would emerge. If the war really was a conflict brought about by the way capitalism had developed on the international arena, then it could be analysed in terms of the evolution of the capitalist system, a progression which might lead eventually to its downfall and its replacement by a higher form of economic system. How the capitalist system expanded, what drove it and how evenly it was spread throughout the various countries became a study of intense interest for socialists. The topic was usually discussed under the heading 'imperialism', a term which tended to confuse later historians as to its connotation.

The question of how capitalism spread throughout the world was a matter Marx had intended to deal with in his 'Critique of Political Economy'. He had originally believed that as it circulated, capital reproduced itself on a progressively wider scale and at the same time adapted to the conditions in which it found itself increasingly to its requirements. But when he tried to show that this expanded reproduction was a necessary feature of capitalism Marx failed. His evidence pointed to the fact that where the ambit of capitalism had been expanded, as for example in colonial countries, this had been accomplished by deliberate government policies. Not being able to find a purely economic imperative for capital's expanded reproduction, Marx left his economic studies unfinished, though Engels gave the manuscripts the appearance of coherence and published them as Volumes II and III of *Das Kapital*. Thus, when Marxist economists in the first decades of the twentieth century tried to study how capitalism developed on a world scale and turned to Marx's work as a starting point, the results were necessarily inconclusive. They could not do what Marx had failed to do, because the real world was constituted differently from the way Marx's causality had envisaged it to be.

Rosa Luxemburg published her study of imperialism, *The Accumulation of Capital*, in 1913. In this work Luxemburg attempted to develop the schemes of the circulation and reproduction that appeared in the second volume of Marx's *Das Kapital*. For Luxemburg the key problem of capitalist development was that of finding markets. She stressed that the capitalist system was characterised by the inability to extend its market to keep pace with its capacity for increased production. The lack of effective markets led to periodic economic crisis and a fall in the rate of growth.

In this situation the factor which gave dynamism to the capitalist system was the acquisition of external markets. Here the non-capitalist environment played a crucial role, as the sphere in which the creation of new capitalist markets was possible. But in this process the natural economy was destroyed and replaced eventually by a new area of capitalist development, which in its turn was obliged to seek external markets. (Here Luxemburg drew upon Kovalevskii's researches.) In this way the non-capitalist environment was constantly reduced. In order to ensure their access to the underdeveloped parts of the world the capitalist monopolies sought to create colonial empires, and the competition for these led to the armed imperialist conflicts of recent times. When all the areas of fresh exploitation had been exhausted, capitalism would have no further markets to sustain it, and at that point the system would collapse.[30]

When Lenin read Luxemburg's book in the spring of 1913 he found it unconvincing. He did not believe that the acquisition of external markets was essential to capitalist development, and recalled that he had argued as much in his *Development of Capitalism in Russia*. He was gratified to note that Luxemburg's critics were saying the same thing as he had said back in 1899 against the Narodniki.[31] Lenin made no systematic critique of Luxemburg's study, and did not refer to it in his own work on imperialism.

Much more important for Lenin's conception of imperialism was the work of the Austrian Marxist Rudolf Hilferding whose book *Das Finanzkapital* appeared in 1910. It was conceived as an extension of Marx's ideas to recent economic developments. Hilferding's starting point was not the question of markets, as it had been for Luxemburg, but the factors which affected the rate of profit which accrued to capitalist enterprise, in particular the way modern industry was financed. It was from this starting point that Hilferding set out to explain the economic phenomena of his own times: the formation of industrial cartels and trusts, the export of capital and the international rivalries to secure spheres of influence in various parts of the world. It was, Hilferding thought, industry's increasing need for finance that had given banks an enhanced importance in the economies of developed countries, and it was this which had caused industrial and finance capital to merge together.

Whereas formerly capital had demanded free trade and non-intervention from the state, finance capital sought to dominate markets, and called upon the state to erect tariff barriers to protect its monopolies. When tariff barriers were raised in other countries finance capital replied by exporting capital in order to set up production behind them. In less developed countries too labour was cheap, and so could be employed to produce value, and thereby counter the tendency of the profit rate to fall.

This export of capital, in Hilferding's view, was an important factor in equalising the level of economic development throughout the world. It was one of the positive developments in the recent evolution of capital with which Hilferding was particularly concerned. For him it appeared that modern capitalism was evolving in a direction which would make the emergence of socialism a distinct possibility. The concentration of the economy had put central regulation and control within easy reach. The fact that industry was controlled by the banks meant that a single bank could 'exercise control over the whole of social production'. The extension of the sphere of influence of finance capital throughout the world also meant extending the sphere of the socialist revolution. Hilferding insisted that 'the proletariat must see that the imperialist policy generalises revolution ... and with it the conditions for the victory of socialism'.[32]

Thus, from Hilferding's analysis it emerged that finance capital was preparing the ground for the socialist society in two ways: (1) intensively – by the rationalisation and centralisation of the economy through monopolies to make it amenable to governmental regulation; and (2) extensively, by spreading the capitalist economy throughout the world, thus making possible a socialist revolution on an international scale. These were aspects of Hilferding's work which Lenin and other radical socialist thinkers of the time found stimulating and encouraging.

One of Hilferding's main critics was Karl Kautsky, who wrote an article of his own on imperialism just before the outbreak of war. Predictably Kautsky's conception of imperialism would be the target for Lenin's scorn when he came to write his book on the subject. Kautsky believed that as capital developed a disproportion would arise since agricultural production would not be able to keep pace with the demands imposed on it by the growth of industry. The way to solve this problem was for a country to acquire agrarian areas abroad. Hence what Kautsky understood by imperialism was the impulse of an industrialised capitalist nation to acquire and annex an increasing quantity of agrarian area.

The competition for agrarian territory had fostered rivalries among the great powers that would culminate in war. But Kautsky did not think that war was the inevitable consequence of imperialism. He could foresee that in the post war era capitalists would have learnt that war was inimical to their interests and must be avoided at all costs. From a purely economic point of view, Kautsky reasoned, capitalism would come to an end only when all the areas for agrarian expansion had been exhausted. This was still far from being the case, and the position would not be changed by the war. The possibility remained, therefore, that after the war the great industrial nations would come to an agreement and bring an end to the arms race. This, Kautsky believed, might usher in a new era of 'ultra-imperialism' in which the danger of war would have been removed. In an essay published in 1915 Kautsky went on to argue that since in modern times capitalism had outgrown national boundaries, the interests of capital would be better served by the formation of free unions of equal states. The peace programme of Social Democracy, Kautsky thought, should be the creation of a United States of Europe.[33] The ideas that modern capitalism had outgrown national boundaries and that socialists ought to demand the formation of a

United States of Europe were ones which Lenin had voiced in his first documents in response to the war. As one might expect, after reading Kautsky's essay his enthusiasm for a United States of Europe cooled rapidly. Trotsky, however, continued to propound these conceptions on the pages of *Nashe slovo*, and argued that the dictatorship of the proletariat would take the form of a republican United States of Europe.[34]

Bukharin's article 'The World Economy and Imperialism' first appeared in the Bolshevik journal *Kommunist* in 1915. It was a polemical work directed against Kautsky and his ideas on 'ultra-imperialism'. In supposing such a development possible, Bukharin considered Kautsky to have overestimated the vitality of the capitalist system. He was insistent that the world economy and imperialism laid the foundations of the socialist order. In his opinion 'by its very existence, an imperialist policy shows that the objective conditions for socialism have ripened'.[35]

Bukharin followed Hilferding in defining imperialism as the 'policy of finance capital'. Like Hilferding too he considered the export of capital to be characteristic of finance capital. Since the export of capital might involve the seizure of foreign territories, and their subjugation to monopolies, the imperialist policy of finance capital brought in its train conflicts on an international scale, which had culminated in the present war. The outcome of a finance-capitalist war, Bukharin reasoned, because it presupposed highly developed and well-organised 'national–economic' organisms, would be the seizure of power by the proletariat and the transformation of the war between nations into a civil war between classes.[36]

Lenin's work *Imperialism, the Highest Stage of Capitalism* was conceived as the introductory volume to a series of booklets on the belligerent countries in the war. The series, which was sponsored by Gorky's journal *Letopis* (Chronicle), was aimed at a mass readership. These circumstances had an influence on the form that Lenin's book was to take. Although intended as a critique of Kautsky, it could not be a purely polemical work. Its educational function demanded that it should have a systematic character, and because the editorial board of *Letopis* was favourably disposed towards Kautsky, adverse comment on the latter could not be a salient feature of the work.[37]

Lenin began his exposition by restating ideas that had become generally accepted by socialists in recent years, namely that free competition had given way to monopoly, and that this had brought with it 'socialisation of production' – a step in the transition towards socialism. This statement, however, was immediately followed by the observation that monopoly had by no means eliminated competition, and that between the two considerable friction was still bound to arise. From the start Lenin was concerned to demonstrate that the monopoly stage of capitalism did not bring with it the end of conflict in the economic sphere.[38]

The next important point that Lenin wished to make was that in the latest stage of capitalism the banks had acquired a new role. Whereas formerly they had functioned as middlemen, now they had become powerful monopolies and had come increasingly to coalesce with industry. Industry in the monopoly stage of capitalism was dominated by the banks and by the financial oligarchies which controlled them. Thus, the driving force behind the new form of capitalism was not industry, as Kautsky believed, but finance. Monopoly capital was finance capital.[39]

A characteristic feature of monopoly capitalism, Lenin stated, was the export of capital. Whereas free-enterprise capital had exported commodities, monopoly capitalism exported capital. The motive was to acquire higher profits than could be earned at home. In more economically backward countries profits were high because labour, land and raw materials were cheap. The world had already been divided up into spheres of interest which were the special preserve of the various international cartels. Lenin was at pains to emphasise, however, that this division was by no means stable, and that as the relative strength of the capitalist groupings altered there would be competition for more advantageous shares.

And like the international cartels, the various nations had already divided up all the territories of the world amongst themselves, so that no area remained unclaimed. What would follow could only be the struggle to redivide the world, once the balance of power changed. This it was bound to do, since Lenin believed that 'finance capital and trusts do not diminish, but increase the differences in the rates of growth between the various parts of the world economy'.[40] Future prospects in this regard gave no hope of lasting stability.

Referring to Kautsky's definition of imperialism as 'the impulse of an industrialised capitalist nation to acquire and annex an increasing quantity of agrarian area', Lenin registered his disagreement with it, since he considered that the characteristic of imperialism was that it strove to gain control not only of agrarian territories, but even of the most highly industrialised regions. Kautsky's mistake had been to think of imperialism as being driven by industrial and not, as was the case, by finance capital.[41]

The same characteristic of imperialism was used by Lenin to counter any prospect of the 'ultra-imperialism' Kautsky had envisaged. He did this by arguing that monopoly capitalism was capitalism in decay. The financial oligarchy was a parasitic class or stratum of society that took no part in any enterprise whatsoever. It made its living by exporting capital and collecting dividends. It had no interest in developing industry, and, indeed, was quite capable of impeding technical innovation in order to safeguard its position. Finance capital was not capital which showed prospects for future development. It was capitalism in decline, the final stage of capitalism before it was transformed into socialism.[42]

Lenin concluded his argument by using his characterisation of imperialism as finance capitalism to explain the failure of the labour movement to oppose the current war. He stated that the receipt of high monopoly profits by the capitalists enabled them to pay relatively generous wages to a minority of the workforce, and so to gain the support of this 'labour aristocracy'. It was this group which fostered opportunism within the working-class movement, an opportunism which found its most characteristic incarnation in the leadership of the Second International.[43]

Although Lenin's book on imperialism was conceived as a popular introduction to the subject, it did not simply paraphrase the ideas of previous writers. Lenin's was a more complex and subtle approach than that of any of his predecessors. The need to achieve his polemical purposes compelled Lenin to examine existing theories critically and to refine the one that he propounded in his book.

The distinctive feature of Lenin's presentation of imperialism is that it does not look forward to a progressive march of capitalism throughout the world which would eventually provide a uniform economic base for the socialist revolution. With Lenin capitalist development is much more patchy and less rational. Finance capital will invest in the undeveloped world or in the industrial world, wherever the dividends are higher. For that reason capitalist development is uneven; there will not be an even spread of the revolution when it occurs and it will not happen in all countries simultaneously. And when revolutions come, they will be of different kinds. Those in the advanced countries will be socialist, but there will be movements for self-determination and rebellions against colonial rule.[44] In this way Lenin's theory of imperialism gave him a distinctive theory of revolution.

The need to show that imperialism or finance capital was the last phase of capitalism prompted Lenin to stress the ways in which finance capital was capitalism in decay. It did not produce, and was quite prepared to impede production if that was a way to extract profit. From a present-day perspective there is an irony here that while Lenin's characterisation of finance capital was extremely perceptive, and gave a better account of capitalist development than Kautsky's theory of imperialism, it underestimated the vitality of finance capital. In fact, Lenin underestimated just how pernicious finance capital could be in the long term. Not only could it impede industrial production, it could even destroy industrial development and productive capacity. But if this were the case, one could not argue that capitalism was laying the foundations for a socialist economy. However, no writer of Lenin's day, certainly no socialist writer, could have predicted just how irrational capitalism would turn out to be. And despite his emphasis on the unevenness of economic development, Lenin continued to believe in the 'civilising mission' of capitalism in preparing the way for the socialist revolution.

Although *Imperialism, the Highest Stage of Capitalism* was not published until 1917, as early as the summer of 1915 Lenin made his views known on the uneven nature of capitalist development and the implications of this phenomenon for the socialist revolution. Commenting on Trotsky's conception of a United States of Europe, Lenin remarked that unequal economic and political development was a necessary law of capitalism. It followed that the victory of socialism was initially possible in a few capitalist countries, even one, taken separately.[45] This was a passage that Stalin was to seize upon to prove that Lenin subscribed to the theory of 'socialism in one country'. It will not bear this interpretation, however, if it is placed in the proper context of Lenin's conception of imperialism and socialist revolution. But Stalin made sure that Lenin's words would not be seen in that context by attributing to Lenin a theory of revolution that he never held, namely that 'the chain of imperialism snapped at its weakest link'. Such is the power of imagery that historians still attribute this aphorism to Lenin, even though it conflicts with the ideas Lenin actually professed.

In 1915 Lenin returned to the topic of national-self determination, this time in the light of the theory of imperialism, stimulated by Bukharin and Pyatakov. They argued that in the era of finance capitalism, when small nations were being absorbed into larger units, it was futile to call for national self-determination. They also contended that the slogan of 'self-determination' was no different from the slogan of 'defence of the fatherland'. The only possible response to finance capital was proletarian revolution. Lenin replied, as he had previously to Rosa Luxemburg, that because economic independence was unattainable, the same thing did not apply to political independence. Lenin likened the ideas of Bukharin and Pyatakov to the mistaken views of the 'Economists' of the 1890s, who had also – allegedly – ignored political questions.[46]

Kienthal

The second international socialist conference was held in the Swiss village of Kienthal in April 1916. It had 43 participants of whom twelve belonged to the Zimmerwald left. These together with their sympathisers among the centrists almost commanded a majority at the conference, indicating a significant shift in the balance of forces since the gathering at Zimmerwald the previous year.

The most heated debates between left and right were on the question of whether the International Socialist Bureau should be reconvened. Lenin and the left took the view that the Bureau was completely discredited by its toleration of chauvinism and should be abandoned. The right argued that the damage done to the International could be repaired and that the existing institution could still be salvaged. The resolution eventually passed was a compromise but one highly critical of the ISB and embodying much of the left's case.

The manifesto issued by the Kienthal conference entitled '*To the Peoples who Suffer Ruin and Death*' was an emotional condemnation of the war. It called for a speedy end to hostilities and stressed that the only way to prevent wars was the seizure of political power by the working classes and the abolition of capitalist property. As such it represented a significant victory for the left. The only shortcoming from Lenin's point of view was that it did not adopt his slogan of turning the war into a civil war.[47]

During the period between the Zimmerwald and Kienthal conferences the position of the left wing had become stronger. Its arguments had been vindicated by the disastrous consequences of the war and the increasing number of anti-war demonstrations in the various belligerent countries. Whereas at the outbreak of the war in 1914 the dissident socialists who had stood out against it were a small and isolated band, by 1916 they had succeeded in becoming a movement with a substantial international following.

Lenin could feel that his position on the war had been justified and that in that respect time was on his side. The war could only become more ruinous and unpopular, and eventually it would end in socialist revolution. The war had also enhanced Lenin's own personal standing. Now instead of fighting such sectarian battles as the one against Liquidators he was involved in a much more substantial campaign against those socialists who were caught up in the patriotic fervour of the war effort. The outcome involved the fate of nations rather than the control of a political party.

The state

The case made by Rosa Luxemburg then by Bukharin and Pyatakov against the right of self-determination for nations was that in the era of imperialism smaller states could not retain their economic independence. Lenin's reply to this argument was that even if economic independence was impossible, it was still feasible to attain political independence. For Lenin 'self-determination concerns only politics'.[48] This argument would hold only if the political and economic spheres remained separate. This separation was, however, questioned by Pyatakov's contention that 'under socialism self-determination becomes superfluous, since the state itself ceases to exist'. In other words, the political sphere would vanish, leaving only economics. Lenin's immediate reply was to claim that under socialism there would be democracy, which was also a form of state, and would in the manner of all states only 'wither away' with time.[49]

This latter proposition was challenged in an article which Bukharin published in the journal *Die Jugend-Internationale* developing his ideas on finance capital in time of war. Bukharin began by pointing out that the slogan 'defence of the fatherland' was misleading, because in fact what was being defended was not the country or the population, but the state organisation. Moreover, the state was a historical entity, an institution which had arisen as an organisation of the ruling class. It was correspondingly destined to disappear with the socialist revolution and the end of class rule. In the era of finance capital, and especially during the war, the economic monopolies had merged with the state apparatus and other organisations of bourgeois society to compose a modern Leviathan predatory state. The proletariat would have to adjust its tactics to combat this formidable adversary and it was the task of Social Democrats, Bukharin maintained, to stress their hostility to the state in principle. In order to dissociate himself from charges of anarchism Bukharin claimed that what distinguished socialists from anarchists was not that the former were in favour of the state while the latter were not, but that socialists advocated a centralised economy whereas anarchists called for a decentralised economy.[50]

In a comment on Bukharin's article in the journal *Sbornik sotsial-demokrata* for December 1916 Lenin disputed Bukharin's distinction between socialists and anarchists. The appropriate distinction to be drawn in the question of the state, he maintained, was that socialists were in favour of utilising the existing state and its institutions to effect the transition from capitalism to socialism. This transitional form was the dictatorship of the proletariat, which was also a state. The anarchists, on the other hand, wanted to abolish the state, to 'blow it up'. For socialists, the state would gradually wither away after the bourgeoisie had been expropriated. Lenin said that he intended to return to this important subject in a further article.[51]

It was the question of the state which preoccupied Lenin in his last months of exile. He began his research in the library at Zurich, collecting quotations on the subject from Marx, Engels, Kautsky, Pannekoek and Bernstein. The culmination of these studies would be the book *State and Revolution* written in 1917. But his writings between December 1916 and his return to Russia in April 1917 show that Lenin's ideas on the subject were in constant flux. It did not take him long, for example, to discover that Bukharin had been right in saying that in the revolution the proletariat ought to 'smash' the existing state machine. But in that case where was the famed 'dictatorship of the proletariat', which was 'also a state'? The problem for Lenin was that the precise way the proletariat came to power was not a theme treated systematically in the works of Marx and Engels. They had said different things at different times, depending on whether they were writing general works, commenting on specific events or making passing remarks in private correspondence.

Even if Lenin could resolve the problem for the advanced industrial countries, he still had to acknowledge that Russia did not number among them. Right until his return to Russia in April 1917 he was still of the opinion that because Russia was a peasant country and one of the most backward of the European countries, 'socialism could not triumph there immediately'.[52] In that case if revolution should break out in Russia, the implication seemed to be that smashing the state machine and establishing the 'dictatorship of the proletariat' would hardly be appropriate. In the context of the actual Russian revolution, however, Lenin chose to ignore the distinctions he had thought important in calmer times.

Lenin and the German General Staff

The First World War was an example of 'total war', a conflict fought out not only on the battlefield, but in all and any sphere which might in some way undermine or destabilise the enemy. The Allies targeted the nationalities of the Austro-Hungarian Empire, encouraging nationalist and separatist movements in order to sap the war effort of the Central Powers.[53] The Germans in their turn fostered the national–separatist movements in the Russian Empire, particularly that of the Poles. They naturally hoped that a revolution might take Russia out of the war. From the German point of view, a government headed by Lenin would be an excellent outcome, because the Bolsheviks were pledged to end the war unilaterally. There is evidence that the Germans took a keen interest in Lenin, and fed him useful information through their agent, the Estonian Alexander Keskküla. There is no evidence that they supplied him with any money. In Keskküla's experience Russians could not be relied upon to use money for the intended purpose of fomenting revolution; they were more likely to embezzle it.[54]

The snag for the Germans was that at the end of 1916, when there were signs of growing social unrest, the only Russian revolution in the offing was one that would sweep away the tsarist regime and replace it with a government of liberals determined to pursue the war more effectively. As early as August 1915 the newspaper *Utro Rossii* (Russia's Morning) had published a list of members for a proposed 'defence cabinet', in which figures like Paul Milyukov and Alexander Guchkov figured prominently.[55] Milyukov, who was the

obvious choice for Foreign Minister, was determined to acquire the
Dardanelles and Constantinople for Russia. Guchkov, who was a
prominent figure in the Moscow business community, was a zealous
proponent of the war and was the chairman of the Central War
Industries Committee, an organisation created to mobilise Russian
industry for the war effort. Guchkov was impatient with the tsarist
government's ineffective pursuit of the war and at the end of 1916
was preparing to stage a palace revolution to install a government
which would secure military victory for Russia.

The German General Staff had obviously learnt something of
Guchkov's intentions because in January 1916 Keskküla obtained a
document which had circulated privately in Moscow suggesting
something of the kind and sent it to the German General Staff for
forwarding to Lenin. The document, entitled 'Disposition No. 1',
outlined a project to establish a 'Supreme Staff Command' whose
nucleus would consist of 'Prince G. Lvov, A. I. Guchkov and
A. F. Kerensky'. Supreme command was to be entrusted to Guchkov,
who had the confidence of the army and the city of Moscow.[56]

The document is significant because, although it was not directly
connected with Guchkov's conspiracy, it had all the hallmarks of
authenticity and listed three people who were in fact to be members
of the Provisional Government in 1917. Although Lvov and Guchkov
might be considered likely candidates for any future Russian government, the same cannot be said of Kerensky, who had not previously been mentioned in this connection.

One use that Lenin made of the document was to predict in the
journal *Sotsial-demokrat* at the end of January 1917 that as a result of
a conspiracy led by Alexander Guchkov Russia would have 'a government of Milyukov and Guchkov if not of Milyukov and Kerenskii'
in the near future.[57] Copies of the journal were sent to the German
General Staff, who were informed by Keskküla that a new journal
being published by Lenin, *Sbornik sotsial-demokrata*, would 'contain
some very interesting material'.[58] The journal in fact contained a
copy of 'Disposition No. 1', thus revealing the source of Lenin's
information about Guchkov's plot and the future composition of the
government to which this would give rise.

It was in the interests of both Lenin and the Germans to prevent
the formation of a liberal regime in Russia. For Lenin such a development would be disastrous, because the constitutional and economic reforms it would institute would take the heat out of popular

discontent and postpone a social revolution indefinitely. For the Germans the prospect of a democratic government which would channel popular enthusiasm into a vigorous pursuit of the war was highly unwelcome. In these circumstances it made sense for both parties to try to sabotage Guchkov's planned *coup d'état* by publishing 'Disposition No. 1'.

What Lenin and the Germans did not know was that the Okhrana had already been alerted to 'Disposition No. 1' and had investigated it thoroughly. They had satisfied themselves that the authors of the document did not pose any serious political threat and had let the matter rest. Lenin's tip-off to the Russian secret police, the Okhrana would not, therefore, have upset Guchkov's plans. What rendered them redundant was the onset of the February revolution and the formation of the Provisional Government, which brought Guchkov and his associates to power by different means. Lenin was able to take some comfort from the fact that he had been able to predict the composition of the new government with considerable accuracy.[59]

On the anniversary of Bloody Sunday in January 1917 Lenin gave a lecture on 1905 to young Swiss workers. He concluded it by observing that people of his generation might not live to see the decisive battles of the coming revolution, but he hoped that the young people in Switzerland would not only live to fight but to win in the coming proletarian revolution.[60] Lenin's biographers have often taken this passage to mean that Lenin did not foresee the impending February revolution, but other sources show clearly that he did. Since Lenin stressed the uneven development of the international economy he naturally envisaged the world revolution as an extended process. Consequently, while he might not live to see the decisive battles of the revolution, he could certainly expect to be present at the initial skirmishes.

On 2 (15) March Lenin first got news of the revolution in Russia. Unlike in 1905 when Lenin had taken his time in returning to Russia, now he desperately sought ways to make his way there. There was no hope of being allowed to pass through Britain or France to Russia, and the scheme to travel there on a Swedish passport was impracticable. The Swiss socialist internationalist Fritz Platten concluded a written agreement with the German ambassador in Switzerland. The terms of the agreement, which Lenin had drawn up, were: (1) all *émigrés* regardless of their opinions on the war be allowed to go; (2) no one be allowed to enter the railway carriage in which the *émigrés* were travelling without Platten's permission – no inspection of passports or luggage; (3) the travellers should undertake to agitate in Russia for the exchange of a number of Austro-German prisoners interned in Russia equal to the number of *émigrés* allowed to travel by the agreement.[61] When the negotiations were successfully completed, Lenin, Krupskaya, the Zinovievs, Inessa Armand, Olga Ravich, Radek – altogether about thirty people – packed themselves into the railway carriage for the journey to Russia. Only Bolsheviks travelled in the first contingent of returnees, but they were followed a month later by more than two hundred *émigrés* including Martov and other Mensheviks travelling under the same agreement.[62] The calculation on the Germans' part was that the bacillus of revolution would be implanted in Russia and relieve pressure on their eastern front.

5

LENIN AS REVOLUTIONARY

'The April Theses'

Four weeks went by between the time Lenin first received news of the revolution in Russia and his arrival at the Finland Station in Petrograd. In those four weeks the tsarist regime had fallen, the tsar had abdicated, the Provisional Government had been established and the Petrograd Soviet had simultaneously come into being, creating the situation of 'dual power' in the country.

The events which culminated in the overthrow of the autocracy began with a demonstration to mark International Women's Day on 23 February (8 March). The demonstrators used the opportunity to protest about the food shortages and to demand an end to the war. On the following day and on the 25th the demonstrators took again to the streets, their numbers increasing on each occasion. By Sunday the 26th the authorities had become worried and troops were deployed to control the crowds. On that day soldiers opened fire on the demonstrators, causing a large number of casualties. On Monday the 27th, however, the tide began to turn in favour of the revolution, as the troops began to go over to the side of the demonstrators. With the help of the soldiers the demonstrators were able to overcome the resistance of the police and take control of the capital. It was at this juncture that people who had hitherto stood aside from the popular movement began to join it and even place themselves at its head.

On the morning of the 27th a group of Menshevik defencists including K. A. Gvozdev, who belonged to the *Samozashchita* circle and now headed the 'Workers' Group' attached to Guchkov's Central War Industries Committee, distributed a leaflet calling for workers'

and soldiers' representatives to meet in the Duma building. This was
to be the first session of the Petrograd Soviet, at which its Executive
Committee was elected.[1] On the same day, members of the recently
dissolved Duma gathered to form a Provisional Committee, which
was to give way on 1 March to the Provisional Government. The new
government, which was headed by Prince G. E. Lvov, had among its
ministers Guchkov, Milyukov and Kerensky, just as Lenin had predicted. The Soviet Executive Committee was anxious that the liberals should take power in order to consolidate the revolution, since it
was by no means certain at that stage that the monarchist forces had
been finally defeated.[2]

During the February revolution the Bolshevik leadership was in the
hands of the Russian Bureau composed of Alexander Shlyapnikov,
Vyacheslav Molotov and Peter Zalutskii. The St Petersburg Committee
had tried to coordinate revolutionary organisations throughout the
city in the mass demonstrations of the February days, but after most
of its members were arrested on Sunday the 26th, this role fell to the
Vyborg Committee. Among the Vyborg Bolsheviks were some experienced activists who had taken part in the 1905 revolution in Nizhnii
Novgorod and were eager to take on the police force in gun battles.
Shlyapnikov was unwilling to sanction this tactic, because it might
lead to armed conflict between the revolutionaries and the army,
which it was essential to win over if the movement was to succeed.
The Vyborg Bolsheviks went ahead in any case, and managed to rout
the police force without antagonising the troops.[3]

Another cause of friction between the Vyborg activists and the
Russian Bureau was that the Vyborg Committee was determined to
stamp an anti-war character on the mass movement and demanded
the publication of a manifesto which would do this. Shliapnikov, on
the other hand, wary of alienating any of the movement's support,
dragged his feet on the issue. The Vyborg Bolsheviks accordingly
drew up a manifesto for themselves and only took it to the Bureau
members for editing. The manifesto was issued on 27 February. Its
contents were reported in *The Times* and praised by Lenin in one of
his 'Letters from Afar' which he sent to *Pravda* for publication.[4]

The manifesto is significant because it shows what the political
stance of the Bolsheviks in Petrograd was at the time of the February
revolution. Besides calling for an end to the war, the document summoned the insurgent populace to form a Provisional Revolutionary
Government, which would later summon a Constituent Assembly.

It did not agitate for the formation of soviets. This was done by the Menshevik leaders, with the result that when the Soviet was established it had a defencist majority.

One of the first acts of the Executive Committee of the Petrograd Soviet was to enter into negotiations with the Provisional Committee of the Duma to negotiate the conditions on which the Soviet would support the Provisional Government. These included a programme of civil rights and the commitment to convene a Constituent Assembly. As the representatives of the Soviet did not want to alienate the Duma liberals, no demands were put to them on the ending of hostilities. In fact, the assumption of Miliukov, Guchkov and their government colleagues, including the socialist Minister of Justice Alexander Kerensky, was that the main *raison d'être* of the Provisional Government was to conduct the war more effectively. They reckoned that with a stake in the new democratic Russia the army would be more motivated to fight. Nevertheless tensions did arise between the Provisional Government and the Soviet on the war issue in the early days of the revolution. Whereas Miliukov and Guchkov wanted to fight the war to a victorious conclusion, the Soviet took a more Zimmerwaldist approach to the war and thought that it should be fought only for defensive objectives, that there should be 'no annexations or indemnities'.[5]

This was also the approach taken by Stalin and Kamenev when they returned from their Siberian exile in the middle of March. Much to the annoyance of Shliapnikov and the Vyborg Bolsheviks, the returnees took over the running of *Pravda* and began to propound the doctrine that the Provisional Government should be supported 'in so far as' it pursued policies in the interests of the proletariat. As far as the war was concerned, Kamenev declared in a *Pravda* article, written in the defencist spirit, that so long as the war continued the Russian soldiers should hold 'their posts and answer a bullet with a bullet, a shell with a shell'.[6]

Lenin returned to Russia via Sweden and arrived at the Finland Station in Petrograd on 3 (16) April. He returned to a vastly different country to the one he had left in 1907. The old oppressive tsarist system had been overthrown. Political prisoners had been freed. The new government had passed laws guaranteeing the freedom of speech, the press, assembly and civil rights in general. They had ended the discrimination against national and religious minorities. These were things Russians had hardly dared dream of in the past.

Lenin himself admitted that Russia was now the freest of all the belligerent nations. In the Petrograd Soviet the majority of the members were Mensheviks or Socialist Revolutionaries; there were relatively few Bolsheviks. These generally supported the Provisional Government, seeing it as incomparably preferable to the old tsarist regime, and well worth making concessions to in order to ensure the success of the new liberal order. The Minister of Justice in the Provisional Government was the Socialist Revolutionary Alexander Kerensky. His presence there was taken to show that the new government was one which was broadly based and sensitive to socialist opinion.

There were other ways in which Russia was a different country from what it had been when war broke out. It was a country whose resources had been sapped by almost three years of war. The economy was disintegrating under the strain, with industry, agriculture and transport approaching a state of crisis. The country had lost an immense expanse of territory as a result of the German advance, and refugees from the occupied territories retreated into the Russian heartland to share the deprivation and despair of the settled population. The Russia in which the February revolution had taken place was one in which quite exceptional circumstances prevailed.

A small delegation led by Chkheidze, the chairman of the Petrograd Soviet, came to welcome Lenin and the other returning *émigrés* at the Finland Station. He was then taken to the Bolshevik headquarters in the mansion of the ballerina Matylda Krzesińska, where in a two-hour-long speech he outlined to his supporters what he thought the policies in the present situation ought to be. The points Lenin made were subsequently published in *Pravda* under the title 'The April Theses'. The Menshevik Internationalist Nikolai Sukhanov was allowed into the meeting, and he later recorded his impressions of Lenin's speech. From what Sukhanov says it is clear that between this speech and the published version of the 'Theses' some modifications were introduced.

A prominent theme in the speech was the familiar one – that the imperialist war would be transformed into a civil war and a world-wide socialist revolution. He criticised the 'revolutionary defencism' of Chkheidze and the other leaders of the Soviet. He said that there was no need for bourgeois democracy, and that the only form of government should be the Soviets of Workers', Soldiers' and Agricultural labourers' Deputies. Sukhanov noted that no mention was made of the Constituent Assembly. Lenin went on to state that since the name of Social Democracy had been disgraced by treason, this should be dropped from the party's title. He thought that there was no need to elaborate legislation for agrarian reform, advocating 'organised seizures' of the land instead.

Sukhanov's reaction to the speech, and one shared by most of the audience, was one of amazement. The point which caused greatest surprise was Lenin's conception of the soviets as a form of government. Despite their importance in the existing political situation no one had considered them as permanent organs of state power. The idea seemed to be one of anarchist inspiration. As Sukhanov points out, it turned out to be impracticable and was never carried out, but for a long time 'even the most erudite Bolsheviks (the proselyte Trotsky in particular) floundered around in it and interpreted the slogan of "Power to the Soviets" quite chaotically'. But the most significant observation Sukhanov made was that in the whole of his speech Lenin made no attempt to analyse what were the objective social and economic conditions that would make socialism in Russia possible.[7] At some point between his leaving Switzerland and arriving in Russia, Lenin had decided that he would orientate himself towards a socialist revolution in Russia, but as yet he had no rationalisation to offer as to why this should be possible.

The question arises: why should Lenin, who had so recently been of the opinion that because of Russia's economic backwardness 'socialism could not triumph there immediately', suddenly change his mind? In fact, there is no sign that Lenin made any radical reassessment of Russia's backwardness and its implications for the establishment of socialism. But one can see from his writings at the time that economic matters were not at the centre of Lenin's attention. He was absorbed with the question of the state and the role he had assigned to the soviets as the form of revolutionary government. This preoccupation suggested to Lenin the political tactics that should be employed in the situation in Russia as he found it, and he was intent on putting these into practice. That these were tactics of a socialist revolution was an implication that Lenin did not confront directly, getting round the problem by denying that socialism was an *immediate* prospect.

After giving his speech at the Krzesinska mansion, Lenin and Krupskaya went to stay at the flat where Anna Elizarova and her husband Mark were living. In the morning Lenin went to the Volkovo cemetery to visit the graves of his mother and his sister Olga. He then addressed a meeting in the Tauride Palace where both the Provisional Government and the Petrograd Soviet were located. The meeting was one of Bolsheviks, Mensheviks and non-fractional Social Democrats called to explore the possibilities of reuniting the party. Lenin gave much the same speech as he had done the previous evening, and was greeted with bemusement and indignation. His audience thought that he had abandoned the principles of Social Democracy and could see no possibility of cooperating with the Bolshevik leader. Of the Bolsheviks present only Kollontai spoke in his support.[8]

When the 'April Theses' were published a week after Lenin's arrival in Petrograd, they showed evidence that Lenin had adapted the printed version to take into account the current mood in the country. As the war still enjoyed widespread support, there was no mention of turning the imperialist war into a civil war. The 'Theses' began by defining the circumstances in which a genuine defensive war would be possible. Under the existing government, a government of capitalists, the war could only be an imperialist war. A truly defencist war could only be fought when the government was in the hands of the workers and the poorest sections of the peasantry. He believed that it was necessary persistently to explain to the masses what the character of the present war was and why the standpoint of defencism was mistaken.

The 'Theses' stated that the revolution was at a transitional stage. Owing to lack of class-consciousness and organisation, the proletariat had allowed political power to be acquired by the bourgeoisie. In the second stage, however, power would pass into the hands of the proletariat and the poorest sections of the peasantry. Lenin was adamant that there should be no support for the Provisional Government. The falsity of its promises should be exposed, so that everyone would understand the futility of 'demanding' that this capitalist government should not act in the interest of the capitalists. Here Lenin had in mind those people, including his fellow-Bolsheviks Stalin and Kamenev, who supported the Provisional Government 'in so far as' it acted in the interests of the proletariat.

In the fourth of the 'Theses' Lenin introduced the idea that the only form of government for Russia should be the soviets, and that all power ought now to pass to the soviets throughout the country. The immediate obstacle to this happening at the present time was that the Petrograd Soviet was dominated by Mensheviks and Socialist Revolutionaries who believed that the Provisional Government should be maintained in power, and that the function of the Soviet was merely to monitor its activities. Accordingly the course of action Lenin advocated was patient persuasion to win a majority to the side of the Bolsheviks. Lenin went on to say that a government of soviets was preferable to a parliamentary republic, and in keeping with the principles of smashing the state apparatus, he demanded 'the abolition of the police, the army and the bureaucracy'.

In agrarian policy Lenin considered that more emphasis should be put on the Soviets of Agricultural Labourers' Deputies. All landed estates should be confiscated and placed at the disposal of these agrarian soviets. As far as economic policy was concerned, the 'Theses' demanded the immediate amalgamation of all banks in the country into a single bank, the activities of which were to be monitored by the Soviet of Workers' Deputies. This demand shows the influence of Hilferding and his conception of finance capital. Hilferding had believed that control of the chief banks in the country would make it possible to regulate the entire economy. It was at this point that Lenin made his only reference to socialism in the entire 'Theses'. It was not, he insisted, 'the *immediate* aim to "introduce" socialism, but only to bring social production and the distribution of products at once under the *control* of the Soviets of Workers' Deputies'.

The 'Theses' concluded with a list of party tasks including: the immediate convocation of a party congress; alteration of the party programme on the questions of imperialism, the state, and the minimum programme; the change of the party's name from 'Social Democrat' to 'Communist'. A more long-term objective was the creation of a new International.[9]

Lenin's 'Theses' were discussed at the Petrograd Conference of the Bolshevik Party on 14 April. They were received favourably on the whole, and one speaker at least, Kalinin, thought that their contents were not particularly novel. He drew attention to the fact that the manifesto the Bolsheviks had issued during the February revolution did not differ substantially in its content from the points Lenin had made in his 'Theses'. In Kalinin's opinion the only thing that was new in Lenin's 'Theses' was the proposition that the Soviet of Workers' Deputies was the only form of government.[10] It was ten days later at the Seventh Congress of the RSDLP that the 'Theses' came under serious fire from Kamenev.

Many contemporaries thought that what Lenin was proposing would consign the Bolsheviks to the political wilderness, and initially most members of the Bolshevik party thought they were wrong-headed. The conception of a 'commune state' based on a hierarchy of soviets, with no police, army or bureaucracy, controlling different sectors of the economy never became reality. But other aspects were powerful motors which would eventually bring the Bolsheviks to power. As the war became increasingly unpopular throughout the year, the Bolsheviks' opposition to it brought them increased support. Their encouragement of immediate land seizures went with the grain of the peasant movement in 1917. And their opposition to the Provisional Government left them untainted by its failures. Unlike the Mensheviks and the Socialist Revolutionaries they never joined any of the coalition governments. But on the negative side, the dismissal of parliamentary government and the encouragement given to violent land seizures served to undermine the very fragile sense of a rule of law in Russia.

The importance of Lenin's 'April Theses' as the document in which the Bolshevik strategy for 1917 was laid down has encouraged some mythology to grow up around it. Trotsky later maintained that while in New York he elaborated in a series of articles in the journal *Novyi Mir* (New World) a strategy comparable to that embodied in the 'April Theses'. The main point made in the 'April Theses', and the main point of similarity, according to Trotsky, was that Lenin had come round to thinking that a socialist revolution in Russia was possible, in this way accepting Trotsky's conception of 'permanent revolution'. Trotsky implies that the differences between Lenin and the 'Old Bolsheviks' revolved around the question of the possibility of socialism in Russia. In actual fact, a perusal of Trotsky's *Novyi mir* articles reveals very little similarity with Lenin's 'April Theses', and on the crucial question of the state, Trotsky remained entirely at odds with Lenin, as indeed Sukhanov indicated in his remarks referred to above.[11] The difference between the 'old Bolshevism' and the 'new Bolshevism' was that the latter accepted Lenin's doctrine that the soviets were the only possible form of a revolutionary government.

The Provisional Government

The opposition to Lenin's ideas led by Kamenev was quickly overcome. The 'Theses' were approved both by the Bolshevik Petrograd City Conference and the Seventh Conference of the RSDLP which took place between 24 and 29 April. The conference passed a number of resolutions on the war, on the soviets, on the agrarian question, on nationalities and so on, which were much in the spirit of Lenin's ideas. On the national question Lenin was as insistent as ever on the right of nations to self-determination. In arguing against Rykov he was adamant that separate states would not disappear, and that even with a soviet government these would remain.[12]

By the time the conference met events had already moved decisively in Lenin's favour. Miliukov's note to the Allies promising to fight the war to a victorious conclusion had been made public, prompting massive demonstrations in protest. Miliukov was forced to resign, and Guchkov resigned with him in protest that General Kornilov, the Commander of the Petrograd Military District, had not been allowed to use force against the demonstrators. The series of events marked the increasing disillusion of the people with the Provisional Government. Among the Bolsheviks S. Ya. Bagdatev called for the overthrow of the government,[13] but Lenin thought the move premature, as he believed that the same result could be achieved by gaining a majority in the Soviet in favour of ending support for the Provisional Government and the transfer of all power to the Soviet.

In the wake of the April crisis a coalition government was established, with some portfolios in the Provisional Government going to the Mensheviks Iraklii Tsereteli and Skobelev and the SRs P. N. Perevertsev and V. M. Chernov. Kerensky moved from the Ministry of Justice to the Ministry of War and Navy. The coalition initially enjoyed wide popularity, but this was gradually dissipated as the government failed to live up to expectations and to deal with the severe problems facing the country.

The most severe problem and the one which exacerbated all the others was the war. This was now in its third year, and was becoming increasingly difficult to sustain. The Russian army had fought well and was holding the line against the Austro-German forces. But the casualties were enormous, and among the troops human endurance was reaching its limit. A constant drain on morale had been the humiliating conditions under which the Russian soldiers served, so that the power of the officers over them perpetuated a master–serf relationship. One of the first measures of the February revolution was Order No. 1, an attempt to rectify this situation and give the soldiers an incentive to fight. Order No. 1, however, came at a time when mistrust between officers and men had already erupted in violence, and only served to diminish further the authority of the officers and undermine military discipline. The main task facing Kerensky as war minister was to restore the fighting capacity of the army and to resume the offensive, as the Allies demanded.

A second problem made more serious by the war was that of supply: how to provide the army and the towns with food. The mobilisation of a large proportion of the peasant population had created a serious imbalance in the perpetually fragile Russian economy. Young peasant men, who had formerly been the main producers of food in the countryside, had now been transferred to the front and had become consumers of agricultural produce. The agricultural workforce now consisted largely of women, elderly men and youths. With less efficient producers, the amount of grain produced diminished and prices soared. The railway network which was overloaded with military traffic could not cope with the task of transporting the grain to the towns. The towns and the army constantly experienced a shortage of foodstuffs. Hunger in the towns caused a drift of urban workers back to the countryside, a movement echoed by the increasing desertion rate from the army as peasant soldiers returned to their villages.

The Provisional Government tried to tackle the food-supply problem by imposing fixed prices for grain to keep them affordable. The result was to encourage the black market in grain and reduce the incentive of the peasants to sell the grain for government prices. In any case there was little to incentive to sell grain if the peasants were unable to use the money they got for their grain to purchase the industrial goods they needed, such as textiles, boots, soap and agricultural implements. Because the country's economy had been directed towards military requirements, consumer goods were now in short supply, and consequently very expensive. It was proposed that the system of fixed prices be extended to a number of consumer goods of prime necessity. The leaders of the Petrograd Soviet favoured increased state regulation for the economy, in accordance with the practice in other belligerent countries, in Germany in particular. But this idea was resisted by those ministers within the Provisional Government who were anxious to see the introduction in Russia of a free market system.

The third major problem facing the Provisional Government was the land question. This was one of long standing, but now made more acute by the wartime conditions and the exodus from the towns. The Provisional Government was committed to agrarian reform, but was not prepared to legislate immediately, considering that this was a matter that should be left until the Constituent Assembly met. In the meantime peasants increasingly took matters into their own hands and confiscated the landowners' estates. Not prepared to condone illegal seizures of land the Provisional Government, where it could, sent troops to protect the landowners' property rights.[14]

The Provisional Government had also failed to ameliorate the condition of Russia's industrial workers, many of whom were engaged in industries producing munitions for the war. Inflation had eroded their wages; they suffered from food shortages and a lack of basic commodities. They had seen the revolution as an opportunity to introduce a new democratic order into the factories, but any gains were short-lived as factories closed and unemployment forced many workers to return to the countryside. In an attempt to keep their workplaces open workers were forced more and more to participate in the running of their factories, trying to obtain fuel, raw materials and new orders.[15]

The February revolution stimulated the demand for autonomy by the non-Russian nationalities which made up the Russian Empire. This was facilitated by the breakdown of central authority in the regions, as the old central institutions were replaced by national assemblies. This process was resisted by the Provisional Government, partly out of a desire to conserve the integrity of the Russian Empire, and partly because the question of national autonomy was one that should be decided by the Constituent Assembly.

This stance began to crumble in June when a delegation led by Kerensky met the Ukrainian Rada and made concessions which the Kadet members of the Provisional Government found unacceptable.[16] Their resignation coincided with Kerensky's unsuccessful offensive on the south-west front, precipitating a political crisis which was accompanied by massive street demonstrations in Petrograd at the beginning of July.

The July Days

On May 10 (23) Lenin along with Zinoviev and Kamenev attended the conference of the Mezhraiontsy and discussed terms by which the organisation would unite with the Bolsheviks. The principle of unification of the groups which accepted the internationalist platform of the Zimmerwald–Kienthal conferences was agreed, and this was formalised at the Sixth Congress of the RSDLP held at the end of July. The union with the Mezhraiontsy brought the Bolsheviks some four thousand additional members as well as some much needed intellectual talent including Trotsky, Lunacharskii, Manuilskii, M. M. Volodarskii, L. M. Karakhan, M. S. Uritskii, A. A. Joffe and Antonov-Ovseenko. It would appear, however, that there was a reluctance on the part of the Mezhraiontsy to dissolve their separate identity within the Bolshevik party, and there are indications that some Mezhraionka organisational links survived the merger.[17]

The First All-Russian Congress of Soviets took place in Petrograd at the beginning of June. Most of the congress delegates were Mensheviks or SRs, reflecting the popularity and influence of those parties at the time. Lenin attended as a member of the Bolshevik delegation. A vote of confidence in the coalition government was passed by 543 votes to 126. Tsereteli had justified the coalition on the grounds that there was not in Russia a single party that was prepared to take power on its own. Lenin at that point intervened to say that the Bolsheviks were just such a party. His speech was greeted for the most part with amusement and derision, since at that particular juncture there did not appear to be any great likelihood that the Bolsheviks would ever come to power.[18]

The Congress of Soviets created a new institution to replace the old Executive Committee of the Petrograd Soviet, the Central Executive Committee. It was still dominated by the Menshevik and SR leadership, which continued to support the Provisional Government. When the Second Congress of Soviets met in October 1917 in a very different political climate, control of the CEC would determine which party held power in the country.

The hectic activity of making speeches, editing *Pravda* and writing articles on developments as they unfolded took its toll on Lenin's strength, and on 29 June he took a trip with his sister Anna to Neivola in Finland to rest for a few days. He was there when mass demonstrations of the July Days threatened to topple the government. Soldiers and sailors from Kronstadt were among those who joined the movement. The Bolsheviks were then put in the position of having to choose whether to lead the movement and attempt to take power there and then or to back away from confrontation with the government. In the event they chose the latter course, and tried to channel the discontent into a peaceful demonstration. Lenin, on learning of the disturbances in the capital, had returned from Finland on 4 July. He addressed the demonstrators from the balcony of the Krzesińska mansion, assuring them that the slogan of 'All power to the soviets!' would eventually triumph, and calling for 'restraint, steadfastness and vigilance'. As Lenin later argued, this was hardly the speech of someone urging the seizure of power, an allegation subsequently made against the Bolsheviks by the Provisional Government.[19] The possibility of seizing power must of course have passed through the Bolsheviks' minds, but it is most unlikely that they made any serious attempt to do so. Of necessity it would have been an enterprise undertaken in Lenin's absence and without preparation. Moreover, a seizure of power in the capital would be pointless if the government could bring troops from the northern front to crush the insurrection, as indeed happened.

From the Krzesińska mansion the demonstrators set out for the Tauride Palace where the Provisional Government was in session. They carried banners demanding 'All power to the Soviets!', 'Down with the capitalist ministers!', 'Peace, bread and freedom!' and so on. On the way there, however, the demonstrators were fired on, causing numerous casualties. This incensed the Kronstadt sailors more than ever against the Provisional Government, so that when Viktor Chernov, the SR Minister of Agriculture, fell into their hands, he only escaped with his life when rescued by Trotsky.

The tide turned on 5 July when the government learnt that troops had been dispatched from the northern front and began its offensive against the Bolsheviks. The *Pravda* offices were ransacked and orders were given for the capture of the Krzesińska villa and the arrest of persons harbouring there. In defiance of the Soviet's prohibition, the newspaper *Zhivoe slovo* (Live Word) carried a story given to it by Aleksinskii, that Lenin was being paid money by the German General Staff through the intermediaries Hanecki and Kozlowski to agitate against the Provisional Government.[20] The story aroused widespread animosity against the Bolsheviks, and created a suitable climate for measures against them. The government ordered the arrest and trial of all those who had been involved in the disturbances. On 7 July a small meeting of Bolsheviks decided that Lenin should not remain in Petrograd and stand trial but should go into hiding. He managed to escape with Zinoviev to Razliv near Sestroretsk on 10 July, but many Bolsheviks and their Mezhraiontsy allies, including Trotsky and Lunacharskii, were arrested and imprisoned.

Following the July Days Lenin now believed that the peaceful phase of the revolution had come to an end. Whereas before July the slogan of 'All power to the Soviets!' could have been implemented peacefully, with the Provisional Government's surrendering power to the Soviet, now this possibility no longer existed. Since the Menshevik and SR leaders of the soviets now collaborated with the counter-revolution and the period of 'dual power' had ended, the demand that all power pass to the soviets had become pointless. Now, Lenin argued, power could no longer be taken by the proletariat by peaceful means, and if the soviets were involved in this process they would not be the soviets that presently existed.[21]

It was in his Razliv retreat that Lenin wrote *State and Revolution*, his main theoretical work of 1917. He had already collected the material he needed to write the pamphlet contained in a notebook which he had entitled 'Marxism and the State'. Lenin attached a great deal of importance to this project, because at the beginning of July, when his life was in some danger, he wrote to Kamenev: '*Entre nous*, if they do me in, I ask you to publish my notebook "Marxism and the State".'[22] *State and Revolution* draws heavily on the research into the question of the state stimulated by Bukharin at the beginning of the year, but it bears clear traces of the political situation in which it was written. It is centred around the conclusions Marx drew from his study of the Paris commune, in particular that 'the proletariat cannot simply lay hold of the ready-made state machinery and wield it for its own purposes'.[23] Lenin took Marx to mean that it was necessary to 'smash the bureaucratic–military machine'. In place of this machine he believed that a state modelled on the Paris Commune would be established in which the police, the standing army and the bureaucracy would be abolished and all public services would be performed at workers' wages. All functionaries would be elected, accountable and revocable.

Some of the main themes in *State and Revolution* were already to be found in the 'April Theses'. But whereas in the 'April Theses' a major role had been allotted to the soviets, in *State and Revolution*, the soviets received only a scant mention. This reflected Lenin's estimation of the soviets in the period after the July Days, when they had been 'prostituted' by the Menshevik and SR leaders. This omission gave the book an abstract and scholastic character. The opinions of Marx and Engels were examined and the views of Kautsky were criticised, but what relation this had to the Russian situation was left unclear.

Although a commune type of state was advocated, Lenin did not explicitly say that a republic of soviets was what he had in mind. He did, however, identify this 'commune state' with the 'dictatorship of the proletariat',[24] though earlier he had noted that, although Engels had equated these two things, Marx had not.[25] He had intended to write a chapter in which he would discuss the soviets in this connection, but this got no further than a preliminary outline.[26] At that stage Lenin had no way of knowing what role the soviets were destined to play in the revolution, and at the time of writing their development seemed to have reached an impasse.

Whereas the 'April Theses' gave a reasonably precise statement of how the proletariat would gain power and what institutions would enable it to do so, *State and Revolution* is much more vague on this issue, and indeed is a very poor guide to how the Bolsheviks actually came to power. But it does give a very good indication of how Lenin believed a revolutionary government would conduct economic affairs. It would, he said, be mainly a matter of calculating in advance the volume of production and systematically regulating it. The functions of accounting and regulating the economy would be fairly uncomplicated since these activities had been simplified by the capitalist system.[27] *State and Revolution* did not appear in print until 1918. It did not play any part in determining the character of the Bolshevik revolution, but it did have a role in influencing how that revolution was perceived.

The Kornilov affair

Following the failure of the June offensive the Provisional Government took measures to restore discipline in the army. As commander-in-chief Kerensky appointed General Lavr Kornilov, a man who attracted round him groups and individuals who believed that the only way to prevent the country sliding into anarchy was the establishment of a dictatorial form of government. They encouraged Kornilov to stage a *coup d'état* and make himself dictator. Believing that he had the tacit support of Kerensky, Kornilov began to move his troops on the capital. There were anxious days in Petrograd at the end of August as Kornilov's forces approached, but the enterprise was soon overtaken by failure. Kerensky dissociated himself from Kornilov, and instead of leading his troops into battle Kornilov remained at the General Headquarters. The troops never reached Petrograd because they were intercepted by agitators sent out from the capital, and sections of railway line were torn up to prevent the movement of their transport trains. Kornilov was arrested and imprisoned and his sympathisers among the officer corps suffered the same fate.

The Kornilov rebellion discredited the Provisional Government and Kerensky in particular. It galvanised the forces of revolution into action. To eradicate the threat posed by Kornilov's supporters within the capital the Petrograd Soviet set up a special committee which carried out searches and made arrests of suspected counter-revolutionaries. Committees for revolutionary defence were set up in the provinces on the model of the Petrograd committee, forming a network throughout the country. Red Guard detachments sprang up in the various districts of Petrograd, arming themselves to protect the workers from Kornilovite counter-revolution. In the debris of the failed Kornilov rebellion the tide turned again in favour of the revolution. On 4 September Trotsky, Lunacharskii and Antonov-Ovseenko and the Baltic sailors' leader P. E. Dybenko were all released from prison, Trotsky immediately being elected chairman of the Petrograd Soviet, while Antonov-Ovseenko became chairman of the Finland Soviet in Helsingfors (Helsinki).

By the autumn of 1917 the situation in the country was becoming critical. There was widespread war-weariness; the army was no longer prepared to fight and deserted in droves. There was a shortage of bread and everyday necessities in the towns, the supply problem worsening as industry ceased to function. As factories closed down unemployment soared, increasing hardship for urban workers and their families. The peasants who had not already seized the landowners' estates waited impatiently for agrarian reform. The Bolshevik slogans demanding 'Peace, bread and land' achieved wide popularity, as they focused on the people's needs and at the same time highlighted those key areas in which the Provisional Government had failed so conspicuously. The Bolsheviks began to be successful in elections to local soviets and municipal assemblies. This opened up the possibility that when the next Congress of Soviets met on 20 October the Bolsheviks would dominate the assembly and might use the congress as a means of taking power, a course of action canvassed by Trotsky.

The October revolution

At the beginning of September Lenin believed he could see an opportunity for compromise with the Menshevik and SR parties who controlled the soviets. He published a proposal in *Rabochii put* that these parties should establish a government which dissociated itself from the bourgeoisie and was responsible to the soviets. This would create freer conditions in which the Bolsheviks could campaign peacefully for the transfer of power to the proletariat and the poorer peasants. In such a political climate the Bolsheviks would have no need to resort to revolutionary methods of action. Lenin believed that such a compromise would be beneficial to both the Bolsheviks and the Menshevik and SR parties, though he cautioned that the moment when such a compromise was still possible would soon pass.[28] To no one's great surprise Lenin's proposal did not meet with any response from the Menshevik and SR leaders.

At the end of September Lenin began to agitate within the Bolshevik party for an insurrection to overthrow the Provisional Government. On 27 September Lenin, then in hiding in Vyborg, wrote to Ivars Smilga, a Bolshevik who in the wake of the Kornilov rebellion had become chairman of the Regional Committee of the Army, Navy and Workers of Finland, asking him to cooperate in enlisting the troops in Finland to march on Petrograd and overthrow the Provisional Government. Lenin was insistent that the time for passing resolutions was over; he was also adamant that the Bolsheviks should not wait until the Second Congress of Soviets to take power.[29]

Lenin's letter reached Smilga during the Second Congress of the Baltic Fleet, chaired by Dybenko. One of the main speakers at the conference was Antonov-Ovseenko, to whom Smilga showed Lenin's letter. Despite the fact that in his letter Lenin stressed that the insurrection should precede the Second Congress of Soviets, both Smilga and Antonov-Ovseenko made military preparations which were not offensive, but defensive in character, ones designed to protect the Second Congress of Soviets and to ensure that Kerensky would not be able to send troops to Petrograd to dissolve it. They would do this by coordinating the activities of the Bolshevik-controlled soviets in the approaches to Petrograd, and to this end they decided to convoke a Congress of Soviets of the Northern Region. According to Antonov-Ovseenko, the idea was that the proposed congress of northern soviets would 'throw around revolutionary Petrograd an iron ring, which would defend the centre of the revolution, the capital, if the need arose'. If successful, this would prevent a repeat of the July Days when government troops had been transferred to Petrograd from the northern front. The proposed congress was organised by Antonov-Ovseenko in Helsingfors, and Karakhan and Trotsky in Petrograd.[30]

Just at that time the political climate in the Baltic region changed dramatically in favour of the defensive tactics that Smilga and Antonov-Ovseenko had initiated. The German fleet made an attack on the Moon Sound in an operation intended to clear Russian defences and to open sea lanes into Riga, in preparation for a renewed German offensive on the northern front. Against a numerically superior and better-armed German opponent the Russian Baltic fleet in its biggest engagement in the whole of the war made a spirited defence, the sailors maintaining discipline and carrying out orders given by their officers. Although the Germans managed to achieve their objective and remove the Russian defences from the Estonian islands, the Baltic fleet was able to inflict serious casualties on the German navy and prevent further German advance. The Baltic sailors were exhilarated by the battle and proud of the success they had in resisting the German attack. They were consequently deeply offended when on 4 October it became known that Kerensky and his ministerial colleagues had discussed the possibility of evacuating the government from Petrograd to Moscow.

On 8 October Lenin wrote two letters concerned with the Congress of Soviets of the Northern Region, 'Advice of an Onlooker' and 'Letter to the Bolshevik Comrades Attending the Congress of Soviets of the Northern Region'. Both of these developed the ideas for an offensive on Petrograd that had been outlined in the letter to Smilga of 27 September, and involved 'a simultaneous offensive on Petrograd, as sudden and rapid as possible, which must without fail be carried out from within and without the working-class quarters and from Finland, from Reval and from Kronstadt, an offensive of the entire navy'.[31] Lenin thought that the opening of the Congress of Soviets of the Northern Region scheduled for 11 October should be the time to launch this major military operation.

On 10 October Lenin came to Petrograd in disguise to address the Bolshevik Central Committee and argue that his plan for an invasion of Petrograd by the Baltic Fleet be put into operation immediately.

He outlined the factors which he believed made immediate action essential. These were the international situation – the growth throughout Europe of the world socialist revolution; the danger that Kerensky would surrender Petrograd to the Germans; the increased support enjoyed by the Bolshevik party; and the increasing momentum of the peasant movement.[32]

Zinoviev and Kamenev were aghast at Lenin's idea of an offensive against Petrograd, pointing out that the invasion force would be cut down by the artillery fanned out around the capital. They believed that an armed insurrection of any kind was inadvisable and that the Bolsheviks ought to concentrate their efforts on the elections to the Constituent Assembly. Trotsky favoured taking power through the Second Congress of Soviets, which, he believed, would have a Bolshevik majority. In the end a compromise was reached by which the Central Committee agreed on an insurrection, but with no particular means or time-scale being specified. While Lenin engaged Zinoviev and Kamenev in an acrimonious polemic on the desirability of an armed insurrection, Trotsky and Antonov-Ovseenko went ahead with their arrangements to create a protective ring of soviet military organisations around Petrograd. When Lenin demanded to know why the Baltic fleet was not being sent to Petrograd, Antonov-Ovseenko made excuses about the Neva's channel being too shallow for the warships.[33]

The Congress of Soviets of the Northern Region which opened the following day provided models for ways in which power could be taken without a shot being fired in anger. First Antonov-Ovseenko, then speakers from Helsingfors, Reval and Kronstadt described how in the aftermath of the Kornilov affair, their local soviets had set up committees to ensure that no order of the Provisional Government was carried out unless it had the approval of the local soviet. In this way, according to Antonov-Ovseenko, 'the committee has in all respects become the organ of revolutionary power'.[34]

During the conference an opportunity arose to establish a committee of this kind in Petrograd itself. On 9 October the Mensheviks on the Executive Committee of the Petrograd Soviet, in an effort to escape the charge of abandoning Petrograd to the Germans, had suggested cooperation between the Soviet and the Petrograd Military District involving the setting up a 'committee of revolutionary defence', which would concern itself with the question of the defence of Petrograd and its approaches, and would draw up a plan for the defence of Petrograd.

Since it was conceived as a propaganda measure, the Bolsheviks were initially unenthusiastic at the proposal. But at the Soviet plenum meeting on the 9th Trotsky and Antonov-Ovseenko changed their tactics and seized upon the idea, drawing up a constitution for the new organisation, to be called the Military Revolutionary Committee, which was more in line with the kind of body they were about to set up at the Congress of Soviets of the Northern Region. What the congress did was to organise the creation of a network of Military Revolutionary Committees throughout the northern region and on the northern front. On 21 October the MRC did in fact send its commissars to demand to countersign orders issued by the Commander of the Petrograd Military District, in the manner the Congress of Soviets of the Northern Region had envisaged.

In fact the way power was seized in Petrograd was that the various strategic points in the city were taken over by the Petrograd Military Revolutionary Committee. The transfer of power, moreover, came about on the day the Second Congress of Soviets met, much in the manner Trotsky had advocated. The great advantage of this means of taking power was made clear by Trotsky on the afternoon of 25 October when he reported to the Petrograd Soviet that so far there had been no bloodshed. He went on to say that he knew of no other example where a revolutionary movement involving such great masses of people had been carried through without bloodshed.[35] It is most unlikely that the same could have been said if Lenin's pre-ferred method of taking power had been adopted. Kerensky tried to bring troops from the northern front, but these were stopped by the local Military Revolutionary Committees. It was Trotsky's method rather than Lenin's which brought the Bolsheviks to power in 1917, though, in order to maintain his claim to be a good Leninist, Trotsky never made this clear. But in 1924 he did recall that as Bolshevik control extended over Petrograd in October 1917 Lenin made the grudging admission: 'Well, I suppose you can do it that way too; just as long as power is taken.'[36] It is also significant that Trotsky's main associates in carrying out his tactic, Antonov-Ovseenko and Karakhan, were, like himself, former Mezhraiontsy. In view of the Mezhraionka affiliations of these key figures in the October revolution, to speak of a 'Bolshevik' seizure of power may be something of a misnomer.

On day two of the Second Congress of Soviets, when the Winter Palace had been captured and the members of the Provisional Government arrested, Lenin appeared on the rostrum to make his

first speech as the leader of the ruling party. He announced that a
Council of People's Commissars was being formed, a list of whose
members would be submitted to the congress. The Council would
propose to the congress three resolutions, upon the basis of which
three decrees would be issued. The first would concern the steps that
should be taken to conclude an immediate armistice on the front,
as a preliminary to peace negotiations. The second decree would
secure for the peasants the right of temporary possession of the
landlords' estates, pending the introduction of detailed agrarian
legislation. The third decree would give the industrial workers power
of supervision over all operations of the employers and managers.[37]

These three decrees had a key importance in the strategy of the
Bolshevik party. They helped it come to power by promising to the
people those things which were most urgently desired at the time
and which they had been denied by the previous government. Peace
was demanded by all sections of the population, and was indeed a
necessity given that the army had lost the will to fight. The peasants
were granted their age-old wish for the land, and the working class
was being given 'workers' control', which was designed to introduce
a democratic order in the running of industry. The decrees also
legitimised the new government and consolidated it in power. The
reckoning was that anyone who dared try to overthrow the government which had promulgated these decrees would have to face the
wrath of the overwhelming majority of the population.

Something Lenin did not mention was the need to smash the state
apparatus, as he had advocated in his *State and Revolution*. In fact the
new People's Commissars took over the existing ministries, or at
least, took them over when the civil servants who staffed the ministries allowed them to do so, for the accession of the Bolsheviks to
power was greeted by a prolonged strike by civil servants and bank
employees, who did everything in their power to obstruct and sabotage the activities of their new masters. Lenin quickly discovered that
it was impossible to dispense with the state apparatus, and it became
clear that running the country would not be such a simple matter as
he had imagined.

6

LENIN IN POWER

The first steps in power

Before the Bolsheviks came to power in Russia, Lenin had been confident that conditions in the country were right for a socialist revolution, and that a socialist economic system could be established on the basis of the structures which Russian capitalism had already laid down. He also expected to be able to implement the conception of a 'commune state' that he had elaborated in *State and Revolution*. Once the Bolsheviks had taken power, however, Lenin's pre-revolutionary vision of Russia's future very rapidly evaporated, and the country gravitated more and more towards the repression and authoritarian rule that Russians had thought superseded with the end of the tsarist regime. One reason for this outcome is that any plans that Lenin had turned out to be entirely inadequate to deal with the situation as it then existed, and the other is that even those plans were based on misconceptions about how capitalism developed and what the nature of Russian society was.

The bulk of Lenin's writings on how he envisaged the socialist system would operate in Russia date from his retreat in Razliv after the July Days. It was then that he worked on *State and Revolution* and shorter works such as *The Impending Catastrophe and How to Combat It* and *Can the Bolsheviks Retain State Power?* All three of these works have in common the belief that modern large-scale capitalist economy, in which industry was subordinated to the banks, was 'socialised economy', in which only slight modifications would have to be made in order to turn it into a socialist economic system. It is a belief that originates in Hilferding's economic writings, and *The Impending*

Catastrophe and How to Combat It contains its most explicit statement. There Lenin insists that: 'Imperialist war is the eve of socialist revolution ... because state-monopoly capitalism is the complete *material* preparation for socialism, the *threshold* of socialism, a rung on the ladder of history between which and the rung called socialism *there are no intermediate rungs*.' The fact that Lenin found monopoly capitalism in Russia implied that Russia too was ripe for socialism.[1]

Lenin developed his ideas on how capitalism had created institutions which could be incorporated in a socialist economic system. He stressed that whereas the oppressive state machinery – the police, the army and the bureaucracy – should be destroyed, the modern state also possessed institutions which had close connections with the banks and syndicates, institutions which performed the functions of accounting and registration. These institutions must not and should not be smashed, but should be wrested from the control of the capitalists. He went on to say that the big banks were the state institutions which were needed to bring about socialism, and which would be taken over as they stood from capitalism. In his opinion: 'Without big banks socialism would be impossible.'[2] Lenin in this period thought that 'socialism is above all else a matter of accounting'.[3] The irony was that in the event the very opposite took place; the Russian banking system was destroyed, while the old tsarist bureaucracy, with its oppressive practices, was preserved.

The main obstacle to destroying the state apparatus was that among the Bolsheviks there were very few who had any knowledge or experience of management or administration. These were skills which they hoped to learn, but in the meantime they had to keep the existing qualified personnel in place. The same was true in industry, where the services of existing managers and technicians, 'bourgeois specialists', had to be retained.[4] The Left Communists and other oppositions within the Bolshevik party regarded this policy as a betrayal of the proletarian revolution, but Lenin rapidly became a firm advocate of employing 'bourgeois specialists'. He also antagonised his left-wing critics by favouring the abandonment of the democratic collegiate principle in the running of industry for that of one-man management, which he believed to be in the interests of efficiency.

In the Soviet period the focus of Lenin's attention shifted from theoretical matters to the practicalities of running the country. He was much less concerned with socialism in the abstract than to find ways to make the system he had inherited work, and having found these ways, to justify them to his critics. Lenin involved himself personally in all levels of policy-making and its implementation. Many of the decrees issued by the Soviet government were drafted by him and bear his signature. He determined not only the general direction of economic policy, for example, but also laid down the policy direction for every single branch of the economy: agriculture, industry, supply, finance and so on. He also followed up the detailed implementation of these policies, sending round a myriad of pointed memos and notes to the relevant officials.[5]

In the spring of 1918 Lenin still held to the principle that no great transformations need be made in the economic sphere. He believed that with the nationalisation of the banks it would be possible to implement accounting and control of the production and distribution of goods. He tried to moderate the enthusiasm of the workers and the left wing of his own party for the nationalisation of industry. It seemed to him that in the course of the revolution more enterprises had been nationalised than the state could handle.[6] He was deeply conscious of the need to increase the productivity of labour in Russia and to this end he encouraged the introduction of the Taylor system to rationalise work practices. To increase grain production he advocated socialist competition in the countryside. Peasant communes would compete with each other in grain production. League tables of commune efficiency would be drawn up, and material rewards would be given to those who were most successful.[7]

Lenin's reluctance to nationalise industry on a wide scale was criticised by the Left Communists, who accused him of fostering not a socialist system, but one of 'state capitalism'. To this Lenin replied that in the present circumstances state capitalism would be a substantial step forward in comparison with what existed. Russia, he maintained, was a country in which small-scale production predominated, and the progression to state capitalism would represent a considerable advance.[8]

Even in terms of what might be considered their most socialist features, there was a high degree of continuity between the economic policies of the Provisional Government and those of the Bolsheviks. The Soviet government extended the state control of the economy which had been initiated by the Provisional Government. The Bolsheviks retained the Provisional Government's monopoly of the grain trade and its fixed prices for grain. When faced with peasant reluctance to sell grain to the state, S. N. Prokopovich, the Minister of Agriculture in the Provisional Government, had proposed to conduct compulsory expropriations[9] and this was in fact implemented by the Bolshevik government. The Provisional Government had established the Economic Council to oversee the regulation of economic matters. A similar body, the Supreme Council of the National Economy (VSNKhA) was set up in December 1917 with similar functions, of regulating and coordinating economic activity.[10]

Writing in 1917 Alexander Bogdanov had noted the measures taken by belligerent governments to establish state control of the economy. He had warned that these measures had been introduced in response to the exigencies of war and should not be mistaken for the emergence of a socialist system. There was, he argued, nothing socialist about the wartime state regulation of industry, a phenomenon which he referred to as 'war communism'.[11] This term was to be applied in retrospect to the economic system which existed in Russia between the summer of 1918 and the beginning of 1921.

The Cheka

The first few weeks were formative ones for the new Soviet regime, and much of its characteristic traits were laid down in that short period. One of the first acts of the Bolshevik government was to try to nationalise the banks and use them to regulate the economy as Lenin had envisaged. The banks, however, refused to cooperate, and their employees, along with civil servants, went on prolonged strike, money from the banks being diverted to support the strikers. Keys to safes were hidden and any accounts made available to the Bolsheviks had figures that were manufactured to conceal the true state of affairs.[12]

The Bolsheviks' response was to set up on 7 December 1917 an All-Russian Extraordinary Commission for the Struggle against Counter-Revolution and Sabotage, the so-called Cheka, headed by Feliks Dzierżyński. As its title suggests, the organisation was created as a temporary measure, to be disbanded as soon as the crisis was over. Continuing opposition to the Soviet regime, however, ensured the longevity of the Cheka and its entrenchment in the political culture of the country. Another measure introduced as an extraordinary one was the restriction on press freedom signed by Lenin on 27 October 1917, which promised complete freedom of the press as soon as circumstances permitted.[13]

Before the Bolsheviks came to power Lenin had not considered in any great detail the implications of crushing any widespread resistance to the new regime. Once in power he subsumed the question under the headings of the 'civil war' and the 'dictatorship of the proletariat'. When he used the term 'civil war' in the early weeks of 1918 Lenin meant by it not the Civil War which was soon to engulf the country, but simply the resistance to the Soviet government by its opponents – 'the Alekseevs, the Kornilovs and the Kerenskys'. It was the civil war into which, as he had promised, the world war would be transformed. He thought of this as being of short duration and completed by the spring of 1918.[14]

It was in connection with the increased use of force that Lenin began to speak of the Soviet Government as the 'dictatorship of the proletariat'. In a pamphlet written in April 1918, *The Immediate Tasks of the Soviet Government*, he defined Soviet power as 'the organised form of the dictatorship of the proletariat',[15] an equation he had avoided making in his *State and Revolution*. There was a need, he said, for 'iron force' for the swift and merciless suppression of both exploiters and hooligans. The campaign would be waged against the external enemies of Soviet power and also against the disruptive elements within it. By characterising the Soviet state in this way Lenin had made terror one of its chief attributes, if not its *raison d'être*. In so doing he was able to convince himself that the use of terror was not something that a socialist state would only resort to in time of dire necessity, but was one of a socialist state's most essential functions.

An 'iron hand', Lenin believed, was necessary in order that the revolution should maintain its momentum. The experience of great revolutions in the past was that initially they had shown salutary firmness in shooting thieves on the spot. Later, however, they had lost their revolutionary enthusiasm and no longer treated disintegrative influences with the necessary ruthlessness. To maintain itself in power the proletariat had to keep up the pressure of revolutionary violence. Hence the need for a dictatorship.[16]

Initially the Cheka had only the right to carry out searches and to conduct preliminary enquiries. But in February 1918 its competence was widened in connection with the German advance into the country and the increase in lawlessness. In the summer of 1918 as the country began to be engulfed in the Civil War the Cheka was permitted to take hostages with a view to preventing hostile action against Soviet power. The practices of the Cheka were attacked not only by groups hostile to the Bolsheviks, but by Steinberg, the SR Commissar for Justice in the Soviet government, and by Bolshevik party members.[17] Lenin staunchly defended the Cheka from all its critics, and encouraged the Cheka to increase both the speed and the strength of its repressions not only against lawlessness and banditry, but against political opponents as well.[18] Ironically, one of Lenin's nephews was among the people arrested by the Kazan Cheka in March 1920 on suspicion of belonging to an anti-Bolshevik organisation. On the intervention of his eminent uncle he was released after two months.[19] Perhaps because of his connections with the Kadet party, Alexander Ulyanov's friend Ivan Chebotarev fell under suspicion. In December 1918 his home was searched by the Kolpino branch of the Cheka, and in the process the notes on Russian economics that Lenin's brother had made were lost.[20] In November 1921 Lenin had to write a letter vouching for Chebotarev's political reliability. The letter is a unique document, as it was the only occasion that a reference to his brother appears in all his writings.[21]

Lenin also encouraged less systematic campaigns of terror. On 26 June 1918 he wrote to Zinoviev complaining that when the Petrograd workers wanted to respond to the assassination of Volodarskii with mass terror, the Petrograd members of the Central Committee and Petrograd Committee prevented them from doing so. Lenin protested strongly against this kind of obstruction. The so-called Red Terror was unleashed in August 1918 following an assassination attempt on Lenin himself by the SR activist Fanya Kaplan. On that occasion Lenin was hit by two revolver bullets, one penetrating the lung and the other the shoulder. He recovered sufficiently rapidly to be able to chair a meeting of the Council of People's Commissars two weeks later. By that time the Red Terror had claimed many innocent lives.

The regime's early resort to coercion was symptomatic of the fact that it could not make its citizens act in the way it required by voluntary means alone. This was particularly the case in the agrarian sphere where the peasants refused to supply grain to the towns at the prices the state offered. In that situation, forcible confiscations were among the alternative means adopted. In this kind of coercion there was a strong element of desperation. A prime example of this is the letter Lenin wrote to communists in Penza on 11 August 1918 demanding that in order to put down a peasant rebellion there, at least a hundred 'unreconstructed kulaks, money-grubbers and blood-suckers' should be hanged publicly to strike fear into the population for miles around.[22] No information seems to have come to light on how the recipients of the letter reacted to Lenin's rather frenetic instructions.

The Constituent Assembly

In his 'April Theses' Lenin had avoided mention of the Constituent Assembly, speaking elliptically instead about a 'parliamentary republic'. A legislative assembly elected by universal suffrage did not accord with his plans at that time for a Soviet republic. *State and Revolution* is more explicit in ruling out such democratic institutions in principle, since democracy is a form of state. Nevertheless, during 1917 Lenin had castigated the Provisional Government with postponing and even trying to sabotage the Constituent Assembly. The elections were held in November 1917 and the Assembly convened in the Tauride Palace on 5 January 1918. The Bolsheviks got 24 per cent of the vote, the SRs 40 per cent, the Kadets 5 per cent and the Mensheviks 2 per cent. The Bolsheviks had garnered most of the urban working-class vote, while the SRs had received most of their support from the rural areas. Lenin declared himself well-satisfied with the result, but after its first session the Constituent Assembly was dispersed, never to meet again.

The action shocked public opinion abroad, and brought the condemnation of both Karl Kautsky and Rosa Luxemburg. Lenin justified the dissolution of the Constituent Assembly on two main grounds. The first was that the elections did not really represent the will of the Russian people, because the electoral lists had been drawn up in the middle of October 1917, before the Socialist Revolutionary Party had split into its right and left wings which stood at opposite poles of the political spectrum. In this way the electorate had been deprived of the opportunity to vote for the SR party of their choice. This was an argument that the Left Socialist Revolutionaries agreed with and they approved the dissolution of the Assembly. The other justification Lenin gave was that a republic of soviets was a higher type of democratic institution than the usual bourgeois republic crowned by a Constituent Assembly.[23]

This latter justification was the one which Lenin developed in his writings of the time, particularly in his pamphlet *The Proletarian*

Revolution and the Renegade Kautsky, written in October–November 1918. A more immediate step to provide a rationale for the dissolution of the Constituent Assembly, however, was to have *State and Revolution* translated into German and distributed abroad, to create the impression that Soviet Russia really was governed by a democratic system of soviets. It was essential to reply to the charges Kautsky had made against the Bolsheviks in order to further the spread of revolution to Germany. Inside Germany itself Lenin's efforts were aided by the left-wing Social Democrat Franz Mehring, who replied to Kautsky's criticisms of the Bolsheviks on the pages of *Leipziger Volkszeitung*.[24]

During 1917 it had been convenient for the Bolsheviks to reproach the Provisional Government with unwillingness to convoke the Constituent Assembly. But once in power Lenin had no inclination to work with an elected assembly that would for the most part express peasant interests. That kind of assembly would doubtless have overwhelmed any attempts to introduce a Bolshevik programme. It would have been just as likely to put paid to any liberal programme as well, so that the survival of the Constituent Assembly would not necessarily have guaranteed the emergence of a democratic regime in Russia. Despite Lenin's assurance that a system of soviets was a superior form of democracy, it soon became clear that the Bolshevik regime was no more compatible with that system than it was with the existence of a Constituent Assembly.

Brest-Litovsk and the Left Communists

Following their accession to power the Bolsheviks were extremely anxious to court the favour of German Social Democrats, because they needed revolution in Germany to extricate them from the need to conclude a humiliating peace with the Austro-German military authorities at Brest-Litovsk. The Decree on Peace had not received the desired response and Trotsky as Commissar for Foreign Affairs had to negotiate peace terms with the Germans. While doing so he was hoping for a revolution that would replace General Hoffmann and Count Czernin with Clara Zetkin, Rosa Luxemburg and other German socialists. The German High Command was eager to end the negotiations quickly and be able to transfer troops to the western front. It also wished to extend Germany's borders in the Baltic provinces and acquire Ukrainian grain to feed the populations starved by the Allied blockade. Trotsky, however, tried to drag out the discussions until such time as the revolution in the West broke out.

Among the Bolsheviks, opinions about how the negotiations ought to be conducted depended on how imminent the European revolution was thought to be. In the Central Committee three points of view emerged on the issue. Bukharin was in favour of launching a revolutionary war against the Germans. He believed that even if this failed militarily it would rouse the proletariat to revolution in the West. Trotsky proposed a tactic of 'neither war nor peace', that is, to declare a halt to the war and demobilise the army, but not to sign a peace treaty. Lenin was firmly of the opinion that, although humiliating, the German peace terms ought to be accepted immediately, because if the Germans recommenced their offensive, then the Soviet government would be forced to sign any peace treaty on offer, and of course the terms would be worse.

Lenin did not think a revolutionary war a feasible proposition. The army was exhausted and its equipment so depleted that in face of a German attack it would be impossible to make an orderly retreat. Since the Bolsheviks had come to power by promising the country peace, support for them would disappear if hostilities recommenced. As far as a revolution in Germany was concerned, Lenin thought that at the present juncture Germany was only 'pregnant with revolution', while Russia had 'already given birth to a completely healthy child, a socialist republic, which might be killed if a war were started'. He believed that Trotsky's suggestion, of 'neither war nor peace', was international political showmanship. It would simply delay the signing of a peace, and sacrifice more territory by doing so. In particular the Soviet republic in Estonia would be overrun.[25]

This prognosis proved correct. On 18 February the German forces began an offensive along the entire front, meeting little or no resistance from the disintegrating Russian army. On the following day the Soviet government signalled its readiness to accept German peace terms. The reply, consisting of new and harsher terms and presented in the form of an ultimatum, was received by Lenin four days later. It demanded the transfer to Germany of the entire Baltic area, Poland and parts of Belorussia. Russia was also obliged to evacuate the Ukraine and Finland. On 3 March a Soviet delegation, demonstratively refusing to enter into negotiations with the Central Powers, signed the peace treaty. The treaty demanded not only territorial concessions, but the cessation of Bolshevik propaganda in the areas occupied by Germany and its allies.

Despite opposition from outside and inside the Bolshevik party, the peace treaty was ratified by the Seventh Extraordinary Congress. The congress was historic in that it resolved no longer to use the old name of the party, the Russian Social Democratic Labour Party, but to adopt the title Russian Communist Party (Bolsheviks). The congress finally made the Bolsheviks into an independent party. It was not, however, a united party. Bukharin and the left wing of the party would not reconcile themselves to the peace with Germany. They regarded it as appeasing imperialism, and in the manifesto which they presented to the congress, 'Theses on the Current Situation', they noted other areas of government policy in which the party leadership had become tainted with capitalist interests. The Left Communists' contention that the revolution had degenerated was one which later opposition groups were to repeat.[26]

The Brest-Litovsk peace complicated relations between the Bolsheviks and the Left SRs. The SR Party had split at the end of 1917, and its left wing, led by Mariya Spiridonova, Boris Kamkov and Mark Natanson, had joined forces with the Bolsheviks and some joined the Soviet government. The Treaty of Brest-Litovsk brought an end to this short-lived cooperation, as the SRs, like the Left Communists, favoured a revolutionary war against the Germans. In order to provoke a resumption of the war against Germany, in July 1918 the SRs assassinated Count Mirbach, the German ambassador in Moscow, and attempted a seizure of power. The rebellion was put down by the Latvian riflemen, the only reliable troops the Bolsheviks had at their disposal. Their commander, Vācietis, recalls Lenin asking him anxiously if the regime could survive until the following day.[27] Mass arrests and reprisals followed the unsuccessful uprising, undermining the SR Party as a political force.

There was no new German offensive following the assassination of Mirbach, because by that time the best German troops had been transferred to the western front, and those that remained were incapable of mounting a major offensive. They were also being harried by guerrilla attacks encouraged by the Soviet government. Although they had agreed to the German terms at Brest-Litovsk, the Bolshevik government soon found ways to circumvent them. From the spring of 1918 ostensibly independent communist parties began to be formed in the occupied territories, such as the Ukrainian, Finnish,

Lithuanian, Belorussian, Polish, and Latvian Communist parties. In August 1918 an Organisational Bureau to coordinate the activities of the new communist organisations was established in Moscow. This task became more urgent in the autumn of 1918 as the German military collapse became imminent, and the prospect opened up of carrying revolution westwards into Europe over the 'red bridge' of the Ukraine.

To decide on tactics for the new communist parties in this situation a Conference of Communist Organisations of the Occupied Territories was held in Moscow between 19 and 24 October 1918. It was referred to by contemporaries as the 'Little International'.[28] In his speech to the delegates of the conference, Lenin emphasised both the dangers and the opportunities of the current situation, the threat posed by an Allied invasion from the south and the possibility of revolution in Germany. Lenin now called a halt to the partisan attacks on the German forces in the occupied territories. Nothing, he emphasised, should be done to prejudice the development of the German revolution. Propaganda should be conducted in the Ukraine and the rest of the occupied territories for a socialist revolution in order to complete the links in the chain between socialist Russia and the emergent socialist Germany.[29]

At the beginning of January 1919, when it seemed that the Russian revolution was about to be exported through the Baltic area into Germany and beyond, Lenin decided to form the Third or Communist International (Comintern). Its first congress was held in March, and its nucleus was formed by the communist parties that had been established in the occupied territories after Brest-Litovsk, such as the Estonian, Latvian, Lithuanian, Belorussian and Ukrainian. The main communist party from abroad was the German Communist Party, but it was the Russians who dominated the new International. The Comintern in its early stages was not something radically new; in essence it was an extension of the kind of Social Democratic party organisation that had existed between 1906 and 1912. In many cases the personalities involved were the same, though the people who would have been key figures in the new organisation, Rosa Luxemburg and Leo Jogiches, had been murdered in Berlin within a few weeks of each other early in 1919.

In June of 1920, at the time the Second Congress of the Comintern met, another occasion arose when the Russian revolution might be carried into Western Europe. This was after the Reds' victory in the Civil War when Józef Piłsudski's Poland invaded the Ukraine and was driven back by Tukhachevskii to the outskirts of Warsaw. Lenin saw the Red Army's victory as a chance to set up a soviet regime in Poland. He later recalled that he and other party leaders had decided informally to 'test with bayonets whether the proletariat in Poland was ready for social revolution'.[30] Apparently they were not, and the fortunes of war were reversed when the Poles rallied and put the Red Army to flight. From then on Lenin and his associates in the Soviet leadership ceased to hope that there would be an international revolution in the near future.

For the Second Congress of the Comintern Lenin elaborated 21 conditions for the entry of socialist parties to the organisation[31] and wrote the pamphlet *Left Wing Communism. An Infantile Disorder*.[32] Both of these documents obliged foreign communist parties to construct themselves on the model of the Russian Communist Party and to adopt the centralisation and discipline that had brought the Bolsheviks to power in Russia. Lenin maintained that some features at least of the Russian revolution were applicable internationally. He was not inclined to consider that what had brought the Bolsheviks to power in Russia was their promise of peace, bread and land to a people exhausted by war and hunger. Lenin was in effect imposing on foreign parties not the pattern of the Russian revolution, but of a mythical revolution that had not occurred anywhere.

The civil war

Although Lenin had spoken repeatedly of turning the world war into a civil war, he was unprepared for the civil war which was unleashed in Russia after the Bolsheviks came to power. The Treaty of Brest-Litovsk provided the context in which the war ignited. It came as the culmination of a number of other Bolshevik actions and policies which alienated the Bolsheviks from other socialist parties, such as the dissolution of the Constituent Assembly, the repressions of the Cheka, the ending of press freedom and the curtailment of civil rights. Attempts by the SRs to win the Latvian Riflemen over to their side had failed. The revolt of the Czechoslovak legion, which was travelling on the Trans-Siberian railway to Vladivostok, in June of 1918, however, had placed an effective fighting force in the hands of the Mensheviks and Socialist Revolutionaries and opened a front of the Civil War in the east. Very soon, however, this 'democratic counter-revolution' began to resort to the same oppressive measures as the Bolsheviks. The moderate socialists, who had initially taken up arms against the Soviet regime, were replaced by leaders, such as Admiral Kolchak in the east and General Denikin in the south, who despised democracy and who did not distinguish the moderate socialists from their Bolshevik opponents.

Russia's withdrawal from the First World War created the conditions in which the Allied powers intervened in the Civil War on the side of the Whites, the intention being to renew the Russian war effort against the Germans. Lenin regarded this intervention as being a coordinated attempt by the imperialist powers, primarily Britain and France, to strangle the revolution in Russia. He viewed the foreign intervention, the Czechoslovak revolt and the peasant rebellions as being constituent parts of a single counter-revolutionary offensive against Soviet Russia. His conclusion was that the whole question of the Russian socialist revolution had been reduced to a question of war.[33]

Despite the Reds being surrounded on all sides, the White armies were never able to make a coordinated assault on the Soviet heartland. Distances were too great and rivalries amongst the White commanders too strong for this to occur. Only in the summer of 1919, when Denikin's forces came within striking distance of Moscow and when Petrograd came under attack from the army commanded by Yudenich based in Estonia, did the Soviet regime find itself in any imminent danger of defeat. But Yudenich's relatively small army was soon driven back to Estonia, and a successful counter-attack was launched against Denikin. By 1920 the main centre of White resistance was the Crimea, the base from which General Wrangel conducted raids along the North Caucasus and into the Ukraine. The campaign to capture Wrangel's Crimean stronghold was to be the final one of the Civil War for a Red Army that had emerged out of the ruins of the old Imperial army to become a formidable fighting force.

Although the main moving spirit behind the creation of the Red Army and the build-up of its fighting capacity was Trotsky, Lenin involved himself in the organisational effort needed to concentrate all possible resources required to secure victory. On 30 November 1918 the Council of Workers and Peasants' Defence was created to coordinate the activities of all organisations on the front and in the rear and to mobilise personnel and resources for an all-out effort in the war. The Council was chaired by Lenin, and had power over economic, military, party and Soviet affairs. It gave Lenin a key role in the conduct of the Civil War. Lenin's article 'All Out for the Fight against Denikin' is an illustration of the way in which Lenin's organisational talents had been directed towards military affairs. Every possible aspect of achieving victory was explored, such as the work among deserters from Denikin's camp, agitation and propaganda against the enemy, the curtailment of work not directly related to the war, and the provision of supplies for the Red Army.[34]

Apart from military considerations, a factor which weighed heavily in the Reds' favour in the Civil War was that the Bolsheviks had a political programme that could attract popular support. The Whites confined themselves to promising to reverse the changes brought about by the Soviet government. The Bolsheviks could promise land to the peasants, whereas the Whites returned the land to its previous owners. And while Denikin and other White leaders wished to restore the integrity of the Russian Empire, Lenin's policy of national self-determination won the Reds the support of the non-Russian nationalities of the Russian Empire. In pursuit of this policy, however, Lenin still had to campaign against those of his associates, such as Pyatakov and Bukharin, who harboured Luxemburgian conceptions of the national question. The Bolsheviks' promise of national self-determination, however, was not unconditional, as they intended to unite the nationalities in a federation of republics. Conflict would arise when the Georgians demanded more national independence than was on offer.[35]

War communism

The Soviet regime inherited the Provisional Government's supply problem. The Bolsheviks had given the peasants the land and they were now able to keep a greater proportion of their produce for themselves than they had in tsarist times. But the peasants had no incentive to supply grain to the towns or to the Red Army, since inflation had reduced the value of money and there were few goods available, as industry continued to decline. When the government tried to requisition the grain by force the peasants responded by concealing their grain stocks. The response from the government was the declaration of a 'Food Dictatorship'. A decree of 9 May 1918 incorporating Lenin's comments ordered an all-out struggle against the kulaks and peasant bourgeoisie who remained unmoved while the village poor starved.[36] In the following month 'committees of the village poor' were set up to extend the class struggle to the country-side and help the local grain collection agencies take surplus grain stocks from the kulaks. The policy did not have the desired results. It did not take into account the traditional solidarity of the peasant community in which poorer peasants were unlikely to enter into con-flict with their comparatively wealthier neighbours. The 'committees of the village poor' were abolished by a decree promulgated on 2 December 1918. Grain thereafter was collected by a system of quo-tas to be supplied by each locality (*prodrazverstka*).

The idea that the peasant community was split along class lines was one which Lenin had propounded since the 1890s. It had been the main theme of his *Development of Capitalism in Russia*. He had suf-ficiently convinced himself of its truth to base his agrarian policy upon it. Practice demonstrated that more than twenty years after Lenin had written his treatise, the peasant commune still retained its vitality and had not divided into antagonistic social classes. Lenin attached great doctrinal significance to the 'committees of the vil-lage poor' and was reluctant to accept that the class polarisation they presupposed had not taken place. In October–November 1918 he was still arguing against Kautsky that if the Bolshevik proletariat had not been able to rally the village poor round itself against the rich peasants, if the peasantry remained an 'integral whole', this would indeed have proved that Russia was 'unripe' for socialist revolution.[37] Needless to say, when the committees of the village poor had to be abolished a month later Lenin did not admit that Russia was not 'ripe' for socialism.

In June 1918 with the intensification of the Civil War there was a wholesale nationalisation of industry. Those enterprises which remained on the territory controlled by the Soviet republic were grouped into branches of industry (*glavki*) and these subordinated to VSNKhA, whose role now became greatly enhanced. The system was top-heavy, bureaucratic and cumbersome. But it did have the appearance of a distinctly socialist institution which controlled the economy in a centralised and rational way. Nevertheless, industry was continually disrupted through lack of raw materials and fuel, particularly when these resources were in areas controlled by the White armies. Improvisation was called for. In the absence of coal and oil for fuel, peat was utilised. Here some of Lenin's old revolutionary associates came in useful. Ivan Radchenko (Stepan Radchenko's brother) had become an expert on the use of peat as fuel for industry, in particular for generating electricity.[38] Gleb Krzhizhanovskii became involved in drawing up a plan for electrifying the country, and in 1920 the ambitious GOELRO scheme was launched to modernise industry and industrialise agriculture.[39] The project gave rise to Lenin's famous saying: 'Communism is Soviet power plus the electrification of the whole country.'[40]

A number of features of the economic system in operation during the Civil War convinced the Bolsheviks that the country was indeed progressing towards communism. The industrial sector had been centralised under VSNKhA; grain was supplied to the state (when it was supplied) under a system of quotas; there seemed to be a movement towards collective forms of agriculture and the high rate of inflation could be interpreted as a step towards a moneyless communist economy. Ideas of this kind appeared in the commentary on the new party programme written by Nikolai Bukharin and Evgenii Preobrazhenskii entitled *The ABC of Communism*.[41] Lenin himself was less inclined to indulge in theoretical speculations of this kind, but he too was of the opinion that Russia was on track for a socialist society. In January 1919 he wrote to the historian N. A. Rozhkov, who had suggested a policy of free trade, that this would be a backward step and that the way forward was through the improvement of the state monopoly towards socialism.[42]

Another characteristic theoretical work of the times was Bukharin's book *The Economics of the Transition Period*. This work reflected the discovery made by the Bolshevik leadership that the transition to communism would not be as smooth and painless as had been imagined in 1917. It admitted that the assumptions on which the Bolshevik revolution had been carried out had been false. It was now clear, for example, that it was impossible to control the economy through the banks, because in the course of the revolution the banking system was destroyed.[43] Because of the wholesale devastation of the country through war, revolution and civil war, it was realised that socialism would not just emerge as the outcome of historical progress, but would have to be consciously constructed. According to Bukharin, in the transition period from capitalism to socialism objective economic processes would be replaced by 'non-economic compulsion'. The proletarian state would use coercion for such purposes as requisitioning grain supplies from the peasants and imposing universal compulsory labour on the workers. Whereas under capitalism, this would mean the enslavement of the workers, under the conditions of the dictatorship of the proletariat it would signify no more than self-organisation by the workers.[44] In his marginal notes Lenin signified his approval of Bukharin's ideas on compulsion and force.

Bukharin concluded his book by accounting for the Russian revolution in the context of the interrelated world economic system. The component parts of this system, Bukharin believed, were joined together like the links of a chain, so that when a crisis occurred it would inevitably assume the character of a world crisis. In Bukharin's view it stood to reason that the collapse of the system was bound to begin precisely 'with those links which were most weakly organised in a capitalist way'.[45] Opposite this passage in Bukharin's book Lenin noted: 'untrue: [it begins] with the moderately weak. Without a certain level of capitalism nothing would have happened here in Russia'.[46] The idea that the chain of imperialism broke at its weakest link was not Lenin's, but Bukharin's, and it was not one that Lenin agreed with.

Oppositions

As the Civil War drew to a close, tensions within the Bolshevik party began to surface. The controversy on the trade unions rekindled some of the old antagonism between Lenin and Trotsky that had been latent since the middle of 1917. In tackling the country's transport problems, Trotsky found that one of the obstacles he encountered was the interference of the railwaymen's union. To obviate this Trotsky created Glavpolitput, whose function was to root out slackness and indiscipline on the railways. When the railwaymen's union objected, the union was replaced by a government creation known as Tsektran.

When the Fifth Conference of Trade Unions met in Moscow from 2 to 6 November 1920, Trotsky urged that the duplication of responsibility between the trade unions and the administrative organs, which had given rise to so much confusion, should be eliminated. This could only be done by the transformation of the trade unions into production unions. If the leaders of the unions objected, they would be 'shaken up' in the same way as the transport unions had been shaken up, by the imposition of military methods. The prospect of the Tsektran model being extended to other trade unions alarmed Communist trade unionists, prompting them to dissociate themselves from Trotsky's ideas. The conference ended by endorsing the theses proposed by the Latvian trade unionist Janis Rudzutaks, which formed the basis for the position of the Central Committee majority. The debate on the trade unions which followed threatened to create a serious split within the Bolshevik party, and placed Lenin and Trotsky on opposite sides of a deep ideological divide.

At the same time views on the role of the trade unions were also being put forward by the 'Workers' Opposition', which had been formed in 1920 by a number of worker Communists, especially trade union leaders, led by Shlyapnikov. Trotsky and the Workers' Opposition represented the opposite ends of a political spectrum. Whereas Trotsky wanted the trade unions to become part of the state apparatus, Shlyapnikov wanted the organs of the state to become part of the trade unions. The Workers' Opposition demanded that the ruling institution of the economy should be the 'All-Russian Congress of Producers'. Provincial, regional and district producers' councils would be elected from below. It also demanded that there should be a unified economic plan for the rational utilisation of economic resources and the distribution of goods. It demanded that a plan be drawn up for achieving the productive levels of 1913 within a set number of years. On immediate practical issues, the Workers' Opposition sought the equalisation of wages, free distribution of food and basic necessities to all workers, and the gradual replacement of money payments by payments in kind.[47]

Alexandra Kollontai put the theoretical case for the Workers' Opposition in a pamphlet distributed to party members during the Tenth Party Congress in 1921. Kollontai's pamphlet *The Workers' Opposition* is significant as an early analysis of the bureaucratic degeneration of the Soviet state. The root causes of this she considered to be the influence of bourgeois specialists. This influence had stifled the initiative of the workers and left them passive and apathetic. Kollontai called for a return to the elective principle, eliminating bureaucracy by making all officials answerable to the public at large. She advocated greater openness within the party, freedom of expression and greater democracy. She also called on the party to purge itself of non-proletarian elements, and make itself truly a workers' party. Kollontai reminded her readers of Marx's dictum that 'the liberation of the working class was the task of the working class itself'.[48]

Lenin's position on the trade unions was an intermediate one between Trotsky's and Shlyapnikov's. He argued that Trotsky was mistaken in thinking that the trade unions did not need to defend the workers, because the state was a 'workers' state'. It was in this context that Lenin conceded that workers might have grievances against the Soviet government. In Lenin's opinion, the existing Soviet state was a 'workers' state with a bureaucratic twist to it' and the workers still required to defend themselves through the trade unions. 'We must', Lenin stated, 'use these workers' organisations for the defence of the workers from their state and for the defence by the workers of our state.'[49] This position was set out in the 'Platform of the Ten' on 14 January 1921, signed by Lenin, Zinoviev, Stalin, M. P. Tomskii, Kalinin, Rudzutaks, S. A. Lozovskii, Petrovskii and Artem. This was to be the approach to the trade union question adopted by the Tenth Party Congress in March 1921. Bukharin initially had held a position midway between Trotsky and Lenin, but latterly allied completely with Trotsky.

Like the Workers' Opposition, the Democratic Centralist group believed that greater rights should be given to the trade unions in the running of the economy. The Democratic Centralists consisted mainly of long-standing members of the Bolshevik party, such as Osinskii and Sapronov, who had been Left Communists in 1918. They thought that after it had come to power, the party had betrayed its own democratic ideals, as set out in Lenin's *State and Revolution*. They opposed the bureaucratic centralism of Lenin's Central Committee and advocated greater freedom within the party, insisting that every important question should be discussed by the party rank and file before decisions were taken. They believed that the function of the Central Committee should not be to manage the party, but only to give it general direction.

Peasant resentment against the system of requisitions gave rise to an outbreak of peasant rebellions in 1920, the most serious being in Tambov and which was eventually put down by Tukhachevskii. Increasingly the Bolshevik leadership began to accept that it would be advisable to replace the *prodrazverstka* by a tax in kind. One of the first to do so was Trotsky in February 1920. The proposal was then rejected and Trotsky did not pursue the matter. But in the course of 1920 the idea must have become widespread because even foreign visitors to Russia like Bertrand Russell and Ethel Snowden voiced the idea.[50] Lenin was late in coming round to the acceptance that requisitions would have to be abandoned. It was only in February 1921, on the eve of the naval mutiny at Kronstadt, that he finally did so.

The demands put forward by the Kronstadt sailors, such as those for freedom of speech and the press for socialist parties, and freedom of assembly for trade unions and peasant associations, were ones which were basic civil rights. They would have been readily accepted by the Bolsheviks before they came to power. Now they were symptomatic of the way the Soviet regime had evolved in its three years in power. It was a political system in which one party had a monopoly of power and expression. It was a system which did not reflect the will of the people, and one which allowed imprisonment for political reasons without trial.

Lenin, however, refused to see the revolt as anything but a threat to the regime, professing to see in it 'the work of Socialist Revolutionaries and white-guard émigrés', a movement inspired by 'petty-bourgeois counter-revolution and petty-bourgeois anarchism'.[51] The tactic of the Soviet leadership was to discredit the Kronstadt rebellion by presenting it as non-proletarian and crushing it with extreme ferocity. Nor did Lenin show any sympathy for the Workers' Opposition, which he subjected to scorn and ridicule at the Tenth Party Congress. He also threatened Shlyapnikov that, as his statements were comparable to ones made by the anarchist Kronstadt mutineers, the Soviet government's response to the Workers' Opposition might be the gun.[52]

The Tenth Party Congress and the beginning of NEP

The replacement of the *prodrazverstka* by a tax in kind at the Tenth Party Congress meant that the peasants now had to pay a tax in grain or other agricultural produce to the state, but after payment of the tax they could do with any stocks they had left as they thought fit. They could use the grain to feed themselves or increase their cultivated area, or they could exchange it for industrial goods. They were also allowed to sell the additional grain on the free market.[53] This last concession prepared the ground for the return of freedom of trade, the dismantling of the 'War Communism' system and the introduction of the New Economic Policy (NEP).

On the question of the trade unions, the Tenth Party Congress gave its overwhelming support to Lenin's 'Platform of the Ten'. During the congress Lenin took steps to consolidate his victory by ensuring that supporters of the Platform would be in control of the party apparatus. At that time, the Secretariat was in the hands of Krestinskii, Serebriakov and Preobrazhenskii – all allies of Trotsky. On the evening of 9 March, therefore, Lenin assembled some trusted delegates and with them drew up a list of approved candidates for the Central Committee. He intended that two-thirds of the Central Committee should consist of supporters of the Platform of the Ten, while the remaining third of the places should be apportioned among the representatives of Trotsky's platform, the Workers' Opposition and the Democratic Centralists. Lenin mentioned in particular that Krestinskii, Serebriakov and Preobrazhenskii should not be elected to the Central Committee, but that he thought that Shlyapnikov and I. I. Kutuzov from the Workers' Opposition and Sapronov from the Democratic Centralists ought to be elected. By including some oppositionists in the Central Committee Lenin hoped to ensure that these groups were not alienated from the regime, and that they would be bound by the collective decisions of the Central Committee. As they could always be out-voted, their presence would not constitute any danger.[54]

But, as an additional safeguard, Lenin thought it prudent to pass a resolution at the congress condemning fractionalism, dissolve all existing fractions, and declare fractional activity incompatible with party membership. He believed that provision should be made for expelling even a member of the Central Committee if he was involved in fractional activities. This would, however, require a two-thirds majority of members and candidate members of the Central Committee.

On the last day of the congress Lenin produced two resolutions – 'On Party Unity' and 'On the Syndicalist and Anarchist Deviation in Our Party'. The first of these resolutions contained the proposal to outlaw fractionalism, as Lenin had planned previously. But as a concession to the opposition groups, it included in addition the undertaking that the party would in the future take measures to respond to the points these groups had made, such as purging the party of non-proletarian and unreliable elements, combating bureaucratic practices, and developing democracy and workers' initiative.[55]

The second resolution echoed arguments Bukharin had advanced against the Workers' Opposition, pointing out that the concept of 'producer' confused proletarians with non-proletarians and small commodity producers. Lenin was emphatic that Marxism taught that only the Communist Party was capable of organising a vanguard of the proletariat that would be able to withstand the vacillations of the petty-bourgeois element which predominated in Russian conditions. To deny this, Lenin considered, was a syndicalist and anarchist deviation.[56] The resolutions, which were approved by the congress, had the effect of reinforcing Lenin's doctrine on the leading role of the party, lessening the scope for intraparty disagreements, and setting in motion the practice of party purges.

The Bolshevik party membership did not accept the New Economic Policy with any great enthusiasm. Although the economic conditions between 1918 and 1920 had been deplorable, the economic system itself had appeared to be in keeping with communist principles. There was widespread nationalisation, private capital had been eliminated, the significance of money was in decline and private trade had been outlawed. If material levels could be raised, it was thought, the result would be highly desirable. When NEP was introduced it was interpreted as capitulation to capitalism and a betrayal of socialist principles.

In combating this attitude Lenin argued that 'War Communism' (he now used Bogdanov's term) had been a temporary measure dictated by circumstances. He asserted that the NEP was a return to the path that had been taken by the party in the first months of Soviet power, before it had been blown off course by the Civil War. Lenin was irritated when local party organisations refused to take NEP seriously, and at the Tenth Party Conference in May 1921 he emphasised that the policy would have to be taken 'in earnest and for a long time'.[57]

After the Tenth Congress decrees were issued to control inflation and stabilise the currency, to privatise some industrial enterprises, to legalise private trade and to offer concessions in Russia to foreign investors. Now, Lenin believed, the peasants had to learn to trade, and to trade in a civilised, European, way. He urged them to enter consumer cooperatives and by this means become 'literate traders' and overcome the Russian legacy of backwardness.

Since state control would remain over most of industry and since the state owned the land, the peasant cooperatives would not threaten a return to capitalist relations in the country as a whole. The cooperatives would function, moreover, within the context of the dictatorship of the proletariat, so that a capitalist restoration would not be likely. NEP, in fact, was accompanied by a tightening of political controls. Lenin now believed that the way to socialism was not by eliminating market relations, but that the country would reach socialism through market relations.

The introduction of NEP coincided with widespread famine in the country. The requisitions of the past three years had served to cause a reduction in sown area, and the collapse of industry had severely reduced the supply of agricultural implements. Combined with a severe drought in the east and south-east the result was a catastrophic reduction of grain on the recently legalised market. Soviet Russia was obliged to accept American aid under the auspices of the American Relief Administration. The loss of life through hunger and disease was enormous.

The General Secretary

The desire of the Soviet leadership to exclude members of opposition groups from being returned as delegates to party congresses and conferences increased the role played by the Secretariat of the Central Committee. It was this institution which acted as the apparatus for filtering delegates. Stalin became the head of the Secretariat, the General Secretary of the party, in April 1922, and in so doing increased his power and influence in the party leadership. Anastas Mikoyan recalls how in preparation for the Eleventh Party Congress he was sent on a mission to Novo-Nikolaevsk by Stalin to ensure that the supporters of Trotsky there would not be included in the delegation to the congress. Mikoyan added that Lenin knew and approved of what Stalin was doing.[58] Lenin had certainly connived in Stalin's accumulation of power, as he had found this convenient. Later, however, he was to have doubts about the wisdom of raising Stalin to such heights.

In April 1922 Lenin underwent an operation for the removal of one of the bullets which had remained since the assassination attempt in August 1918. While convalescing at Gorki outside Moscow a month later he suffered a stroke which left him with a temporary loss of speech and partially paralysed. Lenin's doctors ordered him to have a prolonged rest and, to avoid stress, forbade him to read the newspapers. By October, however, he had recovered sufficiently to resume work and to reenter into the controversies of the time.

An issue which loomed large in the autumn of 1922 was the question of the foreign trade monopoly. A plenary meeting of the Central Committee on 6 October, which Lenin had not attended, had decided to relax the monopoly slightly in respect of certain goods. Lenin thought this decision mistaken and tried to have it reversed. On 16 December, however, he suffered a second stroke and had again to submit to the strict regime of rest ordered by his doctors. Lenin's condition was discussed by a special meeting of the Central Committee on 18 December which gave Stalin the responsibility of seeing that the regime prescribed by the doctors was adhered to. This gave Stalin the right to isolate Lenin from political affairs in Moscow, and to oversee all information going to and from Lenin.

Lenin, however, still kept in touch with events through Krupskaya. When he learnt from her that Trotsky had been able to get the Central Committee to change its mind on relaxing the state monopoly on foreign trade, he got her to send Trotsky a letter expressing his satisfaction at the good news and asking him to make a report at the Twelfth Congress. Doubting whether Lenin was in a position to make such a request, Trotsky consulted Kamenev on the matter and Kamenev in turn told Stalin. Stalin was furious that Lenin had gone behind the back of the Politburo in communicating directly with Trotsky and had done so without his own authority as the person responsible for his medical regime. On discovering that Krupskaya had helped Lenin write his letter, Stalin rebuked her over the telephone and threatened to report her to the Central Control Commission for infringing the doctors' orders.[59]

To avoid distressing him, Krupskaya did not tell Lenin what had occurred, but on the following day (23 December) wrote to Kamenev complaining about Stalin's rudeness and asking him and Zinoviev to protect her from further harassment. Thereafter Krupskaya made no further mention of the incident, and it is most unlikely that she rolled about on the floor sobbing, as Lenin's sister Mariya later alleged.[60]

At the end of December in the short periods his doctors allowed him for dictation to his secretaries, Lenin began to compose a letter to the Twelfth Party Congress in which he discussed who among the present Soviet leadership might succeed him. The letter, which became known as 'Lenin's Testament', is a symptomatic document, because it presupposes a kind of government so centralised and so remote from the public that the outgoing ruler may influence the choice of, if not nominate, his successor.

The letter takes a balanced approach to the people it discusses, in that the strengths and the weaknesses of each are taken into consideration. Nobody is wholeheartedly endorsed. Lenin feared that the rivalry between Trotsky and Stalin might lead to a split in the Central Committee, and for that reason he proposed increasing the number of its members to 50 or 100. Lenin observed that, having become General Secretary, Stalin had 'unlimited authority concentrated in his hands', but that he doubted whether he would use that power with due caution. Trotsky Lenin considered to be perhaps the most capable man in the present Central Committee. But on the other hand, he had displayed excessive self-assurance and had shown 'excessive preoccupation with the purely administrative side of things.' This was an ironic judgement on someone who was later to pose as the great campaigner against bureaucracy.

Bukharin was recognised as being a most valuable and major theorist of the party. But this accolade was tempered if not annihilated by the remark that Bukharin's views could not be classified as fully Marxist and that he had never fully understood dialectics. Zinoviev and Kamenev's opposition to the October revolution was recalled, but Lenin was prepared to overlook it, as he was Trotsky's non-Bolshevism.[61]

When Lenin's secretary Mariya Volodicheva had typed up her shorthand notes she asked her colleague L. Fotieva for advice on what she should do with the typed copy. Fotieva told her that she should show it to Stalin. When she did so Stalin instructed her to burn it. She burnt the copy she had shown to Stalin, but omitted to point out that there were four other copies in a safe. It was only on the following day, when Lenin resumed his dictation, that he told Volodicheva, to her embarrassment, that the letter should be kept strictly secret. Volodicheva, however, did not reveal that Stalin already knew something of its contents. The portions of the letter dictated to Fotieva were probably communicated by her to Stalin, as she was an admirer of the General Secretary. These portions would include Lenin's recommendation that Stalin be removed from his post as General Secretary and replaced by someone with a less abrupt manner.[62]

Lenin had also been following closely the steps which were being taken to unite the territories of the former tsarist Empire into what would become the Union of Soviet Socialist Republics. This was a complex matter, because the union had to be constituted in such a way that the policies of the Russian Soviet Republic would not be undermined by decisions taken in the borderlands. At the same time, however, enough autonomy had to be conceded as would avoid offending national sensibilities. Stalin had the responsibility of working out the constitutional structure for a multinational state, and had managed to get widespread agreement for his proposals. The greatest obstacle he encountered was from the local Georgian communists, who objected to the uncompromising way Moscow's policies were being implemented by Sergo Orjonikidze, the head of the Caucasus party organisation.

Complaints from the Georgian communists to Lenin prompted the Central Committee of the Russian Communist party on 24 November to send a commission of inquiry consisting of Dzierżyński, Manuilskii and V. Kapsukas to Tiflis. The commission exonerated Orjonikidze and condemned the Georgian oppositionists. Lenin, however, who had formerly sided with Stalin and Orjonikidze, began to make common cause with the Georgian communists. In a memorandum written at the end of December he referred to his earlier writings on the national question, stressing that an important distinction had to be drawn between the nationalism of an oppressor nation and that of an oppressed nation. He thought that the treatment of Georgia at the hands of Soviet officialdom was a recrudescence of Great Russian chauvinism. Those whom he held responsible for the campaign of Great Russian nationalism were Orjonikidze, Stalin and Dzierżyński.[63]

On 24 January 1923 Lenin asked his secretaries to gather together all the materials from the Dzierżyński Caucasus commission to compile an independent report. The completed report, which Lenin received on 3 March, took the side of the Georgian communists against Dzierżyński. Three days later he wrote to B. Mdivani and P. Makharadze to inform them that he supported them fully and that he was outraged by the rudeness of Orjonikidze and the connivance of Stalin and Dzierżyński. But as he was too ill to pursue the matter himself, Lenin wrote to Trotsky asking him to undertake the defence of the Georgians on his behalf. Trotsky, however, did not pursue the campaign with any great enthusiasm or robustness, but Lenin's note did prompt Stalin to urge caution in his behaviour to Orjonikidze and to make him come to a compromise with the Georgian communists. Arrangements for the formation of the USSR went ahead as planned.[64]

At the beginning of March Lenin discovered, probably from Kamenev and Zinoviev, about Stalin's abusive treatment of Krupskaya in December. On 5 March he sent Stalin an indignant letter demanding an apology for his conduct and if this was not forthcoming personal relations between Stalin and himself would be severed. Stalin in reply dictated a conciliatory note, in which he denied any blame for what had occurred, saying that he had simply been concerned to see that Lenin's medical regime was strictly observed, and attributing Krupskaya's distress to a misunderstanding. The perfunctory tone of the note would doubtless have seemed unsatisfactory to Lenin.[65] At that point, however, he suffered a third stroke, which deprived him of the power of speech and greatly reduced his mobility. He was moved to Gorki where he lived the remainder of his life in the company of Krupskaya and his sisters Mariya and Anna. He died on 21 January 1924 at the age of 53. Two days later Lenin's body was brought back to Moscow and placed in a mausoleum on Red Square. His name passed into legend.

In his last months Lenin had been concerned about the growth of bureaucracy in the young Soviet state and the survival of tsarist methods and practices. But as regards the Bolshevik revolution and the creation of the Soviet state as a whole Lenin had few qualms. In one of his last articles he noted his impressions of Sukhanov's memoirs of 1917. The aspect of the book which attracted his attention was the argument that Russia was not ripe for socialism. Perhaps he had in mind Sukhanov's observation that when he returned to Russia in April 1917 Lenin was unable to present any economic argument for there being a socialist revolution in Russia. Lenin's comment on this idea is a kind of epitaph on his life and provides an insight into his way of thinking.

He ridiculed people like Sukhanov whose narrow vision precluded them from seeing the infinite possibilities of world history. Revolutions had taken and would take a variety of forms. If the Russian revolution did not conform with Marxist orthodoxy it meant little. Theories should not be allowed to become a fetish. So if for a socialist revolution a certain level of economic development was necessary (though nobody could say what this was) why could not Russia first have its revolution and *then*, with the help of the Soviet system, proceed to construct the advanced economic basis which it allegedly lacked? It was an answer of sorts to the question that had been posed in 1917, but one which Lenin obviously did not insist upon.[66]

7

THE LENIN LEGEND

1st part

The starting point in studying Lenin's intellectual and political biography is the conventional interpretation of Lenin as the man who by his pamphlet *What Is To Be Done?* inspired the creation of the Bolshevik party, a centralised and tightly controlled organisation of professional revolutionaries, which in October 1917 seized power in Russia. This conception was neatly summed up by Merle Fainsod as follows: 'In 1902 in *What Is To Be Done?* Lenin had written, "Give me an organisation of revolutionaries, and we shall overturn the whole of Russia". On 25 October 1917, the wish was fulfilled and the deed accomplished.'[1]

When, however, we look into the matter in more detail, as we have done in the foregoing chapters, it emerges that this interpretation is not supported by the evidence. Lenin did not set out to create the Bolshevik party; he was intent on gaining control over the whole of the RSDLP, and he spent over a decade forming alliances which he hoped would make this possible. In the end he failed in his objective. Even the Bolshevik fraction was never particularly united, and until at least 1912 contained members who did not accept Lenin's ideological leadership. When the Bolsheviks came to power in 1917 it was through a combination of factors, such as the devastation of the country by the war, the promise of peace, bread and land to the Russian people and the organisational abilities of Trotsky and his friends. The centralisation and discipline of the Bolshevik party was not a factor which could have weighed heavily in bringing the Bolsheviks to power, if for no other reason than that in October 1917 the Bolshevik party was not centralised and not well-disciplined, as Lenin knew only too well.

The question therefore arises: how did the conventional picture of Lenin arise? It is an important question to tackle because if the interpretation of Lenin that has been presented in the earlier chapters is right, then it should be possible to document the process by which that picture has been modified to produce the conventional presentation of Lenin as exemplified by Fainsod. In this way the story of how the Lenin legend came about is the counterpart of the investigation to discover the real state of affairs, and a means of verifying the outcome of that investigation.

The problem for biographers of Lenin, which they share with historians of the Bolshevik party, is that right from its inception Soviet historical writing was subordinated to considerations of party policy. Political considerations operated even when the very first history of the Russian revolution was written soon after the event itself. This was Leon Trotsky's pamphlet *The History of the Russian Revolution to Brest-Litovsk*.[2] It was written in the spring of 1918 when Trotsky went to conduct peace negotiations with the Germans at Brest-Litovsk. He used some of the recesses to dictate the text of the pamphlet to the stenographers who accompanied the Soviet delegation.

Trotsky's history was in fact intended for a foreign audience. It was designed to present the acquisition of power by the Bolsheviks in as favourable a light as possible in order that the new Soviet government should gain friends abroad, especially among the Germans. Trotsky hoped that the German workers would make a revolution in their own country. This would remove the military threat from the new Soviet republic and spread the revolution westwards into Europe.

Trotsky had to reckon with the fact that the reaction to the October revolution in the German press, even the socialist press, had been generally unfavourable. The Bolsheviks had been accused of establishing a dictatorship over the workers and peasants, of infringing democratic principles, and of refusing to broaden the base of their government by including representatives of other political parties. In his pamphlet Trotsky set out to answer these charges. He tried to show that the Bolsheviks had not carried out a *coup d'état* behind the backs of the Russian people and had done everything possible to involve all other socialist parties in the government.

In *The History of the Russian Revolution to Brest-Litovsk* Trotsky argued that the acquisition of power by the Bolsheviks had been part of a prolonged process. This had begun in the autumn of 1917 when the Bolshevik party started to enjoy increased support in the country. It looked forward to victory in the forthcoming elections to the Second Congress of Soviets, and expected to come to power in this way. The Bolsheviks' opponents in other political parties, however, tried to prevent this happening and planned to resort to force. The Bolsheviks, in company with some other socialists, responded by taking countermeasures to ensure that the congress would be convened. They collaborated in forming a Military Revolutionary Committee to monitor troop movements in and out of Petrograd. At the congress the Bolsheviks duly secured a majority, but the other socialist parties refused to cooperate with them in forming a government. This forced the Bolsheviks to take power on their own.

In this presentation of events there was no point at which the Bolsheviks took the offensive. They had come to power only as a response to the threat of force by their opponents. It was the latter who had disrupted the elective process because they, unlike the Bolsheviks, did not enjoy popular support. It was they, Trotsky insists, who tried to smear the Bolsheviks by accusing them of seizing power by an armed insurrection. In this way Trotsky explained the Bolsheviks' reputation as insurrectionaries as slander by their opponents.

The pamphlet was quickly translated into several languages, the first of these being German. As part of the same campaign, Lenin's pamphlet *State and Revolution* was translated into German for distribution abroad in order to counter the unfavourable impression made by the dissolution of the Constituent Assembly. It was to show the German workers that Russia intended to establish a superior form of democracy to that enjoyed by parliamentary regimes.

By the time the Second Congress of the Comintern met in July 1920 the political situation had altered and now the Bolshevik party presented itself as the organisation which had planned and led the October revolution. The young Soviet state had now been secured. The Whites had been defeated; the interventionist powers had withdrawn from Russia, and Tukhachevskii was chasing the Poles out of the Ukraine towards Warsaw. The Russian revolution was poised to spread into Western Europe. It was in this heady atmosphere that Lenin wrote his pamphlet *Left Wing Communism. An Infantile Disorder*.

The pamphlet criticised leftist elements in Germany and Britain for neglecting parliamentary tactics and for failure to take advantage of legal means available to them in their respective countries. It was the kind of argument Lenin had deployed against the 'Recallers' over a decade earlier. Now Lenin was generalising his tactics to guide the world revolution. As the party that had brought about the first successful proletarian revolution in history, the Bolsheviks could expect their methods to be emulated by other revolutionary parties. Lenin held that the triumph of the October revolution was a vindication of Bolshevism, which, 'as a current of political thought and as a party, had existed since 1903'. Bolshevism, which consisted in 'the strictest centralisation and iron discipline', had arisen on the 'granite theoretical foundation' of Marxism. It had passed through fifteen years (1903–17) of practical history, which, in wealth of experience 'had no equal anywhere else in the world'.[3] Lenin went on to provide an outline sketch of Bolshevism's history, dividing it up into neat periods, and treating each from his own particular point of view.[4] The impression given was that between 1903 and 1917 a Bolshevik party really had existed as an independent entity, that it had in fact been inspired by the ideas propounded in *What Is To Be Done?* and that it had been governed by Lenin's thinking on whatever issue arose. Even as an outline sketch Lenin's version of the history of Bolshevism was highly fanciful. It was the history of Bolshevism as Lenin would have liked it to have been, and he fully intended that that was how the history of Bolshevism would be written.

Practical steps were taken in this direction in the summer of 1920 when Lenin had discussions with M. N. Pokrovskii and V. V. Adoratskii on the possibility of establishing an organisation specifically concerned with the collection and distribution of materials on the history of the Bolshevik party and the October revolution. The organisation's terms of reference were thus meant to correspond to the scheme elaborated in *Left Wing Communism. An Infantile Disorder*. Pokrovskii, a trained historian, argued in favour of treating the history of the revolution separately from the history of the Bolshevik party, because whereas one could study the revolution from all kind of source materials, the history of the Bolshevik party would have to rely largely on the memoirs of participants. Lenin, however, would not hear of it and insisted that both functions be given to the same organisation. In this way the supposition that the Bolshevik party had brought about the October revolution was built into the very foundations of the institution. This was to be known as the 'Commission on the History of the Russian Communist Party and the October Revolution' or 'Istpart' for short. The Commission was chaired by M. S. Olminskii, who was a veteran of the workers' movement in St Petersburg.[5]

The political importance of Istpart is reflected in the way its organisational affiliation changed in the first months of its existence. When it was first established it had been attached to Gosizdat, the state publishing house and then, a month later, to Narkompros, the Commissariat of Education. At the end of 1921, however, on the insistence of Lenin's sister Anna Ulyanova-Elizarova and presumably with the approval of Lenin, Istpart was attached to the Communist Party Central Committee as one of its departments. Anna wanted to give the organisation more authority, but the Istpart leadership were reluctant to detach themselves from Narkompros. Stalin, however agreed fully with Anna. 'Of course Istpart should come under the Central Committee', he said, 'Where else should it be?'[6] Ultimate responsibility for the activities of Istpart and its local branches rested with the Central Committee and all the decisions it took which had political or ideological implications had to be sanctioned by the Secretariat, the Politburo or the Orgburo. This arrangement provided the mechanism for exercising party control over what was written on the history of the Russian revolution or the Bolshevik party throughout the country. From 1921 onwards Istpart began to issue its monthly journal *Proletarskaya revolyutsiya*, which contained documentary materials, memoirs and scholarly articles on the history of the Russian revolution and the revolutionary movement.

The original membership of Istpart, which included Pokrovskii and Adoratskii and V. I. Nevskii, was joined in April 1921 by Lenin's sister Anna Ulyanova-Elizarova. Anna headed the Lenin section of Istpart and ensured that everything that was published about Lenin was in the spirit that would find approval with her brother. She was assisted in this endeavour by her cousin Ekaterina Veretennikova, who also came to work in Istpart.[7] All the materials about Lenin which were published in *Proletarskaya revolyutsiya* were sifted and processed by Anna. Works which did not show Lenin in the desired light, such as the memoirs of Takhtarev published in 1902 and Ivan Chebotarev's 1922 biography of Lenin for young people, were severely criticised.

The project to which Anna was most dedicated, however, was the collection of memoirs and other materials on her beloved brother Alexander. Through her efforts the collection *Aleksandr Il'ich Ul'ianov i delo 1 marta 1887 g.* was published in 1927. She contacted Ivan Chebotarev, Jozef Lukasiewicz and other friends of her late brother and commissioned them to write reminiscences of Sasha. She used the occasion to set down her own memoirs of her childhood and youth in the household of the Ulyanov family in the carefree times before it was struck by the tragedy of Sasha's death. It is these memoirs which give the best insight into Lenin's family background.

The collection of materials on Alexander Ulyanov was a personal preoccupation of Anna's and it bore the traces of many years of pent-up grief. It was not part of the Lenin cult which Istpart was trying to foster, and dealt with an episode of the past which was outside the main preoccupations of Bolshevik party politics. It is for that reason that Anna's collection is a particularly valuable source. It includes many pre-Soviet memoirs, some of them first published in the historical journal of the Socialist Revolutionaries, *Byloe*. For that reason, the collection contains material on the history of the Russian revolutionary movement which was at variance with the accepted party doctrines on the subject. In particular the collection contains memoir evidence for the coexistence of Marxist views on Russian economic development with terrorist tactics, a combination which would seem unexpected in the light of other sources published by Istpart, including Lenin's *Works*.

The collection avoids the question of the ideological legacy bequeathed to Lenin by his brother. The answer to this question was by then predetermined by Lenin's polemical approach to his predecessors in the Russian revolutionary movement, particularly his campaign against Narodism, a category which included his brother. It was Lenin's younger sister Mariya who voiced the official interpretation of the progression from Alexander Ulyanov to Lenin when she declared at a memorial meeting for Lenin on 7 February 1924 that on receiving the news of his brother's execution Vladimir cried out: 'No, we won't go that way; that is not the way to take.'[8] This was the version that was to enter subsequent Soviet and Western biographies of Lenin.

An important function of Istpart was the publication of Lenin's *Collected Works*. The first edition began in 1920 and was completed in 1926, so that some of the volumes appeared in Lenin's lifetime. The task was facilitated by the fact that Lenin, like Trotsky, with posterity in mind, had preserved as far as he could every scrap of paper relating to himself.[9] The volumes of the first edition of Lenin's works were provided with extensive appendices of related documents and with commentaries by Anna Elizarova and other members of Istpart. The first volume even contained annotations by Martov, as someone who was familiar with the period in question. This kind of documentation was to diminish and disappear entirely in subsequent editions of Lenin's writings.

In 1923 the task of publishing Lenin's works as well as the series of collections of Lenin materials, the *Leninskie sborniki*, was taken over by the newly established Lenin Institute of which Kamenev was director. The Lenin Institute was also something of an Ulyanov family affair, as it included on its staff Anna Elizarova, Mariya Ulyanova and Krupskaya, as well as the Istpart stalwarts Olminskii, Pokrovsii and Adoratskii. Because of the great overlap both in functions and in personnel Istpart was incorporated in the Lenin Institute in 1928. In 1931 the Lenin Institute merged with the Marx and Lenin Institute to form the Marx, Engels and Lenin Institute attached to the Central Committee of the party.[10]

In establishing Istpart it is unlikely that Lenin thought of its function as a purely scholarly one. It is likely that he wanted to use the Commission as an instrument in current politics. Although he himself did not publish a review of Bukharin's *Economics of the Transition Period*, both Olminskii and Anna Elizarova for Istpart published critiques of the book in 1921, presumably at Lenin's instigation. Lenin was also a pioneer in using his earlier writings in current political campaigns. To combat the influence of Alexander Bogdanov and the Proletkult movement in September 1920 he arranged for the reissue of his polemical philosophical work *Materialism and Empiriocriticism*. On Lenin's behest V. I. Nevskii, soon to become head of the section on party history in Istpart, wrote a preface for the new edition denouncing Bogdanov and his ideas in virulent terms. Nevskii's preface, to which Lenin had made editorial corrections,[11] was included in the relevant volume of Lenin's *Collected Works* (Vol. 10) when it came out in 1926. Even in these early stages of historical writing in Soviet Russia the practice was that if something or someone met with the disapproval of those in power that thing or that person would not be mentioned in historical writing. This is what happened to Bogdanov. Trotsky was later to suffer the same fate, as was everyone Stalin designated as an 'enemy of the people'. Those persons at least had the fortune to have been mentioned at some stage in the Soviet period, so that their disappearance could be noticed. But since Bogdanov had fallen foul of Lenin before the Bolsheviks came to power and had been mentioned only fleetingly in Soviet publications, his absence from the history of the Bolshevik party passed for the most part unnoticed.

The publication of Lenin's works was indispensable if events were to be interpreted from a Leninist point of view. K. N. Ostroukhova, for example, the historian of Lenin's campaign against Bogdanov and his associates, in recalling her work for Istpart states that Olminskii advised her that in expounding the theme she should take her cue from the way Lenin had handled it in his writings of the time.[12] Structuring historical events around Lenin's writings in the manner Ostroukhova describes inevitably produced a version of history which ostensibly proved the correctness of Lenin's views.

When Lenin died in January of 1924 his funeral and mourning gave an enormous momentum to the Lenin cult. The preservation of his body in a mausoleum on Red Square was a symptom of the quasi-religious veneration in which he would henceforth be held. Stalin was to find the Lenin cult extremely useful and he did much to foster it. But Stalin did not create the Lenin cult. He found it already in existence and propelled by the momentum that Lenin himself had given it.

Stalin and Lenin

The year of Lenin's death was also to be a landmark in the ideological evolution of the Soviet Union. Stalin gave a series of lectures at the Sverdlov University under the general title 'The Foundations of Leninism', in which he introduced his ideas on 'socialism in one country'. Since the Russian revolution could no longer be explained in terms of Hilferding's economic theories, it was necessary to give a fresh explanation of what the revolution was and what had brought it about. Stalin's lectures were intended to show that in the absence of a world revolution Soviet Russia was not to be understood as an isolated anomaly, but as a phenomenon fully in accordance with the general march of world development.

It was Stalin's contention that according to Lenin's theory of revolution the individual national capitalist systems were linked together in a single chain to form a united front of imperialism. It was generally believed that the proletarian revolution would begin in those countries where industry was more developed, where there was a higher level of culture and where the proletariat constituted the majority of the population. But, according to Stalin, Lenin's theory of revolution held that this was not necessarily the case, and that the front of capital would be breached where the chain of world imperialism was weakest.[13]

Of course Lenin's theory of revolution had stated no such thing. In fact, when Lenin had found the idea in Bukharin's book *Economics of the Transition Period* he had recorded his disagreement with it. The notes in question were published in 1928 when they were used to discredit Bukharin, but in 1924 Stalin was taken at his word. Stalin sought to invest his own ideas with Lenin's authority and prestige. The implication is that he believed that his own authority would be insufficient to secure their acceptance. In this way 'Leninism' became a convenient vehicle for Stalin's political thinking.

One result of Stalin's use of Leninism was that a gulf opened up between Lenin's writings and what Stalin said he had written. Consequently it became impossible to provide commentaries on Lenin's writings and supply them with documentation to show the context in which they were written. The fourth edition of Lenin's *Collected Works* (1941–50), which Stalin supervised, reduced explanatory notes to a minimum, made these as tendentious as possible and removed any reference to Trotsky which could be construed as positive.

Trotsky had an ambivalent attitude towards the Lenin cult. In 1924 he published the book *Reminiscences of Lenin*, which is a unique document of its times in that Trotsky did not place Lenin on a pedestal, but described his own relationship with Lenin as one between equals. In fact, of the two men it is Trotsky who emerges as the more capable and level-headed. In the section on the October revolution there is the hint that it was Trotsky's strategy which triumphed in October 1917, when Lenin is made to say 'Well, I suppose you can do it that way too. Just so long as we take power.'[14] The book is full of picturesque detail, which shows Trotsky's literary skills at their best. No other memoirist of Lenin, not even the professional novelist Gorky, presented such a convincing pen-portrait of Lenin and his personality traits. It was a unique work among the many contributions to the genre, and understandably has been drawn upon widely by Lenin's biographers.

Temperamentally, Trotsky was unsuited to venerate anyone, and his *Reminiscences of Lenin* reflect this healthy attitude. However, for political reasons he found it convenient to make use of the Lenin cult. He found he could exploit the fact that Lenin had become a standard against which other people's behaviour and conceptions were judged because, conveniently, according to that criterion, his political opponents would be found wanting. This was the conception behind Trotsky's essay 'Lessons of October', which appeared in 1924 as the introduction to the volume of his collected works covering 1917.[15] The essay was no dispassionate study of the events of 1917. It was one in which Trotsky used the events of the revolution to discredit his rivals. There were two main focuses in the book. One was Lenin's return to Petrograd in April 1917. The other was the October revolution. The point was that in April when Lenin had presented his 'April Theses', Zinoviev, Kamenev and Stalin had opposed Lenin's ideas. In October Zinoviev and Kamenev had been against the revolution, whereas Trotsky had supported Lenin's call for an armed insurrection. The lesson of October that Trotsky wanted his readers to learn was that Zinoviev, Kamenev and Stalin were very poor revolutionaries and were unworthy to succeed Lenin, whereas he, Trotsky was the real revolutionary and the genuine Leninist, and that by rights he should lead the party.

The Soviet leadership replied to Trotsky in kind, and Istpart was mobilised to produce materials to refute 'Lessons of October'.[16] A collection of Lenin's writings was issued documenting Lenin's former distaste for Trotsky. The collection, edited by Olminskii and entitled *Lenin on Trotsky and Trotskyism: From the History of the RCP(b)* was published in 1925. For good measure it contained a letter from Trotsky to Chkheidze written in 1925, illustrating the antagonism to Lenin at that time.[17] With the growth of the Lenin cult such a document was severely damaging to Trotsky's reputation. The tenth anniversary of the October revolution in 1927 coincided with the defeat of the left opposition to the Soviet leadership and with intensified attacks on Trotsky's version of history. Simultaneously, Trotsky's name began to be removed from the historical record of the Russian revolutionary movement and from the biography of Lenin.

On his expulsion from the Soviet Union in 1929 Trotsky wrote his autobiography, *My Life*. Because of Trotsky's literary talent, the book carries conviction. But it is just as much a political document as 'Lessons of October' whose basic conceptions it incorporates. Because Trotsky is sensitive to the charge of anti-Leninism, his autobiography is evasive about those periods in the history of the

RSDLP when he adopted a non-fractional stance and tried to achieve party unity.

In the spring of 1921 Istpart commissioned Krupskaya to write memoirs of Lenin. Pressure of work prevented her from getting down to the task immediately, and it was only after Lenin's death that she was able to find time to work on the memoirs. The modest aim Krupskaya set herself was to 'give a picture of the circumstances in which Vladimir Il'ich had to live and work'.[18] She wrote the first instalment covering the period 1894–1907 in Gorki, where Lenin had spent the last year of his life. Krupskaya says she wrote this section relying almost entirely on her own memory. This was to be the liveliest part of the memoirs, and was the most rapidly written. It appeared in print in 1925.

By the time Krupskaya came to write the second part of her memoirs the volume of material on Lenin had grown enormously. In dealing with the period 1908–17 she was able to draw upon Lenin's *Works* and other sources concerned with Lenin's life, such as newspapers, proceedings of party congresses and conferences and other people's memoirs. She corresponded with Lenin's former associates such as Stepan Radchenko, Krzhizhanovskii and Lepeshinskii for information to supplement her own recollection of events. The second part of the reminiscences relies less on Krupskaya's own memory and incorporates documentary material which she had available to her. A third part of the memoirs was published in 1934 taking the story up to 1919, but this is noticeably more skeletal and bland than the previous two sections.[19]

One should not expect a wife to be impartial, and in fact Krupskaya's memoirs are invariably sympathetic to Lenin and present events from his point of view. Nevertheless, there is no attempt to imply that Lenin always had it his own way and emerged triumphant from every encounter. Krupskaya is scrupulous in following the twists and turns in Lenin's fortunes, recording his defeats as well as his victories. She presents a full and judicious account of her husband's life and preoccupations. A notable feature of Krupskaya's account is the dispassionate way in which she describes Lenin's political adversaries. Martov, Bogdanov, Trotsky, Takhtarev are all spoken of sympathetically, sometimes even with admiration. The animosity which Lenin displayed to these people at various times in his life is not in evidence in Krupskaya's account.

The change in the quality of Krupskaya's memoirs between the publication of the first section in 1925 and the last section in 1934 was not caused by a decline in Krupskaya's mental powers, but by the change in the political climate of the country during the period in question. As Stalin extended his power and influence he demanded more and more that the printed word should conform to his dictate. He was especially anxious that the image of Lenin which Krupskaya would present should conform with his own ideological requirements.

The evolution of Krupskaya's memoirs is paralleled by a change in Stalin's attitude towards them. When the first section was written Krupskaya sent the manuscript to Stalin for his comments. His response was to inform Krupskaya that he had enjoyed reading her work and that he recommended its publication. The first sign of official disapproval was when Olminskii wrote a critical review of the memoirs in 1930, complaining of its mistakes and distortions, and suggesting that the whole book be reworked.[20]

A better clue to what Stalin wanted a biography of Lenin to look like was supplied when the young historian Petr Pospelov wrote a review of Krupskaya's book in *Pravda* on the occasion of the publication of its third part in 1934. One of Pospelov's criticisms related to the way Krupskaya had treated the Bolshevik/Menshevik split in the first part of her memoirs. There she had recounted how the issue which had caused the division was the vote on the composition of *Iskra*'s editorial board, in which Lenin's supporters had been in the majority. On this matter Pospelov thought that Krupskaya had played down the importance of Plekhanov's disagreements with Lenin on the matter of Clause 1 of the party rules defining who was a party member. In this way Krupskaya was glossing over the divergencies between the 'revolutionary Marxists' and the 'opportunists', while exaggerating the part played in the split by personal sympathies and antipathies. A related criticism was that Krupskaya was too sympathetic to the opportunists and Mensheviks. When she stated that in philosophy Lenin had been a follower of Plekhanov, Pospelov disagreed, asserting that Lenin had been critical of Plekhanov. Pospelov found Krupskaya's treatment of Trotsky too sympathetic and especially objectionable. On this Pospelov remarked that Krupskaya's memoirs failed to reflect the 'ruthless political struggle which Lenin waged against the sectarian Trotsky', pointing out that an omission of this kind would inevitably give the youth a mistaken impression of Lenin's real attitude to Trotsky.

As might be expected, Pospelov found fault with the paucity of references to Stalin in Krupskaya's book. He considered that the leading role of Stalin in the creation of the Bolshevik party and its development and consolidation had been overlooked. The Prague Conference in 1912, following which Stalin had been coopted on to the Central Committee, had been treated, in Pospelov's opinion, much too fleetingly. It was the Prague Conference which Stalin considered to have been the real beginnings of the Bolshevik party. The meetings between Lenin and Stalin during Lenin's exile in Galicia had not been exactly enumerated in Krupskaya's memoirs. In this way they failed to show the close association between Lenin and Stalin that the latter wished posterity to believe had existed.[21]

Pospelov's criticism of Krupskaya's memoirs had been inspired by Stalin's letter to the historical journal *Proletarskaya revolyutsiya* in 1931 entitled 'Some Questions concerning the History of Bolshevism'. This was an important landmark in the imposition of Stalin's will on Soviet historical writing. The pretext was to complain about the publication in the journal of an article by A. G. Slutskii on 'The Bolsheviks on German Social Democracy in the Period of the Pre-War Crisis'. Stalin criticised it for slandering the Bolshevik party by questioning whether Lenin had been sufficiently resolute in his opposition to centrism in German Social Democracy. Stalin's letter set out to do two things: one was to put a stop to independent historical research on the history of the Bolshevik party, and the other was to impose on the writing of history an interpretation of some key episodes which Stalin particularly favoured. The first objective was achieved by declaring that some basic propositions of party history were 'axiomatic' so that anyone who wished to question them must have ulterior purposes, such as smuggling 'Trotskyist contraband' into historical studies. The whole tenor of the article made it clear that Stalin regarded historians who did not adhere to the axiomatic truths as dangerous political enemies who had to be eliminated.

The second element in the letter was the interpretation of the Bolshevik party's history that Stalin demanded be promoted. In the letter Stalin comments on the stages of Bolshevik party history in a manner reminiscent of Lenin in *Left Wing Communism. An Infantile Disorder*. In the initial stage of party history the proposition which was held to be indisputable was the one which stated that the differences between the Bolsheviks and Mensheviks in 1903 were on the question of party membership. According to Stalin the Bolshevik formula on party membership was to prevent the influx of non-proletarian elements into the party; the Menshevik formula, on the other hand, threw the doors of the party wide open to non-proletarian elements. In accusing the Bolsheviks of having centralist and Blanquist tendencies, Rosa Luxemburg had in effect sided with the Mensheviks on that issue. This was a garbled version both of what Lenin's position on party membership had been and of how the Bolshevik/Menshevik split had taken place.

Stalin held that in the period after the 1905 revolution, while the Bolshevik party had put forward the slogan of the 'revolutionary dictatorship of workers and peasants', the German Left Social Democrats, Parvus and Rosa Luxemburg, had invented the utopian and semi-Menshevik scheme of 'permanent revolution', which subsequently was taken up by Trotsky and transformed into a weapon against Leninism. During the last period referred to by Stalin, that before the First World War, the error of the Western Social Democrats had been to oppose the slogan of self-determination for oppressed nations.[22]

Stalin's prescriptions for how the history of the Bolshevik party was to be approached were far cruder than Lenin's had been. Whereas Lenin had wished to imply that throughout its history the Bolshevik party had been centralised and disciplined, Stalin desired to inculcate the idea that this was a party that from its inception had been authoritarian and intolerant. In this he was attempting to align history with present reality. His prescriptions were to have far-reaching implications for how the history of the Bolshevik party was to be conceived. The most fundamental one was that the history of the Bolsheviks was to be interpreted as if they really had existed as a separate party from 1903. The context of their being one of the fractions within the RSDLP was to be ignored. At a stroke this doctrine deprived a great many of Lenin's activities and writings on behalf of the Bolshevik fraction of their true significance.

The doctrine that the Bolsheviks had always existed as a distinct party and that the RSDLP was a kind of synonym for this party was reinforced by the idea that from the very beginning the Bolsheviks had set out to cut themselves off from any 'opportunists', that is, other fractions and groups. The development of the Bolsheviks was now to be presented in a much more unilinear way. The drawing of a clear line of demarcation between the Bolsheviks and the opportunists was held both to characterise the general development of the

Bolsheviks and to be the driving force behind the very creation of the Bolshevik party. Hence Stalin's insistence that the cause of the Bolshevik/Menshevik split had been the issue of Clause 1 of the party statute. Stalin's interpretation of party history also meant glossing over the significance of the Fourth (Unity) Congress when the Bolshevik and Menshevik fractions had reunited. It would be implied that this unity was superficial and ephemeral. It would not be treated seriously or in any systematic way.

If the Bolsheviks' reunification with the Mensheviks in 1906 was disregarded, so too was the fact that at the unity congress the Bund, the SDKPiL and the SDLK had joined the RSDLP and between 1906 and 1910 the Bolsheviks had repeatedly made common cause with the Poles and the Latvians against the Mensheviks and the Bund. From Stalin's letter one can see that this episode in the history of Bolshevism had to be ignored for two reasons. One was that it would disrupt the unilinear pattern of Bolshevik history that Stalin proposed. One could only understand the significance of the Bolsheviks' relationship to the Poles and the Latvians if one took as the unit for investigation not the Bolshevik 'party' in isolation, but the RSDLP as a whole. The other reason why the national parties, the Poles in particular, could not be mentioned was that much of Stalin's letter was devoted to denouncing 'Luxemburgism'. This implied that Luxemburg or 'Luxemburgists' (that is, the national parties) should not appear in the historical record. It would have been heresy, not to say suicidal, to have implied that at any time in its history the Bolshevik party had found common cause with the opportunists.

By the end of the 1930s the number of people and things which Soviet historians could not mention had grown enormously. It was possibly to clarify the situation that in 1938 Stalin supervised the publication of a history of the Bolshevik party containing those things which it was permissible to mention. This was the *Short Course of the History of the RCP(b)*, which contained Stalin's version of the revolution and the revolutionary movement, and the one which all historians of the period were obliged to follow. The *Short Course* was to remain the most authoritative work on party history until Khrushchev's Secret Speech in 1956 created a freer political climate for Soviet historians to work in.

In 1955 the Institute of Marx, Engels, Lenin and Stalin issued a biography of Lenin, which was published in English translation as *Lenin: A Biography* in the same year. It is a work of considerable interest, because it incorporates the directives contained in Stalin's letter and in general embodies the interpretation of Lenin's life which had become accepted at the end of the Stalin era. It is in effect a complete compilation of the ideas on the subject derived from Lenin and subsequently from Stalin.

The tone of the book is highly reverential and partisan. Lenin is always in the right with epithets such as 'brilliant' and 'outstanding' being applied to his writings, whereas any opponents are invariably depicted as wrong-headed or treacherous. Lenin's dealings with them are described as being 'ruthless', 'merciless' or 'relentless'. (But lest the reader gain too stern an impression of Lenin, a passage towards the end of the book explained that although he was merciless towards the enemies of the people, Lenin was otherwise kind, considerate and solicitous about the welfare of the most vulnerable groups in society.) References are made to Stalin on every possible pretext. In accordance with Stalin's precepts, the cause of the Bolshevik/Menshevik split was explained only in terms of Clause 1 of the party rules. The section on the Fourth (Unity) Congress does not mention unity at all, only conflict. On the January plenum in 1910 only Trotsky is mentioned as being in opposition to Lenin, though it is not explained why he should be attending what is presented as an exclusively Bolshevik gathering. On the other hand, in stressing the importance of the Prague Conference in the creation of 'a party of a new type' the book does say that it laid 'the basis for the final recognition of the Bolsheviks as an independent party', the implication being that before this the Bolsheviks were not independent.[23] According to the *Biography* Lenin held that the chain of imperialism broke at its weakest link and that by stressing the unevenness of economic development Lenin originated the doctrine that the victory of socialism was possible in one country. The book left it in no doubt that the October revolution had been planned and led by the Bolshevik party. In particular Lenin had caused a 'party centre' headed by Stalin to be elected for this purpose.

A new edition of the Soviet Lenin *Biography* was published in 1965.[24] It eliminated many of the references to Stalin and supplemented the factual element in the *Biography* with material taken from memoir literature, including the reminiscences of Krupskaya. The result is a more credible and informative work. But only some of the Stalin points of interpretation have been removed. The Bolshevik party is still treated as an autonomous entity. The character of this party is still said to have been determined by Lenin's formulation of Clause 1 of the party rules. In the section dealing with the Fourth (Unity) Congress there is no mention of any actual unification emerging. The Kotka conference is mentioned fleetingly and no hint is given of how Lenin got his majority. As in the earlier version of the *Biography*, only Trotsky is mentioned as being the mover of anti-Leninist resolutions at the January plenum in 1910. Characterisations of the Russian revolution as the breach in the chain of imperialism at its weakest link had disappeared from the book, but Lenin was unambiguously designated as the leader of the October uprising.

A comparison of the two editions gives some indication of what the Soviet compilers thought were the most essential points of interpretation in Lenin's biography. It is probably fair to say that the most essential were also the oldest, the ones set out by Lenin in 1920. According to this scheme Lenin's significance was as the founder of the Bolshevik party in 1903, this party being based on principles Lenin had laid down in his pamphlet *What Is To Be Done?* The party from its inception, whatever its formal position might have been, acted as an autonomous entity. In 1917 under Lenin's leadership in Russia it organised and led the October revolution bringing the proletariat to power in Russia. This scheme of history was of vital importance to the Soviet Communist Party, because it provided that party with its legitimation to rule, and none of the basic premises of that scheme could be open to question.

Trotsky's Lenin

Stalin's infamous letter to *Proletarskaya revolyutsiya* coincided with the publication in the West of Trotsky's classic work *The History of the Russian Revolution*.[25] Trotsky designed his history of the 1917 revolution to counter the charges of anti-Leninism that had been laid against him and to turn the tables on his opponents. His method was to try to show that not only was he, Trotsky, the best Leninist, but that he was the *only* Leninist, since the 'Old Bolsheviks' had found themselves in opposition to him at every critical juncture. Trotsky also argued that Lenin had never accepted the idea of 'socialism in one country' and indeed in April 1917 had come round to accepting the Trotskyist theory of 'permanent revolution'.

As in 'Lessons of October', Trotsky highlights two episodes of the 1917 revolution in his *History*: Lenin's return to Petrograd in April

1917, when he presented his 'April Theses' to the Bolshevik party, and the October revolution. In discussing the 'April Theses' Trotsky maintains that at this point Lenin found himself isolated in the Bolshevik party, but that the ideas put forward by Trotsky at that same time in New York were identical to Lenin's. The other high point in Trotsky's *History* is mid-October 1917, when, according to Trotsky, Lenin's call for an armed uprising was resisted by most members of the Bolshevik leadership, and only he gave Lenin his full support. It was important for Trotsky that the October events should have been a well-organised, once-and-for-all seizure of power by the Bolsheviks, for as leader of this uprising, he had become a historical figure of great importance. And because October was presented as being a critical juncture upon which so much depended, those who had hesitated, those who had turned tail at such a time – Trotsky's adversaries – could be exposed as people of weak character and with little claim to be leaders of a country or, even less, of the international revolutionary movement. The implication was that Trotsky, who had stood firm along with Lenin, had every claim.

In its essentials, Trotsky's book did not challenge the Soviet presentation of Lenin as the leader of the October revolution. It only gave it a rather different slant. It did, however, add a new element of distortion, which was that in April 1917 Lenin had come round to accepting Trotsky's theory of permanent revolution. Though no actual evidence supported it, the idea became a persistent one with historians of the Russian revolution and biographers of Lenin.

Trotsky himself in the 1930s began to write a biography of Lenin of which he only completed the first section which took the story up to 1893, that is just before the young Ulyanov went to St Petersburg. The book was first published in English as *The Young Lenin* in 1972. A major part of the work deals with Alexander Ulyanov and the assassination plot in which he was involved. Although Trotsky did not give references to the sources he was using, it is clear that he drew heavily on Anna Ulyanova-Elizarova's collection *Alexander Ilich Ulyanov and the Case of 1 March 1887*. This work provided Trotsky with the factual material on which much of his book is based. His main contribution as a historian was to rework the material into the lively literary form characteristic of his other writings. He made no attempt to analyse his sources and follow up their implications. He took a narrow view of the episode and found nothing very significant in it. He saw in it 'no seeds of the future' and considered it to be the 'last tragic convulsion of the already doomed claims of the "critically thinking individual" to an independent historic role'.[26] In other words Trotsky interpreted the assassination attempt as the last act of the terrorist Narodniki before the appearance on the scene of the Marxists, who eschewed terrorist methods. This was an interpretation fully in accordance with the Soviet view of the historical stages of the Russian revolutionary movement and the one embodied in the declaration that Mariya Ulyanova had attributed to the young Volodya.

Ironically that particular recollection of Mariya Ulyanova was one source which Trotsky did question. He thought it improbable that Lenin's sister, who was then only eight years old, should have been able to reproduce so exactly her brother's words. And he considered it unlikely that the seventeen-year-old Volodya should have been so well-versed in revolutionary politics as to be able to distinguish one road from another. Trotsky suspected that the story had been concocted to create a different, more perfect, Lenin than the one who had actually existed.[27] Trotsky was right to be sceptical of the story, but he did not question the assumption that lay behind it that there had been Narodnik and Marxist stages in the Russian revolutionary movement, and that whereas the Narodniki espoused terrorist tactics, the Marxists did not. Trotsky's critical approach to Mariya Ulyanova's recollections, however, so impressed all subsequent Western biographers of Lenin that they almost all incorporated his remarks in their accounts of Lenin's youth.

Western biographies of Lenin

By and large Western historians have worked with the same materials as Soviet biographers of Lenin. Seldom do they have access to sources which did not emanate ultimately from Istpart. One such source, however, were the memoirs of Nikolai Valentinov (Volskii) published in Russian in New York in 1953.[28] Valentinov had known Lenin in his Parisian exile during 1904, at the time that Lenin had just formed his alliance with Bogdanov. The picture of Lenin which emerges from Valentinov's memoirs is of an unpretentious man with much personal charm, but with narrow intellectual horizons. The most telling episode for Valentinov was when he tried to interest Lenin in the philosophy of Avenarius and Mach, and Lenin classed the two writers as reactionary without reading their works. Valentinov made the observation that very typical of Lenin was his use of labels to brand his opponents, such as 'Machist', 'Recaller', 'Liquidator' and so on. He also recollected that Lenin quoted with approval Plekhanov's advice on dealing with opponents: 'First stick the convict's badge on him, and only then try his case.' The method of labelling or attaching 'convict's badges' was a characteristic procedure of both Plekhanov and Lenin.[29]

David Shub published his biography of Lenin[30] first in 1948 and brought out a revised edition in 1966. Shub was born in Russia in 1887 and joined the RSDLP in 1903. During 1904–5 he was in exile in Western Europe where he met Lenin and other RSDLP leaders. In 1905 he was arrested and sentenced to exile in Siberia for revolutionary activities. After his escape he settled in the USA in 1908. Shub's biography of Lenin is rich in external detail and contains many passages of direct speech, taken from the documentary sources he uses. Much attention is devoted to Lenin's love life, and Shub tends to focus on the more sensational and picturesque aspects of Lenin's biography. More prosaic topics like what was decided at party congresses and conferences are rather poorly covered. The contents of Lenin's theoretical writings are not revealed.

Adam Ulam's *Lenin and the Bolsheviks*[31] is a very knowledgeable treatment of Lenin's biography, and most aspects of it receive some kind of mention. Practically all of the material available at the time has been consulted. It is to that extent a serious work of scholarship. The weakness of the book is that the approach of the author is superficial. He is not greatly concerned to analyse his material and explore the dynamics of the Russian revolutionary movement of which Lenin was a part. His intention is more to bring out the things that are most incongruous and discreditable about Lenin's life and the revolutionary movement in general. Ulam's book is about 'the intellectual and political history of the triumph of communism in Russia', and as he clearly disapproves of communism, he tries to demonstrate that there is nothing in its triumph that could be thought worthy of emulation. Because his purpose is to discredit whatever Lenin did, he has little incentive to be critical of his sources, and as a result the overall contours of Lenin's biography largely coincide with those of Soviet authors. The difference is that where they would imply approval of the developments, Ulam would add a note of condemnation or ridicule.

Neil Harding's *Lenin's Political Thought*[32] is one of the most valuable books about Lenin to have been written. By concentrating on
his political thought – broadly conceived – Harding is able to make
Lenin's *Collected Works* his principal source. Doing this eliminates
much of the distortion which comes from using memoir materials
emanating from the Soviet Union. In studying the background to
Lenin's thought Harding employs much first-hand material in the
way of contemporary pamphlets and journal articles. Some of these
sources he published separately in translation as *Marxism in Russia*.[33]
The main virtue of Harding's work, however, is the care with which
he has reconstructed the evolution of Lenin's ideas and the depth of
understanding of his exposition.

The disadvantage of this method is that it is Lenin from a Leninist
point of view; it is Lenin in his own terms. His opponents are largely
depicted as Lenin would have his readers believe them to be. There
is no point of reference outside Lenin. Thus, for Harding there
really were Narodniki, there really were Economists, there really were
God-builders and so on who all held the views that Lenin attributed
to them. Lenin, consequently, emerges as the slayer of all these types
of dragon rather than their creator and slayer.

A related weakness is the outcome of concentrating on what Lenin
thought rather than what Lenin did. Harding devotes less attention
to examining the historical context in which Lenin elaborated his
political thought. Therefore the impression is created that the historical context was exactly as Lenin implied it to be. It also conceals
the extent to which Lenin moulded his theorisings to fit particular
political situations. Lenin was not given to theorising for its own sake.

The positive feature of Robert Service's three-volume work *Lenin:
A Political Life*[34] is that it sets out to investigate Lenin's biography
from an independent point of view. It tries to free itself from reliance
on Soviet versions, and is a conscientious effort to give an account of
Lenin's life relying as far as possible on first-hand materials. By and
large the attempt is successful, and Service has produced a readable
and engaging biography of Lenin as a politician and as a person.

Over the three volumes of the book one notices a significant difference in texture, as each came out under different circumstances in
Russia and the Soviet Union. The first volume, which takes the story
up to 1910, was published in 1985, just as Mikhail Gorbachev came
to power, so that it was based on the materials that were available
at that time. These, as Service's source references show, were not

inconsiderable. But by the time the second volume, dealing with the period of the First World War and the Russian revolution, appeared in 1991 the author had been able to draw upon the resources made available by the policy of *glasnost* in the Gorbachev era. The third volume appeared in 1995 and made wide use of archival sources in covering Lenin's life in the Soviet era. No Western biographer of Lenin ever had such a wealth of source material at his disposal.

The use of this material, however, is not always as effective as it might be. Service is at his best when he is describing things which happened. He is less convincing when trying to explain intellectual developments, when for example he is dealing with Russian Marxism before Lenin and Bogdanov's philosophical ideas. A striking example from the First World War period is the treatment of Lenin's *Imperialism*, which Service interprets as an attempt to explain the colonialist policies of the European powers. Lenin, of course, would never have engaged in such a purely academic exercise. Service's one-volume biography of Lenin[35] reduces the theoretical aspects of his subject to a minimum and concentrates on describing the circumstances of Lenin's life in a manner reminiscent of Shub.

Richard Pipes has written and edited several works which have a bearing on Lenin's biography. In 1964 he published a well-researched article, 'Narodnichestvo: A Semantic Inquiry',[36] arguing that until the last years of the nineteenth century 'Narodnik' was a term applied to people who tried to express the wishes and aspirations of the common people, but in the 1890s was a polemical label first attached by Peter Struve to his opponents, who did not believe that Russia was destined to undergo a capitalist phase of development. Pipes also pointed out that the people whom Struve classed as 'Narodniki' did not accept the designation. Pipes was mistaken about who had first coined the term in its modern sense – it was not Struve, but Plekhanov – but in general terms what Pipes said was supported by the evidence.

Because Pipes remained captive to the scheme of Russian intellectual history which Plekhanov invented, he did not see that there was no time when 'Narodniki' in the original sense of the term were not influenced by Marx, that the early Russian Marxists – Plekhanov included – *were* Narodniki. This led Pipes in an influential article on Lenin's early intellectual development[37] to contrast Russian terrorists with Russian Marxists and to argue that before his conversion to Marxism Lenin was a terrorist. But the biographies of Alexander

Ulyanov and his contemporaries show that both Marxists and non-Marxists could be terrorists or non-terrorists. What was decisive was not ideology but practicalities, and terrorism died out after 1887 not because Marxism was adopted but because terrorism was seen to be too costly in human life for the terrorists.

Perhaps Pipes's most valuable contribution to Lenin's biography was the monograph *Social Democracy and the St. Peterburg Labor Movement, 1885–1897* published in 1963.[38] This book was based on the copious memoir material which existed on the workers' groups which appeared in the Russian capital at the end of the nineteenth century. Particularly useful were the memoirs of Takhtarev, supplemented by his wife Appolinaria Yakubova, which first appeared in London in 1902. Some of this material had been appended to the first three editions of Lenin's *Collected Works*, but had been removed in the fourth. Because it challenged the stereotyped presentation of Economism prevalent in Soviet publications of the time, Pipes's book was roundly condemned by Soviet reviewers, and a book was specially written to discredit it.[39]

When access to Russian archives became possible after the fall of the Soviet Union, Pipes compiled a collection of documents relating to Lenin entitled *The Unknown Lenin*.[40] The documents comprise those materials which were never published in any of the editions of Lenin's *Collected Works*, as they tend to show Lenin in a cruel, cynical or devious light. As Pipes concedes, the documents do not fundamentally alter existing perceptions of Lenin's character, but they do offer a new insight into the motivation for some of his policies. The most significant item in the collection is the stenographic record of a speech Lenin delivered in September 1920 to a closed meeting of party officials to report on the circumstances surrounding the unsuccessful campaign against Poland. In the speech Lenin admits to trying to sovietise Poland by force of arms and to carry the Russian revolution through Poland into Western Europe. The document confirms what one can gather from published sources. In the present context, the most interesting document in the collection is the letter Lenin wrote to Janis Berzins in September 1921 to enquire how sales were going of John Reed's book *Ten Days that Shook the World* and Philps-Price's *My Reminiscences of the Russian Revolution*. As these were books which presented the October revolution in a way which he approved of – and probably influenced – Lenin was anxious that they should be distributed as widely as possible.[41]

Lenin: Life and Legacy by Dmitrii Volkogonov, published in 1994, marked a landmark in the history of Lenin biography in Russia.[42] Volkogonov had access not only to materials on Lenin published in the West, but also to the archives of the Central Committee of the Communist Party of the Soviet Union. He was thus able to examine all the material which Istpart and its successors had refrained from publishing. In the Russian context Volkogonov's was a sensational book. From the Western point of view, however, there is less that is surprising. The author's main target is the kind of idealised image of Lenin created over the years in the Soviet Union as a means of legitimising the regime. The impact of this approach is lost on a Western audience who did not have an idealised image of Lenin in the first place. Volkogonov's book is in fact comparable in its approach to Ulam's.

For Volkogonov and his audience it was of great significance to discuss such questions as Lenin's personal life, his receipt of German money, the murder of the tsar's family, the infiltration of the Bolshevik party by police agents. Though these had been topics avoided in Soviet historiography they had been well-aired in Western biographies of Lenin such as David Shub's. The materials which Volkogonov utilised from the party archives were for the most part those documenting examples of Lenin's cruelty and ruthlessness which had not previously appeared in print. The most important of these materials appear in Pipes's *The Unknown Lenin*.

For the Western historian Volkogonov's book contains individual items of information not found elsewhere, but nothing that would influence one's view of Lenin substantially. In other ways Volkogonov's biography owes a great deal to Soviet historical writing. The standard interpretations of the history of the Russian revolutionary movement, and of the February and October revolutions, for example, remain unchallenged. Nor is there any systematic examination of Lenin as a thinker in Volkogonov's book, as theoretical matters are not central to the author's interest.

Volkogonov's book represents a distinct current of opinion in Russia which feels the need to discredit Lenin to counter the decades of adulation in which he was held. It is an approach to Lenin's biography dictated by current politics, an approach typical of the Soviet era, and one not entirely absent from Western historiography.

Lenin, however, deserves to be studied in greater depth, because he was someone who ostensibly set out to change society in accordance with a set of theoretical presuppositions. He himself certainly did his best to convey to posterity that his success in this attempt had vindicated his theories and his methods. Among both Lenin's admirers and his detractors there are many who would agree with E. H. Carr that the Bolsheviks not only made a revolution, but analysed and prepared the conditions in which it could be made.[43] By taking Lenin at his word in this respect and assuming that he was indeed the architect of the Russian revolution, historians have avoided examining the fundamental question of what the relationship was of Bolshevik social and economic theories to the actual conditions of the time.

The evidence suggests, however, that Lenin's revolution was not as self-conscious as Carr implies. There is no doubt that Lenin came to power with abundant theoretical preparation, but in the event none of it proved of any great relevance. If anything, it was a revolution made on false premises. The reason Carr thought that the Russian revolution was one characterised by 'self-consciousness' was that first Lenin and then Stalin had made great efforts to create that impression. Before we can know whether a 'self-conscious' revolution of the kind Carr had in mind is at all possible, it is necessary to clear away the confusion that Lenin and his successors have created.

NOTES

Introduction

1. I have approached this subject in greater detail in J. D. White, *Karl Marx and the Intellectual Origins of Dialectical Materialism* (Basingstoke and London, 1996).
2. V. I. Lenin, *Collected Works*, Vol. 38, p. 180.
3. K. Marx, *Grundrisse*, translated by M. Nicolaus (Harmondsworth, 1973), p. 408.
4. N. I. Ziber, *Teoriia tsennosti i kapitala D. Rikardo v sviazi s pozdneishimi dopolneniiami i raz"iasneniiami. Opyt kritiko-ekonomicheskogo issledovaniia* (Kiev, 1871).
5. N. G. Chernyshevskii, 'Dopolnenie i primechaniia na pervuiu knigu politicheskoi ekonomii Dzhon Stiuarta Millia', *Sochineniia N. Chernyshevskogo*, Vol. 3 (Geneva, 1869); 'Ocherki iz politicheskoi ekonomii (po Milliu)', *Sochineniia N. Chernyshevskogo*, Vol. 4 (Geneva, 1870). Reprinted in N. G. Chernyshevskii, *Polnoe sobranie sochineniy*, Vol. IX (Moscow, 1949).
6. *Arkhiv K. Marksa i F. Engel'sa*, Vols XI–XVI.
7. M. M. Kovalevskii, *Obshchinnoe zemlevladenie, prichiny, khod i posledstviia ego razlozheniia* (Moscow, 1879).
8. Marx to the editorial board of *Otechestvennye zapiski*, November 1877, in *Karl Marx Frederick Engels Collected Works*, Vol. 24, pp. 196–201.
9. Marx to Zasulich, 8 March 1881, in *Karl Marx Frederick Engels Collected Works*, Vol. 24, pp. 346–73.
10. It was published in the journal *Vestnik Narodnoi Voli*, no. 5 (1886).
11. D. Riazanov, 'V Zasulich i K. Marks', *Arkhiv K. Marksa i F. Engel'sa*, Vol. 1 (1924), pp. 269–86.
12. N. F. Daniel'son, 'Ocherki nashego poreformennogo obshchestvennogo khoziaistva', *Slovo*, no. 10 (October 1880), pp. 77–143.
13. N. F. Daniel'son, *Ocherki nashego poreformennogo obshchestvennogo khoziaistva* (St Petersburg, 1893).
14. V. V. Vorontsov, *Sud'by kapitalizma v Rossii* (St Petersburg, 1882).
15. Institut marksizma–leninizma pri TsK KPSS, *Russkie knigi v bibliotekakh K. Marksa i F. Engel'sa* (Moscow, 1979), p. 42.
16. Stepniak, *The Russian Storm-Cloud* (London, 1886), p. 154.
17. G. V. Plekhanov, *Sotsializm i politicheskaia bor'ba* (Geneva, 1883).

18. L. Tikhomirov, 'Chto nam zhdat' ot revoliutsii?', *Vestnik Narodnoi Voli*, no. 2 (1884).
19. G. V. Plekhanov, *Nashi raznoglasiia* (Geneva, 1885).
20. G. V. Plekhanov, *Selected Philosophical Works*, Vol. 1 (Moscow, 1961), p. 73.
21. N. K. Mikhailovskii, *Sochineniia*, Vol. 7 (St Petersburg, 1909), p. 731.
22. Ibid., p. 683.
23. G. V. Plekhanov, *K voprosu o razvitii monisticheskogo vzgliada na istoriiu. Otvet gg. Mikhailovskomu, Kareevu i komp* (St Petersburg, 1895). For commercial considerations the date on the title page was given as 1895 and not as 1894.
24. V. I. Lenin, *Collected Works*, Vol. 1, pp. 133–332.

1 The Making of a Revolutionary

1. A. I. Ul'ianova-Elizarova, 'Vospominaniia ob Aleksandre Il'iche Ul'ianove', in *Aleksandr Il'ich Ul'ianov i delo 1 marta 1887 g.*, edited by A. I. Ul'ianova-Elizarova (Moscow and Leningrad, 1927), p. 36.
2. M. G. Shtein, *Ulianovy i Leniny: Tainy rodoslovnoi i psevdonima* (St Petersburg, 1997), pp. 144–8.
3. Shtein, *Ulianovy i Leniny*, p. 149.
4. A. I. Ul'ianova-Elizarova, 'Kratkaia biografiia Il'i Nikolaevicha Ul'ianova', in *I. N. Ul'ianov v vospominaniiakh sovremennikov* (Moscow, 1989), p. 47.
5. Z. Trofimov, *Otets Il'icha* (Saratov, 1981), pp. 9–14; Ul'ianova-Elizarova, 'Kratkaia biografiia Il'i Nikolaevicha Ul'ianova', p. 47.
6. Shtein, *Ulianovy i Leniny*, pp. 40–2.
7. Ibid., pp. 43–6.
8. Ibid., p. 87.
9. V. Arnol'd, *Sem'ia Ul'ianovykh v Samare* (Kuibyshev, 1979), pp. 7–8.
10. Shtein, *Ulianovy i Leniny*, pp. 80–1.
11. Ibid., p. 84.
12. Ibid., p. 89.
13. Ibid., pp. 92–111.
14. Trofimov, *Otets Il'icha*, pp. 18–50.
15. Ibid., p. 38.
16. Ibid., pp. 101–3; Ul'ianova-Elizarova, 'Vospominaniia ob Aleksandre Il'iche Ul'ianove', p. 55.
17. Trofimov, *Otets Il'icha*, pp. 111–13.
18. *The Unknown Lenin from the secret archive*, edited by R. Pipes and D. Brandenberger, translated by C. A. Fitzpatrick (New Haven, Conn., 1996), p. 119.
19. Ul'ianova-Elizarova, 'Vospominaniia ob Aleksandre Il'iche Ul'ianove', pp. 63–84.
20. Ibid., p. 79; Semen Khlebnikov, 'Vospominaniia ob A. I. Ul'ianove 1886–87', in *Aleksandr Il'ich Ul'ianov i delo 1 marta 1887 g.*, p. 262.

21. J. D. White, '"No, we won't go that way; that is not the way to take": The Place of Aleksandr Ul'ianov in the Development of Social-Democracy in Russia', *Revolutionary Russia*, Vol. 11, no. 2 (December 1998), pp. 86–9.

22. B. Lelewel, 'Przyczynek do dziejów udziału polaków w rosyjskim ruchu rewolucyjnym (1886–1890)', *Niepodległość*, no. 10 (1934), p. 140.

23. M. Brusnev, 'Vozniknovenie pervykh sotsial-demokraticheskikh organizatsii', *Proletarskaia revoliutsiia*, no. 2 (14) (1923), p. 17.

24. L. Aksel'rod-Ortodoks, 'Iz moikh vospominanii', *Katorga i ssylka*, no. 63 (1930), p. 33.

25. Ibid., p. 27.

26. Ibid., p. 33.

27. I. N. Chebotarev, 'Vospominaniia ob Aleksandre Il'iche Ul'ianove i peterburgskom studenchestve 1883–87 gg', in *Aleksandr Il'ich Ul'ianov i delo 1 marta 1887 g.*, p. 241.

28. V. V. Bartenev, 'Vospominaniia peterburzhtsa o vtoroi polovine 80-kh gg. Vyderzhki', in *Aleksandr Il'ich Ul'ianov i delo 1 marta 1887 g.*, pp. 22–3.

29. 'Programma terroristicheskoi fraktsii partii "Narodnaia Volia"', in *Aleksandr Il'ich Ul'ianov i delo 1 marta 1887 g.*, p. 377.

30. A. I. Ul'ianova-Elizarova, 'Vospominaniia ob Aleksandre Il'iche Ul'ianove', p. 106.

31. S. A. Nikonov, 'Zhizn' studenchestva i revoliutsionnaia rabota kontsa 80-kh godov', in *Aleksandr Il'ich Ul'ianov i delo 1 marta 1887 g.*, pp. 150–1.

32. I. D. Lukashevich, 'Vospominaniia o dele 1 marta 1887 goda', *Byloe*, no. 2 (24) (1917), p. 121.

33. Bartenev, 'Vospominaniia peterburzhtsa o vtoroi polovine 80-kh gg. Vyderzhki', p. 27; Lukashevich, 'Vospominaniia o dele 1 marta 1887 goda', p. 129.

34. Bartenev, 'Vospominaniia peterburzhtsa o vtoroi polovine 80-kh gg. Vyderzhki', p. 29; Lelewel, 'Przyczynek do dziejów udziału polaków w rosyjskim ruchu rewolucyjnym (1886–1890)', pp. 138–9.

35. E. Sponti, 'Kratkaia avtobiografiia', in *Na zare rabochego dvizheniia v Moskve* (Moscow, 1932), p. 97.

36. Z. Lukawski, *Polacy w rosyjskim ruchu socjaldemokratycznym w latach 1883–1893* (Cracow, 1970), pp. 68–9.

37. K. Zalewski, 'Isz socializmo istorijos Lietuvoje', *Socialdemokratas*, no. 6/8 (1916), pp. 45–8.

38. Ibid., p. 46; Aksel'rod-Ortodoks, 'Iz moikh vospominanii', p. 37.

39. N. Michta and Jan Sobczak, 'Stanisław Trusiewicz (Kazimierz Zalewski)', *Z pola walki*, no. 1 (69) (1975), pp. 111–14; Walentyna Najdus, *SDKPiL a SDPRR 1893–1907* (Wrocław, 1973), pp. 73–7.

40. Iu. Martov, *Zapiski sotsial-demokrata* (Berlin, 1922), p. 233.

41. L. Trotsky, *The Young Lenin*, translated by Max Eastman (Harmondsworth, 1974), p. 138.

42. V. V. Kashkadamova, 'Vospominaniia', in *Aleksandr Il'ich Ul'ianov i delo 1 marta 1887 g.*, p. 274.
43. V. Alekseev and A. Shver, *Sem'ia Ul'ianovykh v Simbirske (1869–1887)*, edited by A. I. Ul'ianova-Elizarova (Moscow and Leningrad, 1925), p. 64.
44. *Molodye gody V.I. Lenina po vospominaniiam sovremennikov i dokumentam* (Moscow, 1958), p. 236.
45. Ibid., pp. 249–52.
46. G. E. Khait, 'V kazanskom kruzhke', *Novyi mir*, no. 4 (1958), pp. 189–93 (pp. 189–91).
47. *Molodye gody V.I. Lenina*, p. 266.
48. N. Valentinov, *Encounters with Lenin*, translated by Paul Rosta and Brian Pearce (London, 1968), p. 66.
49. *Lenin–Krupskaia–Ulianovy perepiska (1883–1900)*, edited by Iu. A. Akhapkin and K. F. Bogdanova (Moscow, 1981), pp. 46–52; *Sem'ia Ul'ianovykh* (Moscow, 1982), p. 284; Brusnev, 'Vozniknovenie pervykh sotsial-demokraticheskikh organizatsii', p. 23.
50. *Molodye gody V.I. Lenina*, p. 310.
51. Institut marksizma-leninizma pri TsK KPSS, *Vladimir Il'ich Lenin: Biograficheskaia khronika 1870–1924, 1, 1870–1905* (Moscow, 1970), p. 63.
52. *Molodye gody V.I. Lenina*, pp. 342–6.
53. N. K. Mikhailovskii, *Polnie sobranie sochinenii*, Vol. 7 (St Petersburg, 1909), pp. 727–33.
54. D. I. Ul'ianov, 'V Alakaevke', in *Vospominaniia o Vladimire Il'iche Lenine*, Vol. 1 (Moscow, 1968), p. 102.
55. N. Fedoseev, *Stat'i i pis'ma* (Moscow, 1958), p. 174.
56. A. I. Ul'ianova-Elizarova, 'Vospominaniia ob Il'iche', in *Vospominaniia o Vladimire Il'iche Lenine*, Vol. 1 (Moscow, 1968), p. 38; G. M. Krzhizhanovskii, 'Myslitel' i revoliutsioner', in *Vospominaniia o Vladimire Il'iche Lenine*, Vol. 4 (Moscow, 1969), p. 14; R. Pipes, *Social Democracy and the St. Petersburg Labor Movement, 1885–1897* (Cambridge, Mass., 1963), pp. 44–5.
57. V. I. Lenin, *Collected Works*, Vol. 1, pp. 79–125.
58. Lenin, *CW* 1, pp. 139–59.
59. Lenin, *CW* 1, p. 192.
60. K. Marx, *Capital*, Vol. 1, translated by B. Fowkes (Harmondsworth, 1979), p. 91.
61. P. Struve, *Kriticheskie zametki ob ekonomicheskom razvitii Rossii* (St Petersburg, 1894), p. 44.
62. Ibid., p. 46.
63. 'Doklad po delu o voznikshikh v Sankt Peterburge v 1894 i 1895 gg. prestupnykh kruzhkakh lits imenuiushchikh sebia sotsial-demokratami', in *N. Lenin, Sobranie sochinenii, 1, Pervye shagi rabochego dvizheniia 1893–1900*, 1st edn, edited by L. B. Kamenev (Moscow, n.d.), pp. 520–1.
64. Sponti, 'Kratkaia avtobiografiia', p. 99.

65. Institut marksizma–leninizma pri TsK KPSS, *Biograficheskaia khronika 1*, pp. 100–5.
66. 'Doklad po delu', p. 578.
67. Ivan Vasil'evich Babushkin, *Vospominaniia* (Moscow, 1951), pp. 80–4.

2 A Party of a New Type

1. A. Ożóg, *Życie trudne i szczęśliwe. O Nadiezdie Krupskiej* (Warsaw, 1971), pp. 89–96.
2. Institut marksizma–leninizma pri TsK KPSS, *Vladimir Il'ich Lenin: Biograficheskaia khronika 1870–1924, 1, 1870–1905* (Moscow, 1970), p. 115.
3. V. I. Lenin, *Collected Works*, Vol. 3, p. 25.
4. M. L. de Tengoborski, *Commentaries on the Productive Forces of Russia*, 2 Vols (London, 1856).
5. V. I. Lenin, *Podgotovitel'nye materialy k knige 'Razvitie kapitalizma v Rosii'* (Moscow, 1970), pp. 45–6.
6. This point is made in E. Kingston-Mann, *Lenin and the Problem of Marxist Peasant Revolution* (New York, 1983), pp. 43–4.
7. Lenin, *Podgotovitel'nye materialy*, p. 55.
8. N. Harding, *Lenin's Political Thought, 1, Theory and Practice in the Democratic Revolution* (London and Basingstoke, 1977), p. 107; L. Althusser, *Lenin and Philosophy, and other essays*, translated by B. Brewster (1971), p. 43.
9. Institut marksizma–leninizma pri TsK KPSS, *Arkhiv K. Marksa i F. Engel'sa*, Vol. XII (Moscow, 1952), pp. 3–28.
10. R. Pipes, *Social Democracy and the St. Petersburg Labor Movement, 1885–1897* (Cambridge, Mass., 1963), pp. 95–6.
11. K. M. Takhtarev, *Ocherk peterburgskogo rabochego dvizheniia 90-kh godov* (London, 1902), pp. 26–40.
12. Ibid., pp. 66–7.
13. Ibid., pp. 68–72.
14. A. I. Kremer, *Ob agitatsii: s poslesloviem P. Aksel'roda* (Geneva, 1896), p. 28.
15. G. V. Plekhanov, *Sochineniia*, Vol. 12, 2nd edn, 24 Vols, edited by D. Riazanov (Moscow, 1923–7), p. IV.
16. *Marxism in Russia. Key Documents, 1879–1906*, edited by N. Harding, translated by R. Taylor (Cambridge, 1983), pp. 228–40.
17. V. Zasulich, *Ocherki istorii Mezhdunarodnago Obshchestva Rabochikh* (Geneva, 1889), pp. 7–9.
18. Iu. Martov, *Zapiski sotsial-demokrata* (Berlin, 1922), pp. 401–2.
19. Plekhanov, *Sochineniia*, Vol. 12, pp. 500–10.
20. Ibid., p. 512.
21. *Marxism in Russia*, pp. 250–3.
22. A. K. Wildman, *The Making of a Workers' Revolution: Russian Social Democracy, 1891–1903* (Chicago and London, 1967), pp. 175–84.
23. 'Doklad po delu o voznikshikh v Sankt Peterburge v 1894 i 1895 gg. prestupnykh kruzhkakh lits imenuiushchikh sebia sotsial-demok-ratami',

in *N. Lenin Sobranie sochinenii, 1, Pervye shagi rabochego dvizheniia 1893–1900*, 1st edn, edited by L. B. Kamenev (Moscow, n.d.), pp. 664–5.
24. Ibid., p. 667.
25. V. I. Lenin, *Collected Works*, Vol. 4, pp. 171–4.
26. Plekhanov, *Sochineniia*, Vol. 12, pp. 520–1.
27. 'Protest rossiiskikh sotsialdemokratov s poslesloviem ot redaktsii "rabochego dela"', *Rabochee delo*, no. 4–5 (September–December) 1899, p. 24.
28. A. Ascher, *Pavel Axelrod and the Development of Menshevism* (Cambridge, Mass., 1972), p. 162.
29. V. I. Lenin, *Sochineniia*, Vol. 4, 3rd edn (Moscow, 1927), p. vii.
30. I. Rosliakov, 'Kak Ul'ianov stal Leninym', *Argumenty i Fakty*, no. 48 (November 1998), p. 12.
31. Lenin, *CW* 4, pp. 333–49.
32. V. I. Lenin, *Collected Works*, Vol. 5, p. 369.
33. Ibid., p. 375.
34. Ibid., p. 382.
35. Takhtarev, *Ocherk peterburgskogo rabochego dvizheniia*, pp. 68–70.
36. Lenin, *CW* 5, p. 375.
37. Ibid., pp. 383–4.
38. M. Donald, *Marxism and Revolution: Karl Kautsky and the Russian Marxists 1900–1924* (New Haven, Conn. and London, 1993), p. 30.
39. M. Waldenberg, *Wzlot i upadek Karola Kautsky'ego*, Vol. 1 (Krakow, 1972), pp. 314–17.
40. Lenin, *CW* 5, p. 412.
41. Ibid., p. 440.
42. Ibid., pp. 441–2.
43. Ibid., p. 464.
44. Ibid., p. 479.
45. Lenin, *Sochineniia*, Vol. 4, p. 599.
46. N. Valentinov, *Encounters with Lenin*, translated by P. Rosta and B. Pearce (London, 1968), p. 27.
47. *1903 Second Ordinary Congress of the RSDLP*, translated by B. Pearce (London, 1978), pp. 311–12.
48. Ibid., p. 329.
49. Ibid., p. 434.
50. Iu. Martov, *Bor'ba s "osadnym polozheniem" v RSDRP* (Geneva, 1904), p. VI.
51. V. I. Lenin, *Collected Works*, Vol. 7, pp. 267, 387.
52. Lenin, *CW* 7, pp. 322–4.
53. L. Trotsky, *K istorii russkoi revoliutsii*, compiled by N. A. Vasetskii (Moscow, 1990), pp. 76–7.
54. R. Luxemburg, 'Organisationsfragen der russischen Sozialdemokratie', in *Gesammelte Werke*, 1–2 (Berlin, 1972), pp. 422–44.
55. A. A. Bogdanov, *Vera i nauka* (Moscow, 1910), p. 193.
56. Galerka and Riadovoi [A. A. Bogdanov and M. S. Ol'minskii], 'Nashi nedorazumeniia', in *Kak rozhdalas' partiia bol'shevikov: Literaturnaia polemika 1903–04 gg. Sbornik*, edited by Istpart (Leningrad, 1925), pp. 45–59.

3 The 1905 Revolution and its Aftermath

1. V. I. Lenin, *Collected Works*, Vol. 4, pp. 46–54.
2. J. D. White, 'The First *Pravda* and the Russian Marxist Tradition', *Soviet Studies*, Vol. 26, no. 2 (April 1974), pp. 181–204.
3. N. Valentinov, *Encounters with Lenin*, translated by Paul Rosta and Brian Pearce (London, 1968), p. 232.
4. *Tretyi s"ezd RSDRP. Protokoly*, Protokoly i stenograficheskie otchety s"ezdov i konferentsii Kommunisticheskoi partii Sovetskogo Soiuza (Moscow, 1959), p. 191.
5. N. Krupskaya, *Memories of Lenin* (London, 1970), p. 99.
6. J. Biggart, G. Gloveli and A. Yassour (compilers), *Bogdanov and His Work: A guide to the published and unpublished works of Alexander A. Bogdanov (Malinovsky) 1873–1928* (Aldershot, 1998), pp. 121–50.
7. N. A. Rozhkov, *O 1905 g.* Vospominaniia (Moscow, 1925), p. 15; I. I. Skvortsov-Stepanov, *Ot revoliutsii k revoliutsii. Sbornik statei 1905–1917 gg.* (Moscow and Leningrad, 1925), p. 10.
8. D. Grille, *Lenins Rivale: Bogdanov und seine Philosophie* (Cologne, 1966), p. 54.
9. *Tretyi s"ezd RSDRP. Protokoly*, Protokoly i stenograficheskie otchety s"ezdov i konferentsii Kommunisticheskoi partii Sovetskogo Soiuza (Moscow, 1959), p. 262.
10. *Protokoly* III, p. 272.
11. *Protokoly* III, p. 162.
12. *Protokoly* III, p. 337.
13. V. I. Lenin, *Collected Works*, Vol. 10, p. 47.
14. M. N. Liadov, *Iz zhizni partii v 1903–1907 godakh (Vospominaniia)* (Moscow, 1956), p. 117.
15. Lenin, *CW* 10, pp. 19–28.
16. N. K. Krupskaia, 'Vospominaniia o Lenine', in *Vospominaniia o Vladimire Il'iche Lenine*, Vol. 1 (Moscow, 1968), p. 342.
17. W. Najdus, *SDKPiL a SDPRR 1893–1907* (Wroclaw, 1973), p. 256.
18. By the Emancipation Edict of 1861, which liberated the serfs and provided them with allotments of land, landowners were entitled to retain one-third (and in some provinces one-half) of the total land area fit for cultivation on their estates. In exercising this right the landowners were empowered to make reductions (*otrezki*) in peasant allotments. In this way Russian peasants frequently had less land to cultivate than they had had before the Emancipation.
19. Ia. A. Berzin'-Ziemelis, 'Pervye vstrechi s Leninym', in *Lenin v vospominaniiakh revoliutsionerov Latvii*, edited by S. Vons (Riga, 1969), p. 33.
20. A. Ascher, *Pavel Axelrod and the Development of Menshevism* (Cambridge, Mass., 1972), pp. 253–5.
21. Berzin'-Ziemelis, 'Pervye vstrechi s Leninym', p. 36.
22. Valentinov, *Encounters with Lenin*, pp. 235–6.
23. Berzin'-Ziemelis, 'Pervye vstrechi s Leninym', p. 34.
24. Krupskaya, *Memories of Lenin*, pp. 141–2.
25. *Itogi Londonskogo S"ezda R.S.D.R.P.: Sbornik statei* (St Petersburg, 1907), pp. 2–3.

26. *Protokoly Soveshchaniya Rasshirennoi Redaktsii 'Proletariya' Iyun' 1909*,
     edited by G. Swain, Publications of the Study Group on the Russian
     Revolution (New York, London, 1982), p. 264.
27. *Itogi Londonskogo S"ezda R.S.D.R.P.: Sbornik statei*, p. 4.
28. N. A. Vasetskii, *Trotskii: Opyt politicheskoi biografii* (Moscow, 1992), p. 52.
29. V. Shalda, *Za organizatsionnoe edinstvo partii* (Riga, 1989), pp. 89, 90,
     110; Brūno Kalniņš, *Latvijas sociāldemokratijas piecdesmit gadi*
     (Stockholm, 1956), p. 148.
30. W. Najdus, *SDKPiL a SDPRR 1908–1918* (Wroclaw, 1980), pp. 52–61.
31. J. Biggart, '"Anti-Leninist Bolshevism": the *Forward* Group of the
     RSDRP', *Canadian Slavonic Papers*, Vol. 23, no. 2 (June 1981), pp.
     132–53 (p. 136).
32. G. S. Usyskin, 'V. I. Lenin na tret'ei konferentsii RSDRP', *Voprosy istorii*,
     Vol. 4, April 1988, pp. 17–20; A. Kochanski, *Socjal-demokracja Królestwa
     Polskiego i Litwy w latach 1907–1910 (Problemy polityczne i ideologiczne)*
     (Warsaw, 1971), p. 368.
33. A. Yassour, 'Lenin and Bogdanov: Protagonists in the "Bolshevik Center"',
     Studies in Soviet Thought, Vol. 22 (1981), pp. 3–7; A. S. Khalipov, *Bor'ba V.I.
     Lenina protiv likvidatorstva, 1908–1914* (Minsk, 1982), p. 31.
34. Khalipov, *Bor'ba V.I. Lenina protiv likvidatorstva, 1908–1914*, pp. 32–3.
35. *Kommunisticheskaia partiia Sovetskogo Soiuza v rezoliutsiiakh i resheniiakh
     s"ezdov, konferentsii i plenumov TsK (1898–1970), 1, 1898–1917*, 8th edn
     (Moscow, 1970), pp. 236–8.
36. V. I. Lenin, *Collected Works*, Vol. 13, pp. 448–54.
37. *Vladimir Il'ich Lenin: Biograficheskaia khronika 1870–1924, 2, 1905–1912*
     (Moscow, 1971), p. 403.
38. A. V. Lunacharskii, *Religiia i sotsializm*, Vol. 1 (St Petersburg, 1908),
     p. 40.
39. A. V. Lunacharskii, *Religiia i sotsializm*, Vol. 2 (St Petersburg, 1908),
     pp. 395–7.
40. A. M. Gor'kii, 'V. I. Lenin', in *Vospominaniia o Vladimire Il'iche Lenine*,
     Vol. 2 (Moscow, 1969), pp. 249–50.
41. A. A. Bogdanov, *Prikliucheniia odnoi filosofskoi shkoly* (St Petersburg, 1908).
42. Lenin, *CW* 13, p. 16; V. A. Prokof'ev, *Dubrovinskii*, Zhizn' zamech-
     atel'nykh liudei (Moscow, 1969), p. 194.
43. *Biograficheskaia khronika 2*, pp. 413–14; Biggart, '"Anti-Leninist
     Bolshevism": the *Forward* Group of the RSDRP', p. 144.
44. G. Swain, *Russian Social Democracy and the Legal Labour Movement,
     1906–14* (London and Basingstoke, 1983), p. 85.
45. S. V. Tiutiukin, *G. V. Plekhanov: Sud'ba russkogo marksista* (Moscow,
     1997), pp. 262–7.
46. Tiutiukin, *G. V. Plekhanov*, pp. 281, 287.
47. Najdus, *SDKPiL a SDPRR 1908–1918*, p. 84.
48. Biggart, Gloveli and Yassour, *Bogdanov and His Work*, p. 211.
49. A. A. Bogdanov, *Vera i nauka* (Moscow, 1910), p. 210.
50. V. I. Lenin, *Collected Works*, Vol. 38 (Moscow, 1961), p. 179.
51. Ibid., pp. 176–8.
52. Ibid., p. 180.

53. *Protokoly Soveshchaniya Rasshirennoi Redaktsii "Proletariya" Iyun' 1909*, pp. 171–82.

54. S. M. Fal'kovich, *Proletariat Rossii i Pol'shi v sovmestnoi revoliutsionnoi bor'be (1907–1912)* (Moscow, 1975), p. 180; Biggart, Gloveli and Yassour, *Bogdanov and His Work*, pp. 217–19.

55. Najdus, *SDKPiL a SDPRR 1908–1918*, pp. 68, 80; *Protokoly Soveshchaniya Rasshirennoi Redaktsii "Proletariya" Iyun' 1909*, pp. 260–3; Fal'kovich, *Proletariat Rossii i Pol'shi v sovmestnoi revoliutsionnoi bor'be (1907–1912)*, p. 180.

56. Najdus, *SDKPiL a SDPRR 1908–1918*, pp. 71–2, 79–80.

57. *Otchet Pervoi Vysshei Sotsialdemokraticheskoi propagandistsko-agitatorskoi shkoly dlia rabochikh (Avg.–Dek. 1909 goda)* (Paris, 1910), p. 1.

58. Kochański, *Socjaldemokracja Królestwa Polskiego i Litwy w latach 1907–1910 (Problemy polityczne i ideologiczne)*, p. 379.

59. A. S. Khalipov, *Bor'ba V.I. Lenina protiv likvidatorstva, 1908–1914* (Minsk, 1982), p. 81.

60. Prokof'ev, *Dubrovinskii*, p. 203.

61. *KPSS v rezoliutsiiakh*, pp. 288–99; Najdus, *SDKPiL a SDPRR 1908–1918*, pp. 86–7.

62. A. Kochański, *Socjaldemokracja Królestwa Polskiego i Litwy w latach 1907–1910 (Problemy polityczne i ideologiczne)* (Warsaw, 1971), p. 380; Najdus, *SDKPiL a SDPRR 1908–1918*, p. 88.

63. *Otchet vtoroi Vysshei Sotsialdemokraticheskoi propagandistsko-agitatorskoi shkoly dlia rabochikh (Noiabr' 1910–Mart 1911 goda)* (Paris, 1911), p. 3.

64. *Vserossiiskaya Konferentsiya Ros. Sots.-Dem. Rab. Partii 1912 goda*, edited by C. Elwood, Publications of the Study Group on the Russian Revolution (New York and London, 1982), pp. xvi–xvii; Khalipov, *Bor'ba V.I. Lenina protiv likvidatorstva, 1908–1914*, pp. 111–12.

65. Najdus, *SDKPiL a SDPRR 1908–1918*, p. 174.

66. 'Protokoly VI (Prazhskoi) Vserossiiskoi konferentsii RSDRP', *Voprosy istorii KPSS*, no. 5 (May 1988), pp. 49–52.

67. *Vserossiiskaya Konferentsiya Ros. Sots.-Dem. Rab. Partii 1912 goda*, p. xxiv.

68. 'Protokoly VI (Prazhskoi) Vserossiiskoi konferentsii RSDRP', p. 47; 'Protokoly VI (Prazhskoi) Vserossiiskoi konferentsii RSDRP', *Voprosy istorii KPSS*, no. 7 (July 1988), p. 33.

69. 'Obzor partii primykaiushchikh k rossiiskoi sotsial-demokraticheskoi rabochei partii', Russian Revolutionary Literature Collection (Haughton Library, Harvard University, n.d.).

70. Khalipov, *Bor'ba V.I. Lenina protiv likvidatorstva, 1908–1914*, p. 170; I. Thatcher, 'Trotsky and Bor'ba', *The Historical Journal*, Vol. 37, no. 1 (1994), pp. 113–25.

71. I. Iurenev, 'Mezhraionka, 1911–1917 gg', *Proletarskaia revoliutsiia*, 1, no. 24 (1924), pp. 120–38.

72. L. Schapiro, *The Communist Party of the Soviet Union*, 2nd edn (London, 1970), pp. 135–6.

73. R. B. McKean, *St Petersburg between the Revolutions. Workers and Revolutionaries, June 1907–February 1917* (New Haven, Conn. and London, 1990), pp. 80–97.

4 The First World War

1. *Vserossiiskaya Konferentsiya Ros. Sots.-Dem. Rab. Partii 1912 goda*, edited by C. Elwood, Publications of the Study Group on the Russian Revolution (New York and London, 1982), p. 42.
2. V. I. Lenin, *Collected Works*, Vol. 20, pp. 23–33.
3. Ibid., pp. 398–412; Jan Dziewulski, 'Podloze sporu R. Luksemburg – W. Lenin w kwestii narodowej', *Z pola walki*, Vol. 14, no. 1 (1971), pp. 33–61.
4. W. Najdus, *SDKPiL a SDPRR 1908–1918* (Wroclaw, 1980), p. 226; R. C. Elwood, 'The Congress that Never Was: Lenin's Attempt to Call a "Sixth" Party Congress in 1914', *Soviet Studies*, Vol. 31, no. 3 (July 1979), p. 351.
5. J. Augskalns-Aberbergs, *Latvijas socialdemokratiska stradnieku partija. Vesturisks atskats* (Riga, 1929), pp. 131–7; Ia. A. Berzin'-Ziemelis, 'Pervye vstrechi s Leninym', in *Lenin i sotsial-demokratiia latyshskogo kraia*, edited by S. Vons (Riga, 1969), p. 19.
6. Lenin, *CW* 20, pp. 514–15.
7. Ibid., p. 525.
8. *The Bolsheviks and the World War: The Origin of the Third International*, edited by O. H. Gankin and H. H. Fisher, The Hoover Library on War, Revolution and Peace (Stanford, California, 1960), p. 131.
9. Najdus, *SDKPiL a SDPRR 1908–1918*, p. 275.
10. *Bol'sheviki: Dokumenty po istorii bol'shevizma s 1903 po 1916 god byvshego Moskovskogo Okhrannogo Otdeleniia*, 3rd edn (Moscow, 1990), p. 228.
11. Elwood, 'The Congress that Never Was: Lenin's Attempt to Call a "Sixth" Party Congress in 1914', p. 356.
12. S. Iu. Bagotskii, 'V. I. Lenin v Krakove i Poronine', in *Vospominaniia o Vladimire Il'iche Lenine*, Vol. 2 (Moscow, 1969), pp. 328–9.
13. *Lenin's Struggle for a Revolutionary International. Documents: 1907–1916. The Preparatory Years*, edited by J. Riddell, The Communist International in Lenin's Time (New York, 1984), p. 35.
14. M. Waldenberg, *Wzlot i upadek Karola Kautsky'ego*, Vol. 2 (Krakow, 1972), pp. 228–35; *Lenin's Struggle for a Revolutionary International. Documents: 1907–1916. The Preparatory Years*, pp. 123–4.
15. J. Joll, *The Second International 1889–1914*, 2nd edn (London and Boston, 1974), pp. 161–86; *Istoriia vtorogo internatsionala*, Vol. 2, edited by L. I. Zubok (Moscow, 1966), pp. 411–23; N. Milton, *John Maclean* (Bristol, 1973), pp. 76–8.
16. S. V. Tiutiukin, *G. V. Plekhanov: Sud'ba russkogo marksista* (Moscow, 1997), pp. 304–6.
17. Najdus, *SDKPiL a SDPRR 1908–1918*, p. 301.
18. *Men'sheviki. Dokumenty i materialy. 1903–fevral' 1917 gg.*, Politicheskie partii Rossii. Konets XIX – pervaia tret' XX veka. Dokumental'noe nasledie (Moscow, 1996), pp. 351–2.
19. A. Ascher, *Pavel Axelrod and the Development of Menshevism* (Cambridge, Mass., 1972), p. 311.

20. A. V. Rakitin, *V. A. Antonov-Ovseenko: Istoriko-biograficheskii ocherk* (Leningrad, 1989), p. 46; N. Krupskaya, *Memories of Lenin* (London, 1970), p. 249.
21. L. Trotsky, *La guerre et la révolution: Le naufrage de la IIe Internationale. Les débuts de la IIIe Internationale*, Vol. 1, translated by A. Oak (Paris, 1974), pp. 59–61.
22. Ibid., p. 29.
23. V. I. Lenin, *Collected Works*, Vol. 21 (Moscow, 1964), pp. 15–19.
24. Ibid., pp. 27–34.
25. Trotsky, *La guerre et la révolution*, p. 29.
26. *Rosa Luxemburg Speaks*, edited by M.-A. Waters (New York, 1970), pp. 257–331.
27. Ia. G. Temkin, *Tsimmerval'd-Kintal' (Iz istorii bor'by V. I. Lenina za ob"edinenie sotsialistov-internatsionalistov)* (Moscow, 1967), pp. 26–8.
28. S. F. Cohen, *Bukharin and the Bolshevik Revolution: A Political Biography 1888–1938* (London, 1974), p. 36.
29. *Lenin's Struggle for a Revolutionary International. Documents: 1907–1916. The Preparatory Years*, pp. 318–21.
30. J. Dziewulski, *Wokól pogladow ekonomicznych Rozy Luksemburg* (Warsaw, 1972), pp. 288–90.
31. V. I. Lenin, *Collected Works*, Vol. 35, pp. 93–4.
32. R. Hilferding, *Das Finanzkapital* (Vienna, 1923), pp. 218, 471.
33. K. Kautsky, 'Der Imperialismus', *Die Neue Zeit*, Vol. 29 (1914), pp. 919–21.
34. L. Trotsky, 'Nash politicheskii lozung', *Nashe slovo*, 24 February 1915.
35. N. Bukharin, 'Mirovaia ekonomika i imperializm', *Kommunist*, no. 1–2 (1915), p. 44.
36. Ibid., p. 38.
37. M. N. Pokrovskii, 'Kak rozhdalsia "Imperializm"', in *Vospominaniia o Vladimire Il'iche Lenine*, Vol. 2 (Moscow, 1969), pp. 368–72.
38. V. I. Lenin, *Collected Works*, Vol. 22, pp. 205–8.
39. Ibid., p. 268.
40. Ibid., p. 266.
41. Ibid., p. 268.
42. Ibid., p. 300.
43. Ibid., p. 301.
44. V. I. Lenin, *Collected Works*, Vol. 23, p. 60.
45. Lenin, *CW* 21, p. 342.
46. Lenin, *CW* 23, pp. 13–76.
47. *The Bolsheviks and the World War: The Origin of the Third International*, pp. 418–19.
48. Lenin, *CW* 23, p. 49.
49. Ibid., p. 58.
50. V. I. Lenin, *Polnoe sobranie sochinenii*, Vol. 33, p. 333.
51. Lenin, *CW* 23, pp. 165–6.
52. Ibid., p. 371.
53. P. Renouvin, *Histoire des relations internationales, 7, Les crises du XXe siècle. I de 1914 à 1929* (Paris, 1957), pp. 22–3.

54. *Germany and the Revolution in Russia 1915–1918*, edited by Z. A. B. Zeman (London, 1958), pp. 12–13.
55. V. S. Diakin, *Russkaia burzhuaziia i tsarizm v gody pervoi mirovoi voiny (1914–1917)* (Leningrad, 1967), p. 103.
56. *Germany and the Revolution in Russia 1915–1918*, pp. 12–13.
57. Lenin, *CW* 23, p. 264.
58. W. Hahlweg, *Lenins Rückkehr nach Russland: Die Deutschen Akten* (Leiden, 1957), p. 10.
59. J. D. White, 'Lenin, the Germans and the February Revolution', *Revolutionary Russia*, Vol. 5, no. 1 (June 1992), pp. 12–18.
60. Lenin, *CW* 23, p. 253.
61. V. I. Lenin, *Collected Works*, Vol. 24, p. 28.
62. Krupskaya, *Memories of Lenin*, pp. 293–4.

5　Lenin as Revolutionary

1. *The Russian Provisional Government 1917*, Vol. 1, edited by R. Browder and A. Kerensky (Stanford, Calif., 1961), p. 70.
2. N. N. Sukhanov, *The Russian Revolution 1917: A Personal Record* (Princeton, NJ, 1984), pp. 104–5.
3. J. D. White, 'The Sormovo–Nikolaev Zemlyachestvo in the February Revolution', *Soviet Studies*, Vol. 31, no. 4 (October 1979), pp. 475–504.
4. V. I. Lenin, *Collected Works*, Vol. 23, pp. 309–11.
5. Sukhanov, *The Russian Revolution*, p. 125.
6. A. G. Shliapnikov, *Semnadtsatyi god*, Vol. 2 (Moscow and Leningrad, 1925), pp. 183–5.
7. Sukhanov, *The Russian Revolution*, pp. 283–4.
8. Ibid., pp. 285–8.
9. V. I. Lenin, *Collected Works*, Vol. 24, pp. 21–6.
10. *Sed'maia (Aprel'skaia) vserossiiskaia konferentsiia RSDRP (bol'shevikov) Aprel' 1917 goda. Protokoly*, Protokoly i stenograficheskie otchety s"ezdov i konfer-entsii Kommunisticheskoi partii Sovetskogo Soiuza (Moscow, 1958), p. 18.
11. I. Thatcher, 'Russia's Social-Patriotism in Trotskii's Paris Writings during the First World War', *Revolutionary Russia*, Vol. 6, no. 2 (December 1993), pp. 229–76.
12. Lenin, *CW* 24, p. 299.
13. S. I. Gopner, 'Nezabyvaemye dni', in *Vospominaniia o Vladimire Il'iche Lenine*, Vol. 2 (Moscow, 1969), p. 394.
14. S. M. Dubrovskii, *Krest'ianstvo v 1917 godu* (Moscow and Leningrad, 1927), pp. 27–9.
15. S. A. Smith, *Red Petrograd: Revolution in the Factories, 1917–18* (Cambridge, 1983), p. 176.
16. A. Rabinowitch, *Prelude to Revolution: The Petrograd Bolsheviks and the July 1917 Uprising* (Bloomington, Ind., 1968), pp. 142–3.
17. L. Trotsky, 'Lessons of October', in *The Essential Trotsky* (London, 1963), p. 175; A. A. Solov'ev, *S"ezdy i konferentsii KPSS. Spravochnik* (Moscow, 1983), p. 107.

18. Sukhanov, *The Russian Revolution*, p. 380.
19. V. I. Lenin, *Collected Works*, Vol. 25, p. 210.
20. Ibid., pp. 155–9.
21. Ibid., pp. 183–90.
22. V. I. Lenin, *Collected Works*, Vol. 36, p. 454.
23. V. I. Lenin, *Polnoe sobranie sochinenii*, Vol. 33, pp. 128–9.
24. Lenin, *CW* 25, p. 402.
25. Lenin, *PSS* 33, pp. 174–5.
26. Ibid., p. 323.
27. Lenin, *CW* 25, pp. 443, 473.
28. Ibid., pp. 305–10.
29. V. I. Lenin, *Collected Works*, Vol. 26, pp. 69–73.
30. J. D. White, 'Lenin, Trotskii and the Arts of Insurrection: The Congress of Soviets of the Northern Region 11–13 October 1917', *The Slavonic and East European Review*, Vol. 77, no. 1 (January 1999), pp. 117–39.
31. Lenin, *CW* 26, p. 180.
32. Ibid., p. 188.
33. V. A. Antonov-Ovseenko, 'Baltflot v dni Kerenshchiny i Krasnogo Oktiabr'', *Proletarskaia revoliutsiia*, no. 10 (1922), p. 125.
34. *Rabochii put'* no. 35 (13 October 1917).
35. *Rabochii put'*, no. 46 (26 October 1917).
36. A. Lunacharskii, K. Radek and L. Trotskii, *Siluety: Politicheskie portrety* (Moscow, 1991), p. 70.
37. M. Philips Price, *My Reminiscences of the Russian Revolution* (London, 1921), pp. 144–5.

6   Lenin in Power

1. V. I. Lenin, *Collected Works*, Vol. 25, pp. 357–9.
2. V. I. Lenin, *Collected Works*, Vol. 26, p. 106.
3. *The Debate on Soviet Power: Minutes of the All-Russian Central Executive Committee of Soviets 'Second Convocation' October 1917–January 1918*, edited and translated by J. Keep (Oxford, 1979), p. 81.
4. L. A. Fotieva, 'Priemy i metody gosudarstvennoi raboty V. I. Lenina', in *Vospominaniia o Vladimire Il'iche Lenine*, Vol. 4 (Moscow, 1969), p. 114.
5. G. Krumin, 'Lenin i khoziaistvennoe stroitel'stvo Sovetskikh respublik', in *U velikoi mogily* (Moscow, 1924), p. 146.
6. A. Lomov, 'Vladimir Il'ich v khoziaistvennoi rabote', in *Vospominaniia o Vladimire Il'iche Lenine*, Vol. 3 (Moscow, 1969), p. 130.
7. V. I. Lenin, *Collected Works*, Vol. 27, p. 261; R. M. Savitskaia, *Zadachi pobedivshego proletariata: O rabote V. I. Lenina 'Ocherednye zadachi sovetskoi vlasti'* (Moscow, 1981), pp. 144–68.
8. Lenin, *CW* 27, p. 294.
9. *The Russian Provisional Government 1917*, Vol. 2, edited by R. Browder and A. Kerensky (Stanford, Calif., 1961), p. 649.
10. S. Malle, *The Economic Organisation of War Communism 1918–1921* (Cambridge, 1985), p. 203.

11. A. A. Bogdanov, 'Voprosy sotsializma', in *Voprosy sotsializma*, edited by L. A. Abalkin (Moscow, 1990), pp. 335–44.
12. *The Debate on Soviet Power*, p. 206.
13. *Sbornik dokumentov i materialov po istorii SSSR sovetskogo perioda (1917–1958 gg.)* (Moscow, 1966), pp. 50–1, 62.
14. Lenin, *CW* 27, pp. 242, 304.
15. Ibid., p. 265.
16. Ibid., p. 264.
17. A. G. Shlikhter, 'Pervyi otklik Il'icha po adresu levoeserovskoi kontr-revoliutsii', in *Vospominaniia o Vladimire Il'iche Lenine*, Vol. 4 (Moscow, 1969), pp. 104-5.
18. I. S. Unshlikht, 'O Vladimire Il'iche', in *Vospominaniia o Vladimire Il'iche Lenine*, Vol. 4 (Moscow, 1969), pp. 80–1.
19. M. G. Shtein, *Ulianovy i Leniny: Tainy rodoslovnoi i psevdonima* (St Petersburg, 1997), pp. 92–4.
20. A. I. Ul'ianova (Elizarova), Footnote to 'Vospominaniia ob A. I. Ul'ianove, P. Ia. Shevyreve, V. D. Generalove i P. I Andreiushkine', in *Aleksandr Il'ich Ul'ianov i delo 1 marta 1887 g.*, edited by A. I. Ul'ianova-Elizarova (Moscow and Leningrad, 1927), p. 218.
21. V. I. Lenin, *Polnoe sobranie sochinenii*, Vol. 54, p. 14.
22. *The Unknown Lenin from the secret archive*, edited by R. Pipes and D. Brandenberger, translated by C. A. Fitzpatrick (New Haven, Conn., 1996), p. 50.
23. Lenin, *CW* 26, p. 379; I. Z. Steinberg, *Spiridonova, Revolutionary and Terrorist*, edited and translated by G. David and E. Mosbacher (London, 1935), p. 190.
24. F. Mehring, 'Die Bolschewiki und wir', in *Gesammelte Schriften, 15, Politische Publizistik 1905 bis 1918*, edited by T. Höhle, H. Koch and J. Schleifstein (Berlin, 1966), pp. 761–72; E. N. Gorodetskii, 'Pervye trudy V. I. Lenina po istorii Oktiabr'skoi revoliutsii', in *Istoriia i Istoriki. Istoriografiia istorii SSSR. Sbornik statei*, edited by M. V. Nechkina (Moscow, 1965), p. 56.
25. *The Bolsheviks and the October Revolution: Minutes of the Central Committee of the Russian Social-Democratic Labour Party (Bolsheviks) August 1917–February 1918*, translated by A. Bone (London, 1974), pp. 173–5.
26. *A Documentary History of Communism, 1, Communism in Russia*, revised edn, edited by R. V. Daniels (Hanover and London, 1984), pp. 98–102.
27. I. I. Vatsetis, 'Dve vstrechi s Leninym', in *Vospominaniia o Vladimire Il'iche Lenine*, Vol. 3 (Moscow, 1969), p. 267.
28. A. Deruga, 'Z dziejów ruchu rewolucyjnego na ziemiach litewsko-białoruskich w 1918 r', *Z dziejów stosunków polsko–radzieckich*, Vol. 11–12 (1975), p. 306.
29. V. I. Lenin, *Collected Works*, Vol. 28, pp. 114–27.
30. *The Unknown Lenin from the secret archive*, edited by R. Pipes and D. Brandenburger, translated by C. A. Fitzpatrick (New Haven, Conn., 1996), p. 98.
31. V. I. Lenin, *Collected Works*, Vol. 31, pp. 206–12.

32. Ibid., pp. 21–118.
33. Lenin, *CW* 28, p. 30.
34. E. G. Gimpel'son, *Velikii Oktiabr' i stanovlenie sovetskoi sistemy upravleniia narodnym khoziaistvom (noiabr' 1917–1920 gg.)* (Moscow, 1977), pp. 33–4; V. I. Lenin, *Collected Works*, Vol. 29, pp. 436–55.
35. J. Smith, *The Bolsheviks and the National Question, 1917–23* (Basingstoke and London, 1999), p. 20.
36. Lenin, *CW* 27, p. 356.
37. Lenin, *CW* 28, p. 304.
38. I. I. Radchenko, 'Lenin – vozhd' na khoziaistvennom fronte', in *Vospominaniia o Vladimire Il'iche Lenine*, Vol. 4 (Moscow, 1969), pp. 52–60.
39. B. Russell, *The Practice and Theory of Bolshevism* (London, 1962), p. 28; G. M. Krzhizhanovskii, 'O Vladimire Il'iche', in *Vospominaniia o Vladimire Il'iche Lenine*, Vol. 2 (Moscow, 1969), pp. 43–4.
40. Lenin, *CW* 31, p. 516.
41. N. Bukharin and E. Preobrazhensky, *The ABC of Communism*, edited by E. H. Carr (Harmondsworth, 1969).
42. *The Unknown Lenin*, p. 62.
43. N. Bukharin, *The Politics and Economics of the Transition Period*, edited by K. J. Tarbuck, translated by O. Field (London, 1979), p. 89.
44. Bukharin, *The Politics and Economics of the Transition Period*, pp. 93–106.
45. Ibid., p. 169.
46. *Leninskii sbornik*, Vol. 11 (1929), p. 397.
47. *O roli professional'nykh soiuzov v proizvodstve* (Moscow, 1921), pp. 59–61.
48. A. Kollontai, *Selected Writings of Aleksandra Kollontai*, edited and translated by A. Holt (London, 1977), p. 191.
49. V. I. Lenin, *Collected Works*, Vol. 32, pp. 24–5.
50. Russell, *The Practice and Theory of Bolshevism*, p. 48. In an account of her visit to Russia in 1920, published in the same year, Mrs Snowden gives a clear explanation of what the New Economic Policy would involve and why the Bolsheviks were reluctant to implement it: 'In regard to corn and flour, the Government requisitions all that the peasant produces above a certain minimum required for himself and his family. If, instead, it exacted a fixed amount as rent, it would not destroy his incentive to production, and would not provide nearly such a strong motive for concealment. But this plan would have enabled the peasants to grow rich, and would have involved a confessed abandonment of Communist theory. It has therefore been thought better to employ forcible methods, which led to disorder, as they were bound to do.' Mrs P. Snowden, *Through Bolshevik Russia* (London, 1920), p. 115.
51. Lenin, *CW* 32, p. 184.
52. Ibid., p. 206.
53. *Resheniia partii i pravitel'stva po khoziaistvennym voprosam*, Vol. 1 (Moscow, 1967), pp. 200–2.
54. A. I. Mikoian, *Mysli i vospominaniia o Lenine* (Moscow, 1970), pp. 136–8.
55. Lenin, *CW* 32, pp. 241–4.
56. Ibid., pp. 245–8.
57. Ibid., p. 436.

58. A. I. Mikoian, 'V Nizhnem Novgorode', *Novyi Mir*, no. 11 (1972), pp. 188–9.
59. V. A. Kumanev and I. S. Kulikova, *Protivostoianie: Krupskaia – Stalin* (Moscow, 1994), pp. 14–15.
60. Kumanev and Kulikova, *Protivostoianie: Krupskaia – Stalin*, p. 32.
61. V. I. Lenin, *Collected Works*, Vol. 36, p. 594–6.
62. Kumanev and Kulikova, *Protivostoianie: Krupskaia – Stalin*, p. 21.
63. V. I. Lenin, *CW* 36, pp. 606–7.
64. Smith, *The Bolsheviks and the National Question, 1917–23*, pp. 208–10, 224; M. Lewin, *Lenin's Last Struggle*, translated by A. M. Sheridan-Smith (1975), pp. 94–6.
65. Kumanev and Kulikova, *Protivostoianie: Krupskaia – Stalin*, pp. 26–7.
66. V. I. Lenin, *Collected Works*, Vol. 33, pp. 478–9.

7 The Lenin Legend

1.   N. V. Riasanovsky, *A History of Russia* (Oxford, 1963), p. 501.
2.   L. Trotsky, 'The History of the Russian Revolution to Brest-Litovsk', in *The Essential Trotsky* (London, 1963), pp. 21–111.
3.   V. I. Lenin, *Collected Works*, Vol. 31 (Moscow, 1974), pp. 24–6.
4.   Ibid., pp. 26–31.
5.   N. S. Komarov, 'Sozdanie i deiatel'nost' Istparta (1920–1928 gg.)', *Voprosy istorii KPSS*, no. 5 (1958), p. 154; M. N. Pokrovsky, 'O vozniknovenii Istparta', *Proletarskaia revoliutsiia*, no. 7–8 (1930), p. 138.
6.   A. I. Ul'ianova-Elizarova, 'Retrospektivnyi vzgliad na Istpart i na zhurnal "Proletarskaia revoliutsiia"', *Proletarskaia revoliutsiia*, no. 5 (1930), p. 158.
7.   M. G. Shtein, *Ulianovy i Leniny: Tainy rodoslovnoi i psevdonima* (St Petersburg, 1997), p. 54.
8.   M. I. Ul'ianova, 'V Gimnazii', in *Vospominaniia o Vladimire Il'iche Lenine*, Vol. 1 (Moscow, 1968), p. 144.
9.   D. A. Volkogonov, *Lenin politicheskii portret*, Vol. 1 (Moscow, 1994), p. 91.
10. R. M. Savitskaia, 'A. I. Ul'ianova-Elizarova – istorik leninskoi partii', *Voprosy istorii KPSS*, no. 8 (August 1987), pp. 98–112 (p. 110).
11. Iu. P. Sharapov, *Lenin i Bogdanov: Ot sotrudnichestva k protivostoianiiu* (Moscow, 1998), p. 61.
12. K. A. Ostroukhova, 'O rabote v Istparte', *Voprosy istorii KPSS*, no. 6 (June 1967), pp. 92–9 (pp. 94–5).
13. J. Stalin, *Problems of Leninism* (Moscow, 1953), p. 37.
14. A. Lunacharskii, K. Radek and L. Trotskii, *Siluety: Politicheskie portrety* (Moscow, 1991), p. 70.
15. L. Trotsky, 'Lessons of October', in *The Essential Trotsky* (London, 1963), pp. 115–77.
16. 'Vokrug stati L. D. Trotskogo "Uroki Oktiabria" (oktiabr' 1924 g.–aprel' 1925 g.)', *Izvestiia TsK KPSS*, no. 7 (July 1991), pp. 158–77 (p. 159).
17. N. N. Maslov and Z. V. Stepanov, *Ocherki istochnikovedeniia i istoriografii istorii KPSS* (Leningrad, 1974), p. 70.
18. N. K. Krupskaia, 'Vospominaniia o Lenine', in *Vospominaniia o Vladimire Il'iche Lenine*, Vol. 1 (Moscow, 1968), p. 219.

19. V. A. Kumanev and I. S. Kulikova, *Protivostoianie: Krupskaia – Stalin* (Moscow, 1994), pp. 164–8.
20. Ibid., p. 173.
21. P. N. Pospelov, 'K vospominaniiam o Lenine', *Pravda*, 9 May 1934, p. 4; Kumanev and Kulikova, *Protivostoianie: Krupskaia – Stalin*, pp. 176–8.
22. Stalin, *Problems of Leninism*, pp. 483–97.
23. Institut Marksa–Engel'sa–Lenina–Stalina, *Lenin, Vladimir Il'ich: Kratkaia Biografiia* (Moscow, 1955), p. 125; *Lenin: A Biography* (London, 1955), p. 109.
24. *Vladimir Ilyich Lenin: A Biography*, edited by P. N. Pospelov (Moscow, 1965).
25. L. Trotsky, *The History of the Russian Revolution*, translated by M. Eastman (London, 1934).
26. L. Trotsky, *The Young Lenin*, translated by M. Eastman (Harmondsworth, 1974), p. 86.
27. Ibid., pp. 138–9.
28. N. Valentinov, *Encounters with Lenin*, translated by P. Rosta and B. Pearce (London, 1968).
29. Ibid., pp. 124, 182.
30. D. Shub, *Lenin: A Biography* (Harmondsworth, 1966).
31. A. B. Ulam, *Lenin and the Bolsheviks* (London and Glasgow, 1969).
32. N. Harding, *Lenin's Political Thought, 1, Theory and Practice in the Democratic Revolution* (London and Basingstoke, 1977); N. Harding, *Lenin's Political Thought, 2, Theory and Practice in the Socialist Revolution* (London and Basingstoke, 1981).
33. *Marxism in Russia. Key Documents, 1879–1906*, edited by N. Harding, translated by R. Taylor (Cambridge, 1983).
34. R. Service, *Lenin: A Political Life, 1, The Strengths of Contradiction* (Basingstoke and London, 1985); R. Service, *Lenin: A Political Life, 2, Worlds in Collision* (Basingstoke, 1991); R. Service, *Lenin: A Political Life, 3, The Iron Ring* (Basingstoke, 1995).
35. R. Service, *Lenin: A Biography* (London, 2000).
36. R. Pipes, 'Narodnichestvo: A Semantic Enquiry', *Slavic Review*, Vol. 23, no. 3 (September 1964), pp. 441–58.
37. R. Pipes, 'The Origins of Bolshevism: The Intellectual Evolution of Young Lenin', in *Revolutionary Russia*, edited by R. Pipes (London, 1968), pp. 26–52.
38. R. Pipes, *Social Democracy and the St. Petersburg Labor Movement, 1885–1897* (Cambridge, Mass., 1963).
39. R. A. Kazakevich and F. M. Suslova, *Mister Paips falsifitsiruet istoriiu: O knige R. Paipsa "Sotsial-demokratiia i rabochee dvizhenie v S.-Peterburge, 1885–1897"* (Leningrad, 1996).
40. *The Unknown Lenin from the secret archive*, edited by R. Pipes and D. Brandenberger, translated by C. A. Fitzpatrick (New Haven, Conn., 1996).
41. Ibid., p. 134.
42. Volkogonov, *Lenin politicheskii portret*; D. A. Volkogonov, *Lenin: Life and Legacy*, edited and translated by H. Shukman (London, 1994).
43. E. H. Carr, *1917: Before and After* (London, 1969), p. 9.

SELECT BIBLIOGRAPHY

1903 Second Ordinary Congress of the RSDLP, translated by B. Pearce. London: New Park Publications, 1978.

Akhapkin, Y. *First Decrees of Soviet Power*. London: Lawrence & Wishart, 1970.

Althusser, L. *Lenin and Philosophy, and other essays*, translated by B. Brewster. London: NLB, 1971.

Ascher, A. *Pavel Axelrod and the Development of Menshevism*. Cambridge, Mass.: Harvard University Press, 1972.

Balabanoff, A. *Impressions of Lenin*. Ann Arbor: Michigan University Press, 1964.

Baron, S. H. *Plekhanov: The Father of Russian Marxism*. Stanford, Calif.: Stanford University Press, 1963.

Biggart, J. '"Anti-Leninist Bolshevism": the *Forward* Group of the RSDRP'. *Canadian Slavonic Papers*, vol. 23, no. 2 (June 1981), pp. 132–53.

—— G. Gloveli and A. Yassour (compilers), *Bogdanov and His Work: A guide to the published and unpublished works of Alexander A. Bogdanov (Malinovsky) 1873–1928*. Aldershot: Ashgate, 1998.

The Bolsheviks and the October Revolution: Minutes of the Central Committee of the Russian Social-Democratic Labour Party (Bolsheviks) August 1917–February 1918, translated by A. Bone. London: Pluto Press, 1974.

The Bolsheviks and the World War: The Origin of the Third International, edited by O. H. Gankin and H. H. Fisher, The Hoover Library on War, Revolution and Peace. Stanford, Calif.: Stanford University Press, 1960.

Broué, P. *Trotsky*. Paris: Fayard, 1988.

Bukharin, N. *The Politics and Economics of the Transition Period*, edited by K. J. Tarbuck, translated by O. Field. London: Routledge & Kegan Paul, 1979.

—— and E. Preobrazhensky. *The ABC of Communism*, edited by E. H. Carr. Harmondsworth: Penguin, 1969.

Buranov, I. A. *Lenin's Will: Falsified and Forbidden*. Amherst, NY: Prometheus Books, 1994.

Carr, E. H. *The Bolshevik Revolution*, 3 vols, *A History of Soviet Russia*. Harmondsworth: Penguin, 1966.

—— *1917: Before and After*. London: Macmillan, 1969.

—— *The Russian Revolution from Lenin to Stalin 1917–1929*. London and Basingstoke: Macmillan, 1979.

Clark, R. W. *Lenin: The Man Behind the Mask*. London: Faber, 1988.

Cliff, T. *Lenin*, 4 vols. London: Pluto Press, 1975–9.

Cohen, S. F. *Bukharin and the Bolshevik Revolution: A Political Biography 1888–1938*. London: Wildwood House, 1974.

A Documentary History of Communism, vol. 1: *Communism in Russia*, revised edn, edited by R. V. Daniels. Hanover and London: University Press of New England, 1984.

Conquest, R. *Lenin*. London: Fontana, 1972.

The Debate on Soviet Power: Minutes of the All-Russian Central Executive Committee of Soviets 'Second Convocation' October 1917–January 1918, edited and translated by J. Keep. Oxford: Clarendon Press, 1979.

Deutscher, I. *Lenin's Childhood*. London: Oxford University Press, 1970.

Donald, M. *Marxism and Revolution: Karl Kautsky and the Russian Marxists 1900–1924*. New Haven, Conn. and London: Yale University Press, 1993.

Egan, D. R. and M. A. Egan. *V. I. Lenin: An Annotated Bibliography of English-Language Sources to 1980*. Metuchen, NJ and London: Scarecrow Press, 1982.

Elwood, R. C. 'The Congress that Never Was: Lenin's Attempt to Call a "Sixth" Party Congress in 1914'. *Soviet Studies*, vol. 31, no. 3 (July 1979), pp. 343–63.

Fainsod, M. *International Socialism and the World War*. New York: Octagon Books, 1973.

Fischer, L. *The Life of Lenin*. London: Weidenfeld & Nicolson, 1965.

Founding the Communist International. Proceedings and Documents of the First Congress: March 1919, edited by J. Riddell, The Communist International in Lenin's Time. New York: Monad Press, 1987.

Frankel, J. *Vladimir Akimov on the Dilemmas of Russian Marxism*. Cambridge: Cambridge University Press, 1969.

Germany and the Revolution in Russia 1915–1918, edited by Z. A. B. Zeman. London: Oxford University Press, 1958.

Getzler, I. *Martov: A Political Biography of a Russian Social Democrat*. London and New York: Melbourne University Press, 1967.

Gruber, H. *International Communism in the Era of Lenin*. New York: Fawcett, 1967.

Harding, N. *Lenin's Political Thought*, vol. 1: *Theory and Practice in the Democratic Revolution*. London and Basingstoke: Macmillan, 1977.

—— *Lenin's Political Thought*, vol. 2: *Theory and Practice in the Socialist Revolution*. London and Basingstoke: Macmillan, 1981.

—— *Leninism*. Basingstoke: Macmillan, 1996.

Joll, J. *The Second International 1889–1914*, 2nd edn. London and Boston, Mass.: Routledge & Kegan Paul, 1974.

Kalniņš, B. 'The Social Democratic Movement in Latvia'. In *Revolution and Politics in Russia*, edited by A. Rabinowitch and J. Rabinowitch. Bloomington: Indiana University Press, 1972.

Kelly, E. 'Empiriocriticism: A Bolshevik philosophy?'. *Cahiers du Monde Russe et Soviétique*, vol. 21 (1981), pp. 89–118.

Kerzhentsev, P. *Life of Lenin*. Moscow: Co-operative Publishing Society of Foreign Workers in the USSR, 1937.

Kingston-Mann, E. *Lenin and the Problem of Marxist Peasant Revolution*. New York: Oxford University Press, 1983.

Kochan, L. *Lenin*. London: Wayland, 1974.

Kolakowski, L. *Main Currents of Marxism: Its Origins, Growth and Dissolution*, 3 vols., translated by P. S. Falla. Oxford: Oxford University Press, 1981.

Kollontai, A. *Selected Writings of Aleksandra Kollontai*, edited and translated by A. Holt. London, 1977.

Krupskaya, N. *Memories of Lenin*. London: Panther, 1970.

Late Marx and the Russian Road. Marx and 'the Peripheries of capitalism', edited by T. Shanin. London, Melbourne and Henley: Routledge & Kegan Paul, 1984.

Le Blanc, P. *Lenin and the Revolutionary Party*, Introduction by Ernest Mandel. New Jersey and London: Humanities Press International, 1990.

Lenin and Leninism: State, Law and Society, edited by B. W. Eissenstat. Lexington, Mass.: Lexington Books, 1971.

Lenin, the Man, the Theorist, the Leader: A Reappraisal, edited by L. Schapiro and P. Reddaway. London: Pall Mall Press, 1967.

Lenin, V. I. *Collected Works*. Moscow: Foreign Languages Publishing House, 1960–70.

Lenin: A Biography. London: Lawrence & Wishart, 1955.

Lenin's Struggle for a Revolutionary International. Documents: 1907–1916. The Preparatory Years, edited by J. Riddell, The Communist International in Lenin's Time. New York: Monad Press, 1984.

Lewin, M. *Lenin's Last Struggle*, translated by A. M. Sheridan-Smith. Pluto Press, 1975.

Liebman, M. *Leninism under Lenin*, translated by B. Pearce. London: Cape, 1975.

Low, A. D. *Lenin on the Question of Nationality*. New York: Bookman Associates, 1958.

Lukács, G. *Lenin: a study on the unity of his thought*, translated by N. Jacobs. London: NLB, 1970.

Malle, S. *The Economic Organisation of War Communism 1918–1921*. Cambridge: Cambridge University Press, 1985.

Marx, K. *Grundrisse*, translated by M. Nicolaus. Harmondsworth: Penguin, 1973.

—— *Capital*, vol. 1, translated by B. Fowkes. Harmondsworth: Penguin, 1979.

Marxism in Russia. Key Documents, 1879–1906, edited by N. Harding, translated by R. Taylor. Cambridge: Cambridge University Press, 1983.

Maxton, J. *Lenin*. London: Daily Express Publications, 1932.

McKean, R. B. *St Petersburg between the Revolutions. Workers and Revolutionaries, June 1907–February 1917*. New Haven, Conn. and London: Yale University Press, 1990.

McNeal, R. H. *Bride of the Revolution Krupskaya and Lenin*. London: Gollancz, 1973.

The Mensheviks in the Russian Revolution, edited by A. Ascher, Documents of Revolution. London: Thames & Hudson, 1976.

Meyer, A. G. *Leninism*. Boulder, Colo: Westview Press, 1986.

Milton, N. *John Maclean*. Bristol: Pluto Press, 1973.

Naimark, N. *Terrorists and Social Democrats*. Harvard, Mass.: Harvard University Press, 1983.

Nettl, J. P. *Rosa Luxemburg*, 2 vols. London: Oxford University Press, 1966.

Pipes, R. *Social Democracy and the St. Petersburg Labor Movement, 1885–1897*. Cambridge, Mass.: Harvard University Press, 1963.

—— 'Narodnichestvo: A Semantic Enquiry'. *Slavic Review*, vol. 23, no. 3 (September 1964), pp. 441–58.

Pipes, R. 'The Origins of Bolshevism: The Intellectual Evolution of Young Lenin'. In *Revolutionary Russia*, edited by R. Pipes. London: Harvard University Press, 1968.

—— *The Formation of the Soviet Union: Communism and Nationalism 1917–1923*, revised edn. Cambridge, Mass. and London: Harvard University Press, 1997.

Plekhanov, G. V. *Selected Philosophical Works*, vol. 1. Moscow: Foreign Languages Publishing House, 1961.

Possony, S. T. *Lenin: The Compulsive Revolutionary*. London: Allen & Unwin, 1966.

Price, M. P. *My Reminiscences of the Russian Revolution*. London: George Allen & Unwin, 1921.

Rabinowitch, A. *Prelude to Revolution: The Petrograd Bolsheviks and the July 1917 Uprising*. Bloomington, Ind.: Indiana University Press, 1968.

—— *The Bolsheviks Come to Power*. London: NLB, 1976.

Renouvin, P. *Histoire des relations internationales*. vol. 7: *Les crises du XXᵉ siècle. I de 1914 à 1929*. Paris: Librairie Hachette, 1957.

Revisionism: Essays on the History of Marxist Ideas, edited by L. Labedz. London: George Allen & Unwin, 1962.

Riasanovsky, N. V. *A History of Russia*. Oxford: Oxford University Press, 1963.

Rosa Luxemburg Speaks, edited by M.-A. Waters. New York: Pathfinder Press, 1970.

Russell, B. *The Practice and Theory of Bolshevism*. London: Unwin Books, 1962.

The Russian Provisional Government 1917, 3 vols, edited by R. Browder and A. Kerensky. Stanford, Calif.: Stanford University Press, 1961.

Resolutions and Decisions of the Communist Party of the Soviet Union, vol. 1: *The Russian Social Democratic Labour Party 1898–October 1917*, edited by R. C. Elwood. Toronto and Buffalo: University of Toronto Press, 1974.

Schapiro, L. *The Communist Party of the Soviet Union*, 2nd edn. London: Methuen, 1970.

—— *The Origin of the Communist Autocracy: Political Opposition in the Soviet State. First Phase 1917–1922*. Houndmills and London: Macmillan, 1977.

Schlesinger, R. *History of the Communist Party of the USSR*. Bombay, Calcutta, Madras, New Delhi: Orient Longman, 1977.

Schorske, C. E. *German Social Democracy 1905–1917: The Development of the Great Schism*. Cambridge, Mass. and London: Harvard University Press, 1983.

Senn, A. E. 'The Myth of German Money During the First World War'. *Soviet Studies*, vol. 28, no. 1 (January 1976).

Service, R. *Lenin: A Political Life*, vol. 1: *The Strengths of Contradiction*. Basingstoke and London: Macmillan, 1985.

—— *Lenin: A Political Life*, vol. 2: *Worlds in Collision*. Basingstoke: Macmillan, 1991.

—— *Lenin: A Political Life*, vol. 3: *The Iron Ring*. Basingstoke: Macmillan, 1995.

—— *Lenin: A Biography*. London: Macmillan, 2000.

Shub, D. *Lenin: A Biography*. Harmondsworth: Penguin, 1966.

Shukman, H. *Lenin and the Russian Revolution*. London: Batsford, 1966.

Smith, J. *The Bolsheviks and the National Question, 1917–23*. Basingstoke and London: Macmillan, 1999.

Smith, S. A. *Red Petrograd: Revolution in the Factories, 1917–18*. Cambridge: Cambridge University Press, 1983.

Snowden, M. P. *Through Bolshevik Russia*. London, 1920.

Sochor, Z. A. *Revolution and Culture: The Bogdanov–Lenin Controversy*. Ithaca, NY: Cornell University Press, 1988.

Stalin, J. *Problems of Leninism*. Moscow: Foreign Languages Publishing House, 1953.

Stepniak. *The Russian Storm-Cloud*. London: Swan Sonnenschein & Co., 1886.

Stites, R. *The Women's Liberation Movement in Russia*. Princeton, NJ: Princeton University Press, 1978.

Sukhanov, N. N. *The Russian Revolution 1917: A Personal Record*. Princeton, NJ: Princeton University Press, 1984.

Swain, G. *Russian Social Democracy and the Legal Labour Movement, 1906–14*. London and Basingstoke: Macmillan, 1983.

Tengoborski, M. L. d. *Commentaries on the Productive Forces of Russia*, 2 vols. London: Longman, 1856.

Thatcher, I. 'Perspectives on the Russian Revolution from New York, L. D. Trotsky'. *Journal of Trotsky Studies*, vol. 1 (1993), pp. 95–122.

—— 'Russia's Social-Patriotism in Trotskii's Paris Writings during the First World War'. *Revolutionary Russia*, vol. 6, no. 2 (December 1993), pp. 229–76.

—— 'Trotsky and *Bor'ba*'. *The Historical Journal*, vol. 37, no. 1 (1994), pp. 113–25.

Theen, R. H. W. *Lenin: Genesis and Development of a Revolutionary*. London: Quartet Books, 1974.

Trotsky, L. *The History of the Russian Revolution*, translated by M. Eastman. London: Victor Gollancz, 1934.

—— 'Lessons of October'. In *The Essential Trotsky*. London: Unwin Books, 1963.

—— *On Lenin: Notes towards a Biography*, edited by L. Kochan, translated by L. Kochan. London: George G. Harrap, 1971.

—— *La guerre et la révolution: Le naufrage de la IIe Internationale. Les débuts de la IIIe Internationale*, 2 vols, translated by A. Oak. Paris: Editions Tête de Feuilles, 1974.

—— *The Young Lenin*, translated by Max Eastman. Harmondsworth: Penguin, 1974.

Tumarkin, N. *Lenin Lives: The Lenin Cult in Soviet Russia*. Cambridge, Mass. and London, England: Harvard University Press, 1983.

Ulam, A. B. *Lenin and the Bolsheviks*. London and Glasgow: Fontana, 1969.

The Unknown Lenin from the secret archive, edited by R. Pipes and D. Brandenberger, translated by C. A. Fitzpatrick. New Haven, Conn.: Yale University Press, 1996.

Valentinov, N. *Encounters with Lenin*, translated by P. Rosta and B. Pearce. London: Oxford University Press, 1968.

—— *The Early Years of Lenin*, Introduction by Bertram D. Wolfe, translated by R. H. W. Theen. Ann Arbor: University of Michigan Press, 1969.

Vladimir Ilyich Lenin: A Biography, edited by P. N. Pospelov. Moscow: Progress Publishers, 1965.

Volkogonov, D. A. *Lenin: Life and Legacy*, edited and translated by H. Shukman. London: HarperCollins, 1994.

—— *The Rise and Fall of the Soviet Empire*. London: HarperCollins, 1998.

Weber, G. and H. Weber. *Lenin: Life and Works*, edited and translated by M. McCauley, Macmillan Chronology Series. London and Basingstoke: Macmillan, 1974.

White, J. D. 'The First *Pravda* and the Russian Marxist Tradition'. *Soviet Studies*, vol. 26, no. 2 (April 1974), pp. 181–204.

—— 'The Sormovo–Nikolaev Zemlyachestvo in the February Revolution'. *Soviet Studies*, vol. 31, no. 4 (October 1979), pp. 475–504.

—— 'Early Soviet Historical Interpretations of the Russian Revolution 1918–24'. *Soviet Studies*, vol. 37, no. 3 (July 1985), pp. 330–52.

—— 'Lenin, the Germans and the February Revolution'. *Revolutionary Russia*, vol. 5, no. 1 (June 1992), pp. 1–21.

—— 'Theories of Imperialism in Russian Socialist Thought from the First World War to the Stalin Era'. *Co-Existence*, vol. 30 (1993), pp. 87–109.

—— 'National Communism and World Revolution: The Political Consequences of German Military Withdrawal from the Baltic Area in 1918–19'. *Europe–Asia Studies*, vol. 46, no. 8 (1994), pp. 1349–69.

—— *Karl Marx and the Intellectual Origins of Dialectical Materialism*. Basingstoke and London: Macmillan, 1996.

—— '"No, we won't go that way; that is not the way to take": The Place of Aleksandr Ul'ianov in the Development of Social-Democracy in Russia'. *Revolutionary Russia*, vol. 11, no. 2 (December 1998), pp. 82–110.

—— 'Lenin, Trotskii and the Arts of Insurrection: The Congress of Soviets of the Northern Region 11–13 October 1917'. *The Slavonic and East European Review*, vol. 77, no. 1 (January 1999), pp. 117–39.

Wildman, A. K. *The Making of a Workers' Revolution: Russian Social Democracy, 1891–1903*. Chicago and London: The University of Chicago Press, 1967.

Williams, B. *Lenin*. London: Longman, 2000.

Williams, R. C. *The Other Bolsheviks: Lenin and His Critics, 1904–1914*. Bloomington and Indianapolis: Indiana University Press, 1986.

Wolfe, B. D. *Three Who Made a Revolution*. London: Thames & Hudson, 1956.

Yassour, A. 'Lenin and Bogdanov: Protagonists in the "Bolshevik Center"'. *Studies in Soviet Thought*, vol. 22 (1981), pp. 1–32.

Biographical Notes

Antonov-Ovseenko, Vladimir Aleksandrovich (1884–1939). Revolutionary, military commander and diplomat. A native of Chernigov in the Ukraine, Ovseenko attended the St Petersburg Military Engineering Academy. During the First World War he collaborated with Trotsky in publishing the anti-war newspaper *Nashe Slovo*. He returned to Russia in 1917 and joined the Bolshevik party. In 1919 he commanded the Ukrainian front. In 1923 he joined the Trotskyist opposition, breaking with it in 1928. In 1937 while serving as Soviet consul in Barcelona he was recalled and died in Stalin's purges in 1939.

Armand, Inessa (1874–1920). A Bolshevik party activist and close associate – allegedly mistress – of Lenin, Armand (née Stefan) was born in Paris of a French actor father and an Anglo-French mother. She was brought up in Moscow in the household of a wealthy industrialist and married one of his sons. In 1903 she joined the RSDLP, meeting Lenin in Paris in 1909. In 1912 Armand went to Russia to campaign in the elections to the Fourth Duma. She was arrested but managed to escape, reaching Switzerland in 1913. In 1917 Armand returned to Russia along with Lenin. She died of cholera after a visit to the Caucasus and was buried in the Kremlin wall.

Bogdanov, Alexander Alexandrovich (1873–1928). Revolutionary activist, philosopher, scientist and physician, Bogdanov (real name Malinovskii) studied at the universities of Moscow and Kiev, beginning his revolutionary activities in Tula in the 1890s. Simultaneously, he began to develop his ideas on philosophy and economics in a series of publications culminating in his three-volume collection *Empiriomonism*. Bogdanov collaborated with Lenin between 1904 and 1908 in establishing the Bolshevik fraction of the RSDLP. From 1907 onwards the viewpoints of the two men diverged increasingly, particularly on the matter of Bolshevik representation in the Duma. After Bogdanov was expelled from the Bolshevik fraction in 1909 he remained within the RSDLP in his own group 'Vpered' which organised the party schools on Capri (1909) and Bologna (1910). Bogdanov left 'Vpered' in 1911 and returned to Russia in 1913, serving in the army as a doctor during the First World War. After the Bolsheviks came to power Bogdanov was prominent as the main ideologist of the Proletkult movement, but from 1920 onwards devoted himself increasingly to scientific work. He died in 1929 as a result of an unsuccessful experiment in blood transfusion.

Bukharin, Nikolai Ivanovich (1888–1937). Leading Bolshevik theoretician. He was a participant in the 1905 revolution in Moscow, emigrating to Germany in 1911. In 1915 he published 'The World Economy and Imperialism' in Lenin's journal *Kommunist*. The following year Bukharin moved to New York and became editor of the journal *Novyi mir*. He returned to Moscow in May 1917 and became a member of the Bolshevik Central Committee in August 1917. In opposition to the Treaty of Brest-Litovsk he became a left communist. In 1919, along with E. A. Preobrazhenskii, Bukharin wrote *The ABC of Communism* and in the following year published his analysis of War Communism, *Economics of the Transition Period*. Bukharin was an upholder of NEP and opponent of Stalin's forced collectivisation of agriculture. He was put on trial and shot in 1938.

Chernyshevskii, Nikolai Gavrilovich (1828–89). Literary critic and leader of the radical intelligentsia during the 1850s and 1860s. Much of his writing was published in the journal *The Contemporary* in the decade between 1854 and 1864. His many writings include the novel *What Is to Be Done?*, the Commentary to J. S. Mill's *Principles of Political Economy*, and *The Aesthetic Relations of Art to Reality*, which was inspired by Feuerbach's philosophy. In 1862 Chernyshevskii was arrested and sentenced to fourteen years' penal servitude and exile for life in Siberia; he was allowed to return only in 1883.

Chkheidze, Nikolai Semenovich (1864–1926). A Georgian Social Democrat and Menshevik leader. Chkheidze was a member of the Third and Fourth Dumas. In 1917 he was chairman of the Petrograd Soviet between February and August 1917. He also chaired the Central Executive Committee (CEC). After the Bolsheviks came to power Chkheidze emigrated to France in 1921, where he committed suicide.

Danielson, Nikolai Frantsevich (1844–1918). Collaborator with Marx, translator of *Das Kapital* into Russian and writer on Russian economic development. Danielson began to correspond with Karl Marx in 1868, and took up the translation of *Das Kapital* into Russian that had been begun by his friend Herman Lopatin. The translation of the first volume appeared in 1872, and the remaining two volumes appeared in Russian translation by him in 1885 and 1896 respectively. Danielson also sent Marx materials on Russian economic development. Using the same materials Danielson himself carried out research on the Russian economy, first publishing the results in the article 'Studies in Our Post-Reform Social Economy' (1880) which was later expanded into a book (1893). Although Marx found Danielson's writings of great value, they were condemned as 'Narodnik' by Plekhanov and Lenin.

Dzierżyński, Feliks (1877–1926). Of Polish gentry parentage from the Vilna province, Dzierżyński was a founder member of the SDKPiL. He was repeatedly imprisoned and exiled to Siberia for revolutionary activities. Dzierżyński was one of the main advocates of the SDKPiL's union with the RSDLP in 1906. Following his release from prison in Moscow at the time of the February revolution, he became a member of the Bolshevik Central

Committee. When the Cheka was established in December 1917 Dzierżyński was appointed its chairman. From 1924 until his death he was chairman of the Supreme Council of the National Economy (VSNKh).

Fedoseev, Nikolai Evgrafovich (1871–99). A pioneer of Marxism in Russia, Fedoseev was born in the Vyatka province, the son of a nobleman. After being expelled from school for reading illegal literature, Fedoseev established a number of study circles in Kazan, to one of which Lenin belonged in 1888–9. In July 1889 Fedoseev was arrested along with 35 members of his organisation. During his term of imprisonment he made a study of Russia's economic development, which Lenin commented upon. At the end of 1893 Fedoseev was exiled to Siberia, where, in a fit of depression, he committed suicide.

Gorky, Maxim (1868–1936). Real name Aleksei Maksimovich Peshkov. Russian author and playwright.

Guchkov, Alexander Ivanovich (1862–1936). Businessman and politician, Guchkov belonged to a Moscow merchant family. He was an organiser for the Red Cross during the Russo-Japanese War (1904) and in 1905 was founder member and leader of the Octobrist party. He was a member of the Third Duma and acted as chairman (1910–11). During the First World War he was chairman of the Central War Industries Committee, 1915–17. In March 1917 he became Minister of War and Navy in the Provisional Government. He resigned on 2 May 1917 and emigrated from Russia in 1918.

Jogiches, Leo (Pseudonym Tyszka) (1867–1919). Prominent activist in the Polish and German workers' movements. The son of a wealthy Jewish Vilna merchant, Jogiches early made contact with the People's Will organisation in Vilna. Unlike other members of the group, he did not take part in the plot to assassinate Tsar Alexander III in 1887, and escaped arrest when the plot was discovered. After forming a Marxist circle and conducting propaganda among the Vilna workers he was arrested in 1888. In 1890 Jogiches emigrated to Switzerland, where, along with Rosa Luxemburg in 1893, he became a founder member of the SDKP, which became the SDKPiL in 1900. In December 1905 he helped organise the Warsaw workers' strike. Jogiches was arrested in March 1906 and sentenced to eight years' penal servitude, but succeeded in escaping and going abroad in 1907. During the First World War Jogiches was a leading figure among the German left Social Democrats, and was involved in establishing the Spartakus League in 1916. He was imprisoned in March 1918 for anti-war agitation, but was freed during the November revolution. Together with Rosa Luxemburg and Karl Liebknecht, Jogiches formed the German Communist Party (1918). He was murdered in prison in Berlin on 10 March 1919.

Kamenev [Rosenfeld], Lev Borisovich (1883–1936). Bolshevik activist. Between 1909 and 1914, along with Lenin and Zinoviev, Kamenev directed the Bolshevik organisation from abroad. He was exiled to Siberia in 1915 and returned to Petrograd after the February revolution. Along with Stalin he took over the editorship of *Pravda*, publishing articles which propounded defencism, and gave conditional support to the Provisional Government. In October 1917 Kamenev and Zinoviev opposed an armed uprising by Bolsheviks, advocating a coalition of all socialist parties. After the October revolution Kamenev became chairman of the Central Executive Committee and chairman of the Moscow Soviet (1918–26). He sided with Stalin against Trotsky in 1923–4, but later, along with Zinoviev and Trotsky, headed the opposition to Stalin (1926–7). He was arrested following Kirov's assassination in 1934, sentenced to death and executed.

Kautsky, Karl (1854–1938). Leading theoretician of the German Social Democratic Party and the Second International.

Kerensky, Alexander Fedorovich (1881–1970). Son of the headmaster of Simbirsk high school, which Alexander Ulyanov and Lenin attended. He graduated in Law from St Petersburg University in 1904 and frequently acted for the defence in trials of revolutionaries. He was a member of the Fourth Duma (1912) and chairman of the Trudovik fraction. Following the February revolution in 1917 Kerensky became vice-chairman of the Petrograd Soviet and Minister of Justice in the Provisional Government. He served as Minister of War and Navy in May–June 1917, becoming prime minister in July 1917. He left Russia after the Bolsheviks came to power, emigrating to France in 1918, and moving to the USA in 1940. Kerensky was the author of many memoir works on the revolutionary period.

Kollontai, Alexandra Mikhailovna (1872–1952). Revolutionary activist, campaigner for women's rights and Soviet diplomat. Along with Alexander Shlyapnikov, Kollontai was one of the leaders of the Workers' Opposition in 1920.

Kornilov, Lavr Georgevich (1870–1918). General. After the February revolution he was Commander of Petrograd Military District, but resigned this post to be Commander of the Eighth Army on the SW front. He was appointed Supreme Commander-in-Chief by Kerensky on 18 July 1917. When Kornilov's troops advanced on Petrograd he was dismissed by Kerensky on 27 August, placed under arrest and imprisoned. In September 1917 Kornilov escaped to Novocherkassk, where he participated in the formation of the Volunteer Army. He was killed during an attack on Ekaterinodar on 13 April 1918.

Krupskaya, Nadezhda Konstantinovna (1869–1939). Lenin's wife, Bolshevik political activist and educationalist. Krupskaya was born in St Petersburg, the daughter of an army officer. Her early childhood was spent in Warsaw, where her father was posted, the family returned to the capital in 1874. In 1887 Krupskaya qualified as a governess and in 1889 enrolled in the Bestuzhev Courses. She made contact with the members of the Social Democratic circle led by Mikhail Brusnev and began to study Marxism. In the following year she devoted herself to working for the Brusnev organisation, teaching workers in evening classes. In 1894 she met Lenin, and after Lenin's arrest in 1895, as a leading member of the Union of Struggle for the Liberation of the Working Class, Krupskaya helped organise the textile workers' strikes in 1896. For this activity she was arrested and sentenced to three years' exile in Siberia. She joined Lenin in Shushenskoe and married him in 1898. At the end of her exile in 1901 Krupskaya joined Lenin abroad and worked as secretary for the editorial board of *Iskra*. After taking part in the Second Congress of the RSDLP in 1903 she acted as secretary for the Bolshevik publications *Vpered* and *Proletarii* and maintained correspondence with party organisations inside Russia. She returned to Russia in 1917 with Lenin, and after the October revolution worked in the Commissariat of Education. In October 1923 Krupskaya became a member of the Academic Council of the Lenin Institute. She wrote her memoirs, *Reminiscences of Lenin*, between 1924 and 1929.

Kuskova, Ekaterina Dmitrievna (1869–1958). Famous for her Economist manifesto, the 'Credo', against which Lenin organised a protest of Social Democrats in 1899.

Liebknecht, Karl (1871–1919). Left-wing German Social Democrat and member of the German Reichstag. Liebknecht was the only Deputy to oppose war credits in the Reichstag in 1914. Drafted during the war, he was imprisoned (May 1916 to November 1918) for anti-war activity. Leader of the International Group and, later, the Spartacus League, Liebknecht was one of the leaders of the Berlin uprising in 1919. He was murdered along with Rosa Luxemburg in Berlin on 15 January 1919.

Lunacharskii, Anatolii Vasilevich (1875–1933). Playwright, philosopher and literary critic, Lunacharskii was a close friend and associate of Alexander Bogdanov. He was a participant in the 1905 revolution, contributing to a number of Bolshevik newspapers. He emigrated in 1906, publishing his *Religion and Socialism* in 1908. During the First World War he was associated with Trotsky's newspaper *Nashe slovo* (Our Word). He returned to Russia in May 1917, and joined the Bolshevik party along with the Mezhraionka. After the Bolsheviks came to power he became Commissar of Education.

Luxemburg, Rosa (1871–1919). Political leader and theoretician of the Polish and German Social Democratic parties. Luxemburg was born in Zamość, in Russian Poland, the daughter of a Jewish merchant. Through her connections with the Polish revolutionary organisation, the 'Proletariat', she was forced to move to Switzerland in 1889. In Zurich she studied economics, receiving her doctorate in 1897. Her dissertation *The Industrial Development of Poland* was published the following year. In 1893, along with Leo Jogiches, Luxemburg was a founder member of the Social Democracy of the Kingdom of Poland (SDKP), which became the Social Democracy of the Kingdom of Poland and Lithuania (SDKPiL) in 1900. In 1898 she moved from Switzerland to Germany and became a member of the German Social Democratic Party, becoming one of the leading opponents of Eduard

Bernstein's reformist views. In 1905 she returned to Russian Poland along with Leo Jogiches and took part in organising the workers in Warsaw, serving a term of imprisonment from March to August 1906 for these activities. In August she took part in the Stuttgart Congress of the Second International and along with Lenin formulated a resolution against militarism. In 1913 she published her major work on economic theory, *The Accumulation of Capital*, expounding her conception of imperialism. On the outbreak of the First World War her anti-war stance brought her continual terms of imprisonment between January 1915 and November 1918. In prison she wrote the *Juinius Pamphlet*, which condemned the SPD leadership for its accommodation with the German government during the war. In November 1918 Luxemburg was released and resumed revolutionary agitation, along with Karl Liebknecht founding the German Communist Party (KPD). On 15 January 1919, while under arrest, Luxemburg and Liebknecht were killed, and their bodies thrown into a river.

Malinovskii, Roman Vatslavovich (1876–1918). Police spy, trade unionist and member of the Fourth State Duma.

Martov [Tsederbaum], Iulii Osipovich (1873–1923). For his involvement in radical student politics Martov was arrested and sent into exile in Vilna in 1892, where he joined the local Social Democrats, and ran study circles for Jewish workers. From Vilna Martov took the tactic of 'agitation' which he promoted on his return to St Petersburg in October 1895 when he joined Lenin's Social Democrat group. After Lenin's arrest in December 1895 Martov gave the group the name of the 'Union of Struggle for the Liberation of the Working Class'. In 1900 Martov, together with Lenin and Potresov, founded the journal *Iskra* and campaigned against 'Economism'. After the Second Congress of the RSDLP, however, Martov, repelled by Lenin's methods and his creation of a 'state of siege' within the party, formed a separate, 'Menshevik' fraction. In the years that followed Martov was a constant opponent of Lenin and the Bolsheviks. During the First World War Martov cooperated with Antonov-Ovseenko and Trotsky in editing the anti-war Parisian newspaper *Nashe Slovo*. He returned to Russia in May 1917, but after the Bolsheviks came to power he left the country in 1920. In exile he edited the journal *Sotsialisticheskii vestnik* (Socialist Herald).

Mikhailovskii, Nikolai Konstantinovich (1842–1904). Socialist thinker and literary critic, Mikhailovskii was a constant contributor to *Otechestvennye zapiski* (Notes of the Fatherland) for which he wrote articles on current affairs, sociology and literary criticism, acquiring the position of one of the leading ideological influences of his day for the radical youth. After *Otechestvennye zapiski* was closed down in 1884, he published his articles from 1892 onwards in the radical journal *Russkoe bogatstvo* (Russian Wealth), of which he became the chief editor in 1894. In the 1890s Mikhailovskii polemicised in this journal against the Russian Marxists, accusing them of fostering the development of capitalism and industrialisation at the cost of impoverishing and expropriating the small peasant producers.

Milyukov, Pavel Nikolaevich (1859–1943). Historian and liberal politician. Milyukov lectured in Russian History at Moscow University between 1886 and 1895. He was a founder member of the Constitutional Democratic (Kadet) Party (1905) and editor of its newspaper *Rech* (Speech). He was a prominent member of the Third and Fourth Dumas. After the February revolution in 1917, Milyukov became Minister of Foreign Affairs in the Provisional Government. In face of popular opposition to his territorial war aims and lack of support in the government, he resigned on 2 May 1917. In 1918 he helped found the Volunteer Army. He emigrated to England in 1920 and moved to Paris the following year, where he edited the *émigré* newspaper *Poslednie novosti* (Latest News). Milyukov was the author of numerous works on Russian history and politics.

Plekhanov, Georgii Valentinovich (1856–1918). 'The Father of Russian Marxism'. In 1876 Plekhanov joined the Bakuninist anarchist group of 'Rebels', which later merged with 'Land and Liberty'. When in 1879 Land and Liberty split into 'People's Will' and 'Black Repartition', Plekhanov became a founder member of Black Repartition. Forced to emigrate from Russia in 1880, Plekhanov settled in Switzerland and formed a new political group based on Marxist principles, the 'Liberation of Labour' group (1883). To explain the new group's political standpoint and how it differed from 'People's Will', Plekhanov published *Socialism and the Political Struggle* in 1883. This was followed in 1885 by *Our Differences*, a book criticising 'People's Will' and terming as 'Narodniki' those socialists who believed Russia might avoid a capitalist stage. In response to N. K. Mikhailovskii and other critics of Russian Marxism, Plekhanov published *On the Development of the Monist View of History* in 1895. Along with Lenin, Martov and others he became an editor of *Iskra*, in 1901. Following the Second Congress of the RSDLP he sided with the Mensheviks. During the First World War he was editor of the pro-war newspaper *Edinstvo* (Unity). Plekhanov returned to Petrograd on 13 April 1917. He died in Finland the following year.

Prokopovich, Sergei Nikolaevich (1871–1955). After leaving Russia with his wife, E. D. Kuskova, in 1896, Prokopovich studied at Brussels University, graduating in 1899. In 1897 he and Kuskova joined the Union of Social Democrats Abroad, conducting polemics against Akselrod and Plekhanov. In 1905 Prokopovich became a member of the Central Committee of the Kadet Party, but soon resigned. In July 1917 Prokopovich became Minister of Trade and Industry in the Provisional Government, and on 25 September, Minister of Supply. In 1921, along with Kuskova, Prokopovich was involved in famine relief in Russia.

Radek [Sobelsohn], Karl Berngardovich (1885–1939). Political activist and journalist. An internationalist during the First World War, Radek took part in the Zimmerwald and Kienthal conferences. He returned with Lenin from Switzerland to Russia in April 1917. In 1918 he was arrested in Germany for revolutionary activity. He returned to Moscow in 1922 and took up the post of secretary of the Comintern. He joined Trotsky's opposition to Stalin and was expelled from the party in 1927. After he was reinstated, he was for several years a leading party commentator on foreign affairs in the Soviet press. He was put on trial during the purges in 1937 and probably died in a concentration camp.

Shlyapnikov, Alexander Gavrilovich (1885–1937). Bolshevik activist, leader of the 'Workers' Opposition' and memoirist. Shlyapnikov was a native of Vladimir province, born into a working-class family. He joined the RSDLP in 1901, becoming a member of the St Petersburg Committee of the RSDLP in 1907. At the time of the February revolution in 1917 Shlyapnikov participated in the creation of the St Petersburg Soviet. During 1917 he was chairman of the All-Russian Union of Metal-Workers. Following the October revolution he became People's Commissar of Labour. Along with Alexandra Kollontai, he led the Workers' Opposition (1920–2). At the Tenth Party Congress Shlyapnikov was elected to the Bolshevik Central Committee. He was expelled from the party in 1933 and executed in 1937.

Spiridonova, Mariya Alexandrovna (1884–1941). Born in Tambov into a family of minor nobility, Spiridonova joined the Socialist Revolutionary Party in 1901 while still at school. In 1906 she attempted to assassinate the governor of Tambov, G. N. Luzhenovskii, as a reprisal for his brutal suppression of local peasant disturbances. The initial sentence of death she received at her trial was commuted to one of indeterminate imprisonment. Spiridonova was released in March 1917 after the fall of tsarism. She joined the left wing of the SR Party and became a founder member of the Left SR Party in November 1917. Spiridonova was an advocate of a Left SR coalition with Bolsheviks. She supported the Brest-Litovsk peace until April 1918. She was arrested following the assassination of the German ambassador Mirbach on 8 July 1918. She was released in December 1918, but for the rest of her life was repeatedly arrested, imprisoned and exiled. She was sentenced to death by a military tribunal in 1941.

Stalin [Jugashvili], Iosif Vissarionovich (1879–1953). Bolshevik leader and head of the Soviet government. Stalin was born in the Georgian town of Gori, the son of a cobbler. He was educated at the Orthodox seminary in Tiflis and joined the local Social Democratic group *Mesame Dasi* (Third Section) in 1898. He then worked as a political organiser and agitator for the Social Democrats in Transcaucasia. When the Social Democratic Party split in 1903, Stalin joined the Bolshevik fraction. In 1912 he moved to St Petersburg and became an editor of the Bolshevik newspaper *Pravda*. With Lenin's encouragement Stalin wrote a work on the nationalities question which was published in 1913. He was repeatedly imprisoned and exiled, and was in Siberia at the time of the February revolution. He returned to Petrograd on 12 March 1917 and rejoined the editorial board of *Pravda*. His advocacy of qualified support for the Provisional Government and for a defensive war attracted Lenin's criticism in April. After the Bolsheviks took power Stalin became Commissar for Nationality Affairs. During the Civil War he organised the defence of Tsaritsyn (later renamed Stalingrad).

In 1922 he became General Secretary of the Russian Communist Party's Central Committee. He presided over the industrialisation of the USSR and initiated the forced collectivisation of agriculture. During the 1930s, especially in 1937–38, Stalin ordered the mass imprisonment and execution of perceived 'enemies of the people', including many from the generation that had been active in the Russian revolution.

Struve, Peter Berngardovich (1870–1944). Economist, historian and philosopher. Struve studied law at St Petersburg University, graduating in 1895. In 1894 he published his influential book *Critical Remarks on Russia's Economic Development*. He collaborated with Lenin in the publication of *Iskra*, but the two soon diverged, as Struve increasingly became dissatisfied with the absence of ethics in Marx's 'economic materialism'. It was Struve, however, who wrote the RSDLP's manifesto in 1898. From 1902 to 1905 he edited the liberal–constitutionalist *Liberation* in Stuttgart. In 1905 he joined the Constitutional Democratic Party (Kadets) and became a member of the Second State Duma in 1907. He was a contributor to the collection of articles *Vekhi* (Landmarks), published in 1909, criticising the Russian intelligentsia for its radicalism. He was Minister of Foreign Affairs in Wrangel's government during the Civil War, but left Russia and spent the rest of his life in emigration.

Sukhanov [Gimmer], Nikolai Nikolaevich (1882–1940). Radical journalist and memoirist of the Russian revolution. Born in Moscow into a family of impoverished nobility, Sukhanov joined the Socialist Revolutionary Party in 1903. He was editor of the journal *Sovremennik* (Contemporary) in 1914 and of *Letopis* (Chronicle), an anti-war paper financed by Gorky (1915–17). In the February revolution Sukhanov became a member of the Executive Committee of the Petrograd Soviet. He joined the Mensheviks in May 1917 and contributed to Gorky's newspaper *Novaya Zhizn*. Between 1918 and 1921 he wrote his *Notes on the Revolution*, which were published in seven volumes in 1922–23, and reviewed by Lenin in one of his last articles.

Trotsky [Bronstein], Lev Davydovich (1879–1940). Leading figure in the Russian revolutionary movement and prominent member of the Soviet government. Trotsky was the son of a Jewish farmer from Yanovka in the Ukrainian province of Kherson. For his membership of a workers' circle in Nikolaev he was exiled to Siberia in 1898. He managed to escape and joined Lenin in London in 1902. Trotsky was the delegate of the Siberian Social Democrats at the Second Congress of the RSDLP in 1903, at which he sided with the Mensheviks. He returned to Russia and played a prominent part in the 1905 revolution as chairman of the St Petersburg Soviet. On 3 December 1905 he was arrested and again exiled to Siberia, but he escaped *en route* and made his way abroad. Between 1908 and 1912 he published the non-fractional newspaper *Pravda* in Vienna. After the Sixth Conference of the RSDLP organised by Lenin in Prague, Trotsky participated in the August conference in Vienna which formed the 'August Bloc' in an attempt to unite the anti-Leninist forces. During the First World War Trotsky edited the newspaper *Nashe slovo* (Our Word) in Paris, but was deported from France for anti-war agitation. In New York he edited the Russian-language newspaper *Novyi mir*, in which he published commentaries on the February revolution in 1917. He arrived back in Petrograd on 5 May 1917. Along with Mezhraionka Trotsky joined the Bolshevik party in July. After the July Days he was arrested and imprisoned until 2 September. On 25 September he was elected chairman of the Petrograd Soviet and played a prominent part in setting up the network of Military Revolutionary Committees which brought the Bolsheviks to power in October. Trotsky became Commissar for Foreign Affairs, leading the Soviet delegation at the Brest-Litovsk peace negotiations. He served as Commissar for Military Affairs during the Civil War. From 1923 onwards Trotsky became a critic of the increasing centralisation of the Soviet regime. He was expelled from the Communist Party in 1927 and deported from the USSR the following year. In exile Trotsky continued to criticise the Stalin dictatorship. In exile too, he published his monumental *History of the Russian Revolution* (1931–3). He settled in Mexico in 1937 and on 20 August 1940 was assassinated by one of Stalin's agents.

Ulyanov, Alexander Ilich (1866–87). Lenin's elder brother, who was executed for his part in the assassination attempt on Tsar Alexander III.

Ulyanov, Dmitrii Ilich (1874–1943). Lenin's younger brother. Dmitrii Ulyanov trained as a doctor at Moscow University. He was a delegate at the Second Congress of the RSDLP (1903). Between 1905 and 1907 he worked as a doctor in Simbirsk. During the First World War he served as a military doctor in Sevastopol, Odessa and the Romanian front. In 1917 he took part in establishing Soviet power in the Crimea. From 1921 he worked in the People's Commissariat for Health. He was also a director of the Central Lenin Museum.

Ulyanov, Ilya Nikolaevich (1831–86). Lenin's father, mathematician, schoolteacher and educationalist. In the 1850s and 1860s he taught at schools in Penza and Nizhnii Novgorod, becoming an inspector of schools in 1868 and the director of primary education for the Simbirsk province in 1874. In 1882 he was awarded the Order of St Vladimir 3rd Class, which entitled him to hereditary nobility.

Ulyanova, Mariya Alexandrovna (1835–1916). Lenin's mother. Born in St Petersburg, the daughter of the physician Alexander Dmitrievich Blank and Anna Johannovna Grosschopf. She qualified as a primary schoolteacher in 1863.

Ulyanova, Mariya Ilinichna (1878–1937). Lenin's youngest sister. Mariya joined the RSDLP in 1898 and between 1900 and 1903 worked for the newspaper *Iskra*. From 1904 she was active in the St Petersburg Bolshevik organisation, and as a result was arrested and imprisoned on several occasions. From March 1917 until the spring of 1929 Mariya was a member of the editorial board of *Pravda*, thereafter working for the Lenin Institute for which she collected Lenin's letters to his relatives.

Ulyanova, Olga Ilinichna (1871–91). Lenin's younger sister and childhood companion. Olga was a student at the Bestuzhev Courses in St Petersburg, where she died of typhoid.

Ulyanova-Elizarova, Anna Ilinichna (1864–1935). Lenin's elder sister. Anna was arrested on 1 March 1887 in connection with her brother Alexander's attempt on the life of the tsar. In 1889 she married Alexander's university friend Mark Elizarov. From 1893 she became involved in the Social Democratic movement in Moscow, and in 1898 became a member of the first Moscow Committee of the RSDLP. After the October revolution, Anna worked in the Commissariat of Education and Istpart. She was a member of the editorial board of *Proletarskaya revolyutsiya* and took part in the establishment of the Lenin Institute of which she became an associate.

Vorontsov, Vasilii Pavlovich (1847–1918). Economist and writer on Russia's post-1861 development. Vorontsov (pseudonym V. V.) practised medicine before devoting himself entirely to the study of economics. He contributed articles on economics to the journals *Russkoe Bogatstvo* (Russian Wealth), *Novoe Slovo* (New Word) and *Vestnik Evropy* (The Herald of Europe). In these articles and in his more extended publications Vorontsov focused on the obstacles to the development of capitalism in Russia and the human costs it involved. His most influential book, *The Fate of Capitalism in Russia* (1882), evoked critical responses from, among others, Plekhanov, Struve and Lenin.

Zasulich, Vera Ivanovna (1849–1919). One of the founders of Russian Social Democracy. Zasulich joined the Land and Liberty organisation in 1877, and on 24 January 1878 made an assassination attempt on the governor of St Petersburg. Following the split in Land and Liberty in 1879, Zasulich sided with Plekhanov's Black Repartition. She emigrated to Switzerland, from where she sent a letter to Marx in February 1881 inquiring whether Russia would be obliged to pass through the capitalist phase. In 1883 Zasulich took part in the formation of the Liberation of Labour group. She became a member of the editorial board of *Iskra* in 1900 and, following the Second Congress of the RSDLP in 1903, sided with the Mensheviks.

Zinoviev [Radomyslskii], Grigorii Evseevich (1883–1936). Bolshevik activist and head of Comintern. During the First World War, along with Lenin, Zinoviev was active in the anti-war movement. He returned to Petrograd with Lenin in April 1917. Along with Kamenev, Zinoviev opposed an armed uprising by the Bolsheviks in October 1917. From December 1917 to January 1926 he was chairman of the Petrograd Soviet, serving as chairman of Comintern between March 1919 and October 1926. In the internal party conflict which followed Lenin's death, Zinoviev first sided with Stalin and Kamenev against Trotsky, but subsequently allied with Trotsky against Stalin in 1926–7. Following Kirov's assassination in 1934 Zinoviev was a defendant at a show trial and executed in 1936.

CHRONOLOGY

1861	Liberation of the serfs in Russia.
1863 January	Polish uprising.
1870 10 April	Birth of Vladimir Ilyich Ulyanov (Lenin).
1872	Publication of the Russian translation of Volume I of Marx's *Capital*.
1874	The 'going to the people' movement.
1876	Foundation of the Land and Liberty revolutionary organisation.
1878 January	Vera Zasulich's assassination attempt on General D. F. Trepov, the governor of St Petersburg.
1879 June 16 August	Land and Liberty divides into the two groups: People's Will (*Narodnaia Volya*) and Black Repartition (*Cherny Peredel*). Lenin is accepted into the first class of Simbirsk classical *gimnaziia* (grammar school).
1881 February 1 March	Vera Zasulich writes to Marx asking him whether Russia is obliged to pass through a capitalist stage. Assassination of Alexander II by People's Will.
1882 1 January	Foundation of the Polish workers' party 'Proletariat'. Ilya Ulyanov is awarded the Order of St Vladimir 3rd class, which gives him the right to hereditary nobility.
1883	Formation in Geneva of the Liberation of Labour group, including Plekhanov, Pavel Akselrod and Vera Zasulich.

1883	Publication of Plekhanov's *Socialism and the Political Struggle*.
	Death of Karl Marx.
1885	Publication of Plekhanov's book *Our Differences*.
1886	
12 January	Death of Lenin's father Ilya Ulyanov from a brain haemorrhage.
1887	
1 March	Arrest of Lenin's elder brother Alexander for taking part in an attempt on the life of Tsar Alexander III.
8 May	Execution of Alexander Ulyanov, along with four others, for his part in the assassination attempt on Alexander III.
12–29 May	Lenin sits his leaving-certificate examinations.
10 June	Lenin graduates from the Simbirsk *gimnaziia*, receiving a gold medal.
End of June	The Ulyanov family moves to Kazan.
13 August	Lenin is accepted into the Law Faculty of Kazan University.
7 December	Lenin expelled from the University of Kazan and placed under police surveillance at the family estate at Kokushkino.
1888	
1888–89	Fedoseev's Social Democratic group in Kazan.
October	Lenin returns to Kazan. First contact with Marxist groups.
1889	
1889–92	Mikhail Brusnev's Social Democratic group in St Petersburg.
3 May	Lenin moves to Alekaevka, near Samara.
1890	Krupskaya joins Brusnev's Social Democratic group in St Petersburg.
1891	Famine in Russia.
4–24 April	Lenin sits his law examinations as an external student at the Law Faculty of St Petersburg University.
8 May	Lenin's younger sister Olga dies of typhoid in St Petersburg. After the funeral Lenin returns with his mother to Alekaevka, where he spends the summer.
16 September–9 Nov.	Autumn diet of law examinations in St Petersburg.
1892	
14 January	Lenin is awarded a first-class degree in law by the St Petersburg Board of Education.

1893	Foundation of Social Democracy of the Kingdom of Poland (SDKP).
31 August	Lenin moves to St Petersburg.
1894	Death of Alexander III; accession of Nicholas II. Lenin joins the group of Social Democrats led by S. Radchenko in St Petersburg and writes his first major work: *What the 'Friends of the People' Are and How They Fight the Social-Democrats*. Publication of Plekhanov's *The Development of the Monist View of History*.
1895	Death of Friedrich Engels.
May	Lenin takes his first journey abroad. In Switzerland Lenin establishes contact with Plekhanov's Liberation of Labour group.
8–9 December	Lenin is arrested.
1896	
April	*On Agitation* published in Geneva. Foundation in Vilna of the Lithuanian Social Democratic Party.
May–June	Strike of textile workers in St Petersburg.
11–12 August	Krupskaya is arrested for her part in organising the textile workers' strike.
1897	
13 February	Lenin is sentenced to three years' exile in Siberia.
14–17 February	Lenin attends a meeting of members of the St Petersburg Union of Struggle attended by the 'elders', the members of the Union of Struggle arrested along with him (Vaneev, Kzhizhzanovsky, Zaporozhets etc.) and the 'youngsters', who remained at liberty.
September	Foundation in Vilna of the General Jewish Workers' Union in Lithuania, Poland and Russia, known as the 'Bund'.
December	Krupskaya is sentenced to three years' exile in Siberia.
1898	
1–3 March	First Congress of the Russian Social Democratic Labour Party in Minsk.
10 July	Lenin and Krupskaya marry.
1899	The first Social Democratic groups appear in the Latvian territories.
March	Publication of Lenin's *The Development of Capitalism in Russia*.

1899
August

Lenin writes the 'Protest of Russian Social Democrats directed against the Manifesto of the "Economists" – the "Credo" '.

1900

The Social Democracy of the Kingdom of Poland unites with Lithuanian Social Democrats to form the Social Democracy of the Kingdom of Poland and Lithuania (SDKPiL).

January
Lenin's term of exile ends.

February
Publication of Plekhanov's *Vademecum*.

16 July
Lenin goes abroad. This first exile lasts for five years.

11–13 August
Negotiations with Plekhanov at Corsier near Geneva.

11 December
First issue of *Iskra* published in Munich.
Second Congress of the Union of Russian Social Democrats. The Union splits Liberation of Labour leaves the Union and sets up its own organisation 'Sotsial-Demokrat'.

1901
11 March
End of Krupskaya's term of exile.

1902
March

Foundation of the Socialist Revolutionary (SR) Party.
What Is To Be Done? published in Stuttgart.

1903
17 July–10 August
Second Congress of the Russian Social Democratic Labour Party.

19 October
Lenin leaves the editorial board of *Iskra*, on which the Mensheviks have the majority.

1904
May

One Step Forward, Two Steps Back published in Geneva.

7–9 June
First Congress of the Latvian Social Democratic Labour Party in Riga.

August
Conference of 22 Bolsheviks convened near Geneva.

Dec.–May 1905
Publication of the Bolshevik newspaper *Vpered*.

1905
9 January

Bloody Sunday. Beginning of revolutionary developments in Russia.

12–27 April
Third Congress of the RSDLP held under Lenin's chairmanship and without the participation of the Mensheviks.

May–November	Publication of the Bolshevik newspaper *Proletarii*.
June–July	*Two Tactics of Social Democracy in the Democratic Revolution* published.
October	General strike.
October–December	Soviet of Workers' Deputies in St Petersburg.
27 October–3 Dec.	Publication of the Bolshevik newspaper *Novaya zhizn*.
8 November	Lenin arrives in St Petersburg; Krupskaya follows ten days later.
13 November	Lenin's article 'Party Organisation and Party Literature' is published in *Novaya zhizn*.
12–17 December	First Conference of the RSDLP in Tammenfors chaired by Lenin. It resolves to call a congress to unite the separate party fractions. It is decided to boycott the Duma.

1906

March–April	Conference of the Latvian Social Democratic Labour Party in Riga resolves to unite with the RSDLP and change its name to 'Social Democracy of the Latvian Region' (SDLK).
10–25 April	Fourth (Unity) Congress of the RSDLP held in Stockholm with the participation of both fractions.
27 April–8 July	First State Duma.
20 August	Lenin takes up residence in the 'Vasa' villa in the Finnish village of Kuokkala.
August–Nov. 1909	Publication of the Bolshevik journal *Proletarii*.
Summer	Lenin reads the third part of Bogdanov's *Empiriomonism*. He drafts a critique of it.

1907

20 February–2 June	Second State Duma.
30 April–19 May	Fifth Congress of the RSDLP in London.
3 June	Election Law amended.
25 June	The Central Committee elected at the Fifth Party Congress delegates Lenin to represent the Russian Social Democrats on the International Socialist Bureau.
26 June	Lenin writes 'Against the Boycott'.
1907–12	Third State Duma.
21–3 July	Third Conference of the RSDLP held in Kotka, Finland.
3–11 August	Lenin participates in the Stuttgart Congress of the Socialist International.
5–12 November	Fourth Conference of the RSDLP in Helsingfors.
25 December	Lenin takes up residence in Geneva, where he remains until November 1908.

1908

1908–12	Publication of *Pravda* edited by Trotsky in Vienna.
January–March	Lenin reads the collection of articles *Studies in the Philosophy of Marxism*, published in St Petersburg at the beginning of 1908. He sends his unfavourable impressions of the collection to Gorky.
25 January	In a letter to Gorky Lenin says that he has been reading the articles by Lunacharskii and Bogdanov in *Studies in the Philosophy of Marxism* and he has become convinced that in matters of philosophy Plekhanov is correct.
February	Lenin works on his book *Materialism and Empiriocriticism*, which is published in Moscow in May.
10–17 April	On Gorky's invitation Lenin goes to Capri and spends several days there in the company of Gorky, Bogdanov, Lunacharskii, Bazarov and Ladyzhnikov.
3–28 May	Lenin is in London to gather material for his book *Materialism and Empiriocriticism* in the Library of the British Museum.
Before 15 May	In London Lenin writes 'Ten Questions to the Lecturer', which he sends to I. F. Dubrovinskii to use in his intervention at Bogdanov's lecture in Geneva on 15 May.
27–8 September	Lenin participates in the session of the ISB at Brussels.
21–7 December	Fifth Conference of the RSDLP.
November–Dec.	Lenin moves from Switzerland to Paris.

1909

1 February	At a meeting of the editorial board of *Proletarii* Lenin insists on a campaign against 'God-building', allegedly propounded by Lunacharskii.
February	Personal relations between Lenin and Bogdanov are broken off.
8–17 June	Lenin chairs meeting of the extended editorial board of *Proletarii*. Bogdanov is expelled from the Bolshevik Centre.

1910

2–23 January	Tenth Plenum of the Central Committee.
18–30 June	Lenin visits Gorky on Capri.
15–21 August	Lenin takes part in the Copenhagen Congress of the Socialist International.

1911

Summer	Lenin organises a party school at Longjumeau near Paris.

1912

5–17 January	The Sixth Conference of the RSDLP held in Prague with Bolshevik and party Menshevik delegates.
4 April	Shooting of workers on the Lena goldfields.
9 June	Lenin moves to Crakow to exercise closer editorial control over the new party paper, *Pravda*.
15 Nov.–25 Feb. 1917	Fourth State Duma.

1913 Publication of Rosa Luxemburg's *The Accumulation of Capital*.

1914

25 July	Lenin is arrested by the Austrian authorities on suspicion of espionage; he is released on 6 August.
23 August	Lenin moves to Switzerland and takes up residence in Berne.
24–6 August	Lenin sets out his attitude to the war in 'The Tasks of Social Democracy in the European War'. St Petersburg renamed Petrograd.
27 September	Conference of Italian and Swiss socialists at Lugano.
November	Arrest of the members of the Bolshevik fraction of the Duma. They are tried in February 1915.

1915

March	International Women's Conference.
April	International Youth Conference.
23–6 August	International Socialist Conference in the Swiss village of Zimmerwald.

1916

11–17 April	International Socialist Conference in the Swiss village of Kienthal.
June	Lenin completes his book, *Imperialism, the Highest Stage of Capitalism*.
12 July	Death of Lenin's mother in Petrograd.

1917

9 January	Lenin delivers a lecture on the 1905 revolution.
23 February	Street riots begin in Petrograd.
27 February	Defection of troops of the Petrograd garrison. Petrograd Soviet of Workers' and Soldiers' Deputies formed.
1 March	Army Order No. 1.
2 March	Nicholas II abdicates in favour of his brother Mikhail. Provisional Government formed.
3 March	Grand Duke Mikhail refuses to become ruler; the future form of Russia's government to be decided by a Constituent Assembly.

27 March	Lenin leaves Switzerland for Russia.
3 April	Lenin arrives in Petrograd.
4 April	Lenin's 'April Theses'.
24–9 April	Seventh (April) Conference of the Bolshevik fraction of the RSDLP.
April	Demonstrations against the foreign policy of the Provisional Government.
1–2 May	Milyukov and Guchkov resign their posts in the Provisional Government.
May	First All-Russian Congress of Soviets of Workers' and Soldiers' Deputies.
May–June	First Coalition Government.
June–July	Russian offensive in Galicia ends in failure.
2 July	Second Congress of Petrograd Mezhraionka organisation. It is resolved to unite with the Bolsheviks.
3–4 July	Street disturbances in Petrograd. Lenin goes into hiding.
7 July	Prince Lvov resigns as prime minister and is succeeded by Kerensky. The Provisional Government issues warrants for the arrest of Lenin and other leading Bolsheviks.
18 July	Kerensky appoints General Lavr Kornilov commander-in-chief.
23 July	Trotsky and Lunacharskii are arrested.
26 July–3 August	Sixth Party Congress of the Bolsheviks held in Lenin's absence.
10 August–7 October	Lenin in hiding in Finland.
26–31 August	The Kornilov revolt.
August–September	Lenin works on the book *State and Revolution.*
4 September	Trotsky released from prison.
23 September	Trotsky elected chairman of the Petrograd Soviet.
8 October	Lenin writes the article 'Advice of an Onlooker' and 'Letter to the Bolshevik Comrades attending the Congress of Soviets of the Northern Region' demanding that the Bolsheviks should launch an immediate armed insurrection.
10 October	Meeting of Bolshevik Central Committee in Petrograd attended by Lenin at which it is resolved to prepare for an armed insurrection.
11–13 October	Congress of Soviets of the Northern Region.
25 October	Opening of the Second All-Russian Congress of Soviets. Assault on Winter Palace.
26 October	Lenin issues Decrees on Peace and on Land and announces the formation of a Council of People's Commissars. Lenin is elected chairman of the Council.
27 October	Decree on the Press.

14 November	The Soviet Government issues Regulations on Workers' Control.
2 December	Establishment of the Supreme Council of the National Economy (VSNKh).
7 December	Establishment of the Cheka headed by Dzierżyński.

1918

5 January	Constituent Assembly meets and is dissolved.
14 February	Russia introduces the Gregorian calendar to replace the old-style Julian calendar. All subsequent dates are given in new-style.
3 March	Peace Treaty of Brest-Litovsk signed.
6–8 March	Seventh Extraordinary Congress of the Russian Communist Party ratifies the Brest-Litovsk treaty.
10–11 March	Capital transferred to Moscow.
March	Left Socialist Revolutionaries withdraw from the government.
11 June	Establishment of 'committees of the poor peasants'.
28 June	Nationalisation of large industrial enterprises.
6 July	Count Mirbach assassinated.
30 August	Attempted assassination of Lenin by Fanya Kaplan.
October–November	Lenin works on the pamphlet *The Proletarian Revolution and Renegade Kautsky*.

1919

2–6 March	Foundation Congress of the Communist International.
18–26 March	Eighth Congress of the Russian Communist Party. Publication of *The ABC of Communism* by N. I. Bukharin and E. A. Preobrazhenskii.

1920

	The first edition of Lenin's *Collected Works* begins to appear.
April–May	Lenin works on the book *Left Wing Communism. An Infantile Disorder*.
May	Publication of Bukharin's *Economics of the Transition Period*.
19 July–7 August	Second Congress of the Communist International.
21 September	Lenin signs a decree establishing a commission for the collection and study of materials on the history of the October revolution and the history of the Russian Communist Party (Istpart).
Autumn	Discussion on the trade unions.

1921

8–16 March	Tenth Congress of the Russian Communist Party. Introduction of the New Economic Policy (NEP). Suppression of the Kronstadt rising.
March–April	Lenin writes the pamphlet *The Tax in Kind*, justifying the New Economic Policy.

1921   Tenth Conference of the Russian Communist Party.
26–8 May   Third Congress of the Communist International.
22 June–12 July   The Istpart journal *Proletarskaya revolyutsiya* begins
October   to appear.

1922
23 April   Lenin has an operation to remove one of the
                                  bullets lodged in his body as a result of the assas-
                                  sination attempt.
26 May   Lenin is partially paralysed.
2 October   Lenin returns to work.
23–6 December   Lenin dictates the first part of 'Letter to the
                                  Congress' ('Testament').

1923
4 January   Lenin adds a note to his 'Testament' on Stalin's
                                  rudeness and the desirability of removing him
                                  from the post of General Secretary.
4–6 January   Lenin dictates 'On Co-operation'.
16–17 January   Lenin dictates the article 'On Our Revolution' in
                                  regard to N. N. Sukhanov's book *Notes on the
                                  Rovolution*.
2–9 February   Lenin dictates the article 'Better Fewer, But Better'.
31 March   Establishment of Lenin Institute in Moscow.

1924
21 January   Death of Lenin.
                                  Petrograd renamed Leningrad.
                                  Krupskaya begins to write her reminiscences of
                                  Lenin.

1931
October   Stalin's letter to the editorial board of *Proletarskaya
                                  revolyutsiya*, 'Some Questions concerning the
                                  History of Bolshevism', is published.

1939
27 February   Death of Krupskaya.

GLOSSARY

Agitation and Propaganda. The terms emerged in the 1870s during the 'going to the people' movement. The followers of Lavrov engaged in 'propaganda', that is; the long-term thorough education of the peasants to incline them towards socialism. The supporters of Bakunin, on the other hand, believed that all that was needed was 'agitation' – since the peasants were socialists by nature, all the revolutionaries had to do was to call upon them to rebel. In the 1890s the teaching of a small number of workers in study circles over a prolonged period was thought of as 'propaganda', whereas addressing large meetings and producing leaflets calling on the workers to strike was termed 'agitation'.

Barshchina. The labour service performed by Russian serfs for the landowner.

Black Repartition. Russian: *Chernyi peredel*. The name implies the expropriation of the land from the landowners and its redistribution among the peasants in an egalitarian fashion. A revolutionary organisation formed in 1879 as a result of the split in the Land and Liberty (*Zemlya i Volya*) organisation, it was led by G. V. Plekhanov and P. B. Akselrod, both of whom soon emigrated. Black Repartition defended the Narodnik tradition of basing its revolutionary tactics on the peasants and, in pursuit of the social revolution, abstained from political activity.

Bund. The General Jewish Workers' Union of Lithuania, Poland and Russia, founded in Vilna in 1887.

Cheka. Russian acronym for the All-Russian Extraordinary Commission for the Struggle against Counter-Revolution and Sabotage. It was established on 7 December 1917, its first head being Feliks Dzierżyński.

Comintern. The Communist or Third International founded in March 1919.

Constitutional Democrat (Kadet) Party. Founded in October 1905, the Constitutional Democrat Party (commonly known as the Kadets, from its acronym) was the main liberal party in Russia. Its objective was to establish a constitutional monarchy and a parliamentary regime in Russia. The party was led by the Moscow historian Paul Milyukov.

Economism. The name applied by their opponents to the trends in Russian Social Democracy which subscribed to the principle formulated by Marx that 'the liberation of the working class is the task of the working class itself'. To these trends were attributed the idea that the social democrats should concentrate their efforts on improving the economic conditions of the people, but should leave the political struggle against the autocracy to the the liberals. No Russian Social Democrat actually admitted to holding these views; the only written statement of them was the rough note by E. D. Kuskova, the so-called 'Credo'.

Land and Liberty. Russian: *Zemlya i Volya*. A revolutionary organisation formed in 1876 in St Petersburg, its main organisers being A. D. Mikhailov, M. A. Natanson, S. M. Kravchinskii, G. V. Plekhanov and L. A. Tikhomirov. The organisation believed that it was possible to base a socialist society in Russia on the peasant commune. One of its main forms of activity was to send its members to live among the peasantry. The organisation split in 1879 into People's Will and Black Repartition.

Left Socialist Revolutionaries. A radical current within the Socialist Revolutionary Party which first appeared during the First World War, and whose leaders included B. D. Kamkov, M. A. Natanson and M. A. Spiridonova. The split in the party deepened in the course of 1917, when the left wing criticised the party leadership for its moderate stance on a number of issues, including the war and the agrarian question. On 2 December 1917 the left SRs formed themselves into a separate party at their First Congress. Their party newspaper was *Zemlya i Volya* (Land and Liberty).

Liberation of Labour. Russian: *Osvobozhdenie truda*. The organisation of Russian Marxists founded in Geneva in 1883 by G. V. Plekhanov and including V. I. Zasulich, P. B. Akselrod and L. G. Deich.

Liquidators. The pejorative name applied by the Bolsheviks and adherents of Plekhanov among the Mensheviks ('party Mensheviks') to the current within Russian Social Democracy (led by Potresov) which wished to concentrate on work in the State Duma, trade unions, cooperatives, workers' educational associations and other legal institutions. It was averse to reviving the old conspiratorial party apparatus.

Mezhraionka. The Social Democratic group headed by K. K. Yurenev which was formed in St Petersburg in 1913 by people belonging to neither the Bolshevik nor Menshevik fractions of the RSDLP. It adopted an internationalist position during the First World War. After the February revolution in 1917 the group attracted many Social Democrats returning from exile abroad, such as Trotsky, Lunacharskii, Pokrovskii, Antonov-Ovseenko and so on. The Mezhraionka joined the Bolsheviks at the Sixth Congress in July 1917.

Mir. The Russian word meaning 'world' and 'peace'. It was also applied to the peasant village communities.

Narodnichestvo. A term derived from the Russian word *narod* – people. Originally the term '*narodnichestvo*' meant the tendency to base the revolution on the immediate desires and aspirations of the peasants. In 1895, however, G. V. Plekhanov in his book *Our Differences* began to class as 'narodniki' those people who did not accept that Russia would pass through a capitalist stage before socialism could be established. In later writings Plekhanov attributed further ideological characteristics to his conception of Narodism (*Narodnichestvo*).

NEP. New Economic Policy (*Novaya ekonomicheskaya politika*). The policy adopted by the Bolshevik government in March 1921, originally as a tax in kind, which allowed peasants to trade with whatever agricultural produce remained to them after the tax had been paid. Subsequently the policy was extended to allow market forces to play a major part in the economy.

Obrok. The payment of goods or money by Russian serfs to the landowner.

Otrezki. Literally 'cut-offs'. When the serfs were liberated in 1861 and the holdings which they had been cultivating were allotted to them, the landowners were allowed to retain one-third or, in the steppe provinces, one-half, of the cultivable land of their former estates, even if it meant appropriating part of the peasant allotments. These 'cut-off' portions often included pastures, woodlands, streams and so on to which the peasants formerly had access, but which subsequently were made available only for the payment of rent.

People's Will (*Narodnaya Volya*). Revolutionary organisation formed in August 1979 following the schism in Land and Liberty. Its founder members were A. I. Zhelyabov, A. D. Mikhailov and N. Morozov. The organisation believed in the admissability of terrorism as a political weapon against the autocracy. In 1881 members of People's Will succeeded in assassinating Tsar Alexander II.

Prodrazverstka (pronounced 'prodrazvyorstka'). The system of requisitioning foodstuffs during the period of 'War Communism'.

Proletkult. Contraction of the name '*Proletarskaya kultura*' (Proletarian Culture), a movement established in 1918 to develop workers' education and culture. Alexander Bogdanov was one of the movement's leading figures. In 1920, on Lenin's insistence, it was subordinated to the Commissariat of Education, and abolished in 1930.

RSDLP. The Russian Social Democratic Labour Party, formed in 1898.

SDKPiL. Social Democracy of the Kingdom of Poland and Lithuania. It was founded in 1893 first under the name of Social Democracy of Poland, then Social Democracy of the Kingdom of Poland (SDKP), and finally in 1900 as Social Democracy of the Kingdom of Poland and Lithuania (SDKPiL). Its founders dissented from the programme of the Polish Socialist Party (PPS), founded in 1892, which demanded Polish independence.

SDLK. Social Democracy of the Latvian Region. The first Social Democratic organisation appeared in the Latvian provinces in 1899, but the Latvian Social Democratic Labour Party (LSSP) was only formed in 1904. Its newspaper was *Ciņa* (Struggle). When it joined the Russian Social Democratic Labour Party in 1906 as an autonomous territorial organisation it changed its name to Social Democracy of the Latvian Region – SDLK.

Socialist Revolutionary Party (PSR or SRs). A socialist party formed in 1902 by uniting groups of varied ideological inspiration. The leading figures in the party were V. M. Chernov, N. D. Avksentiev, G. A. Gershuni and E. E. Breshko-Breshkovskaya, its main publications being the newspapers *Revolyutsionnaya Rossiya* (Revolutionary Russia) and *Vestnik russkoi revolyutsii* (Herald of the Russian Revolution). The party programme demanded a democratic republic, civil rights and a welfare state. The SR land programme advocated the socialisation of the land, that is, giving it to peasant communities. Unlike the Social Democrats, the SRs did not believe that class conflicts existed among the peasantry.

Union of Social Democrats Abroad. Founded in Geneva in response to demands from recent Social Democrat émigrés for a share in the Liberation of Labour's publication work. The purpose of the organisation was to produce popular and semi-popular literature for dissemination among the workers within Russia. Among the Union's members were E. D. Kuskova, S. N. Prokopovich and T. M. Kopelzon.

Union of Struggle for the Emancipation of the Working Class. The name given by Yu. O. Martov in December 1895 to the organisation uniting several social democratic groups in St Petersburg, including that of S. I. Radchenko, Martov himself and the Central Workers' Circle.

VSNKhA. The Supreme Council of the National Economy, known by its Russian acronym VSNKh or Vesenkha.

War Communism. A term coined by Alexander Bogdanov in 1917 and the name given in retrospect to the series of economic policies and measures, some inherited, some introduced, by the Bolsheviks after June 1918. They were characterised by wholesale nationalisation of enterprises, devaluation of the currency and centralised control of the economy. They were widely regarded at the time as embodying socialist principles.

War Industries Committees. Formed in May 1915, the War Industries Committees were voluntary associations intended to mobilise Russian industry for the war effort and to make good the deficiency in munitions that was experienced at that time. Originally the Central War Industry Committee was controlled by the largely foreign-owned Petrograd firms, but in July at the First Congress two prominent Moscow businessmen, A. I. Guchkov and A. I. Konovalov, were elected chairman and vice-chairman respectively of the Central Committee. The War Industries Committees became associated with the liberal opposition to the tsarist regime. To exercise some influence over the workers' movement, Workers' Groups were attached to the WICs, the most prominent of their leaders being the Menshevik defencist K. A. Gvozdev.

Workers' Opposition. The opposition within the Bolshevik party which was formed in 1920 by a number of prominent worker Communists, especially trade union leaders, headed by A. G. Shlyapnikov and A. M. Kollontai. The Workers' Opposition criticised the bureaucratic control of industry and advocated the establishment of an All-Russian Congress of Producers to run the country's economy. The opposition was condemned by the Tenth Party Congress.

Zemlyachestvo (plural *zemlyachestva*). From the Russian '*zemlya*' (land), a *zemlyachestvo* was an association of people from the same town or locality. Peasants who came to work in the city or students from the provinces attending a university would form *zemlyachestva*. They gave support to their members and pooled resources.

INDEX